LITERARY INTERVENTIONS IN THE CAMPAIGN BIOGRAPHY

Literary Interventions in the Campaign Biography considers campaign biographies written by major authors including Nathaniel Hawthorne, William Dean Howells, Lew Wallace, Jacob Riis, and Rose Wilder Lane. Whereas a number of cultural historians have previously considered campaign biographies to be marginal or isolated from the fictional output of these figures, this volume revisits the biographies in order to understand better how they inform, and are informed by, seismic shifts in the literary landscape. The book illuminates the intersection of American literature and politics while charting how the Presidency has developed in the public imagination. In so doing, it poses questions of increasing significance about how we understand the office as well as its occupants today.

Michael J. Blouin, PhD, is an Associate Professor in English and the Humanities at Milligan University. His areas of interest include nineteenth-century American literature, politics, and popular culture. He and co-author Tony Magistrale were recently awarded the Carl Bode prize for best essay from the *Journal of American Culture* in 2019. He was also invited to serve as guest editor for a special issue of the *Journal of Popular Culture* entitled "Neoliberalism and Popular Culture" (2018). Blouin's other works include *Stephen King and American Politics* (2021), as well as *Mass-Market Fiction and the Crisis of American Liberalism, 1972–2017* (2018). He received his doctorate in American Studies from Michigan State University in 2012. He currently resides in East Tennessee with his wife and two daughters.

LITERARY INTERVENTIONS IN THE CAMPAIGN BIOGRAPHY

Michael J. Blouin

NEW YORK AND LONDON

First published 2022
by Routledge
605 Third Avenue, New York, NY 10158

and by Routledge
2 Park Square, Milton Park, Abingdon, Oxon OX14 4RN

Routledge is an imprint of the Taylor & Francis Group, an informa business

© 2022 Michael J. Blouin

The right of Michael J. Blouin to be identified as author of this work has been asserted by them in accordance with sections 77 and 78 of the Copyright, Designs and Patents Act 1988.

All rights reserved. No part of this book may be reprinted or reproduced or utilised in any form or by any electronic, mechanical, or other means, now known or hereafter invented, including photocopying and recording, or in any information storage or retrieval system, without permission in writing from the publishers.

Trademark notice: Product or corporate names may be trademarks or registered trademarks, and are used only for identification and explanation without intent to infringe.

Library of Congress Cataloging-in-Publication Data
A catalog record for this title has been requested

ISBN: 978-0-367-67703-9 (hbk)
ISBN: 978-0-367-67694-0 (pbk)
ISBN: 978-1-003-13244-8 (ebk)

DOI: 10.4324/9781003132448

Typeset in Bembo
by Taylor & Francis Books

In Memory of
Basil "Bumpa" Day
1934–2021

CONTENTS

Acknowledgments   *viii*

Introduction: The Campaign Biography as American Literature   1
1 Presidential Biographies and the Knickerbockers   24
2 Nathaniel Hawthorne and the (Im)perfect President   43
3 William Dean Howells and the Real American President   62
4 Interlude: Wolcott Balestier and the Candidate's Secret   83
5 Lew Wallace, Benjamin Harrison, and the Historical Romance   99
6 Jacob Riis, Theodore Roosevelt, and the Art of Adoration   123
7 Rose Wilder Land and the Frontier Candidate   150
8 The Campaign Autobiography   173

Index   *197*

ACKNOWLEDGMENTS

I am grateful to Tim Dillon, a thoughtful historian and good friend, for encouraging me to pursue this project. Many thanks to my family – my partner, Kate Emmerich, who loves me unconditionally; my daughters, Emerson and Willow, for holding my hand through a pandemic and reminding me of what truly matters; and my mother, Melissa Perley, who raised me to think democratically. Additional thanks to my colleagues and teachers – Heather Hoover, Amy Edmonds, and Lee Blackburn, for their unwavering support; Joseph Baker, for always lending a sympathetic ear; Tony Magistrale and Todd McGowan, for their wisdom and lifelong commitment to education. This book has also greatly benefited from the astute comments of reviewers as well as editors at Routledge.

Finally, I lost my grandfather during the completion of this project. Basil "Bumpa" Day was a proud man, a storyteller, and a lover of American history. I dedicate the book in his honor. Love you, Bump.

INTRODUCTION

The Campaign Biography as American Literature

American democracy and American literature are both restless sorts of things. In few places is this innate restlessness more evident than in the campaign biography. And yet, despite their ubiquity through much of American history, campaign biographies continue to be summarily ignored. Scholars typically dismiss these unusual texts as mere propaganda, or curios from a fleeting moment in time and therefore unworthy of sustained critique. The few critics that do consider the campaign biography at any length are almost always cultural historians with little interest in the so-called literariness of the genre. Yet a number of important literary figures, including most prominently Epes Sargent, Nathaniel Hawthorne, William Dean Howells, Charles Wolcott Balestier, Lew Wallace, Jacob Riis, and Rose Wilder Lane have contributed to the tradition.[1] Why, then, have there been so few analyses of these works as literature?[2]

The genre of the campaign biography originates at a specific moment in which nineteenth-century American "men of letters" actively lobby for political appointments; in turn, the celebrities of American literature provide aspiring politicians with a "dignifying effect." The two parties benefit from an arrangement that bridges a perceived divide between America's literary and political spheres. Consequently, during the 1800s, more than 45 influential writers receive political appointments with varying degrees of importance (Brubaker 556, 558). This spoils system produces uneven results: whereas critically acclaimed aesthetes like Washington Irving effectively curry political favor, other writers rise to prominence thanks to their name recognition rather than their assumed merit as artists. For example, the relatively high-brow Herman Melville angles for a plum post to no avail, while Warren Harding employs a popular writer of crime stories, Richard Washburn Child, to write materials for his 1920 campaign before rewarding him with a position as ambassador to Italy. In short, although there has always existed an

DOI: 10.4324/9781003132448-1

imbrication of American literature and politics – not only in the arena of ideas, but in the daily operation of government – campaign biographies composed by literary figures in pursuit of patronage have yet to garner much scholarly attention.

To begin to rectify this issue, let us establish the degree to which even the most open-minded critics dismiss the campaign biography as a worthy object of study. Naysayers tend to treat these works as singularly hagiographic and classify them as the brainchild of sycophants or desperate amateur politicos in search of cushy government gigs. In one of the initial analyses in this vein, William Burlie Brown surveys the genre with a preconceived notion of what he will (or, more to the point, will not) discover. He contends that campaign biographies, "quite naturally, are neither subtle nor learned" (88). In his introduction to a vast catalog of Presidential biographies, William Miles agrees with Brown's assessment that these texts stand uniformly "devoid of what could be terms literary excellence," in part because as promotional tools they display a high degree of "sameness" (v–vi).[3] Scott E. Casper adds that the campaign biography has "remained in shadow... because nothing about it seems subversive. It seems the paramount genre of dominant liberal individualism and self-made manhood" (11). Enforcing a similar degree of separation between America's literature and its politics, Irving Howe defines literariness as a "moral order beyond ideology." To avoid placing their novel's "liveliness" in peril, Howe contends that American writers must "resist reduction to formula" (21–24). In other words, since literariness apparently requires subtlety, learnedness, an emphasis upon difference instead of sameness, and a healthy degree of subversion over complicity, its detractors insist that the campaign biography cannot be deemed literary and so it must be relegated to the status of trivial miscellany. However, I will argue that this dismissal says more about the dominant mode of modern literary criticism than it does about the works under review, which is to say, it reveals a good deal about how many critics codify American literature within rigid parameters and therefore fail to unpack fully its complex bond with American politics, in theory or praxis.[4]

Denigrators of the campaign biography insist that by ignoring the fixed framework for what is supposedly literary, we risk muddying the proverbial waters. However, while a writer can certainly conduct her work for a variety of purposes, and employ distinctive styles to appeal to distinctive audiences, why should readers automatically isolate Hawthorne's campaign biography of Franklin Pierce (1851) from, say, his novel *The House of Seven Gables* (1852) – two books published a year apart from one another?[5] Why wouldn't Hawthorne's reader explore the much-maligned ending to Hawthorne's novel – much maligned in part due to its problematic political vision – in conversation with his problematic vision of Pierce's candidacy, a tract that led to his exile from the literary circle in Concord? To foreclose these kinds of unorthodox conversations sustains a short-sightedness among Americanists, to which William Spengemann responds by advocating for a greater willingness to reconsider otherwise marginalized artifacts like the campaign biography:

> Letters, diaries, memoirs, histories, polemical and devotional writings are all conventional forms with their own characteristic assumptions and literary strategies, and hence their own possibilities for literary innovation. The boundaries we now draw between fiction and "nonfiction," artifact and "usifact," did not exist in most of the periods we study. Why we continue to insist upon them in the present age of generic confoundment remains a mystery. (23)

Said another way, a number of Americanists treat the campaign biography as strict nonfiction and, more derisively still, as overtly "political" in nature, and so they hesitate to read the genre through what they consider to be a literary lens. The reality that most pundits preclude such lines of inquiry may come as no surprise to students of American literature, since a wide range of scholars have historically viewed American literature as apolitical. Because literature must remain disinterested by design, or so the story goes, a range of self-proclaimed gatekeepers find "political writing" to be too shrewd and calculating – hardly noble work for the oft-fabled "man of letters." In response to this renunciation, Anthony Hutchison denounces what he views as a false demarcation between the "man of letters" and "political writers." He acknowledges "a complex but nonetheless distinguishable cross-fertilization between American political and literary cultures" (xxiii). According to Hutchison, imposed partitions between literature and politics prove to be quite permeable:

> There is no absolute difference between political and literary language … if we assume that a literary work has both aesthetic and political capacities, we may respect the difference between political and aesthetic motivation and at the same time allow for their intermingling within a work of art. (Whalen-Bridge 4)

That is, once we unpack the different motivations as well as intermingling capacities of the campaign biographies in question, and effectively tear down the artificial divide between politics and literature, we might return to canonical works like *The House of Seven Gables* with novel insights. Hawthorne very well may have written his parallel texts with dissimilar agendas, under acute pressures of differing degrees, and with more or less investment of his mental energy – but we need not catalog these texts as completely distinctive specimens. In each case, Hawthorne deploys some of the same responses to aesthetic quandaries and reaches some of the same political dead-ends.

Built into the critic's all-too-familiar rejection of the literary qualities of the campaign biography is a set of assumptions that these works are rushed, hackneyed, formulaic, and unsophisticated. Yet, instead of rejecting the campaign biography as one-dimensional and disposable, readers might reclaim these eclectic contributions as important elements within a given author's corpus as well as within the broader body of American letters.[6] Each of the chapters that follow demonstrate how the campaign biography provides keen insights into larger literary movements and, concurrently, how literary movements provide keen insights into campaign biographies. If we set aside the eternally thorny, contentious question of whether these productions are "good" or "bad," we can uncover in the campaign biography intriguing avenues for exploration concerning a plethora of cultural concerns, such as generic hybridity, the blending of Romance and realism in American thought, and perhaps most significant of all, the illusory split of American literature from American politics.

In a word, these candidate portraits recall formulas and fetishes that occupy the attention of American politicians and "men of letters" alike (closed) as well as the fragility, and raw potential, of a democratic society that endlessly re-invents itself (open).[7] As Russ Castronovo points out, "Even complacent and affirming texts such as patriotic biographies ... have stood uneasily upon a foundation of dissent" (*Fathering* 23). The fact that the majority of these publications are unpolished as well as stylistically uneven need not dissuade critics from attending to their internal complexities. Indeed, to revisit the genre of the campaign biography provides an alternative space in which to rethink long-standing preconceptions about American life. By reevaluating the campaign biography in dialogue with genre studies as well as reflections upon the long arc of realism (two areas of inquiry that remain uniquely within the bailiwick of literary critics), readers might come to understand better the role of democratic candidacies as a dominant trope in the American imagination.

Reclaiming the Campaign Biography

We ought to define the genre of the campaign biography first and foremost by its readerly situation: democratic campaigns conducted in the United States.[8] Hermione Lee states that biographies remain "always an index of (their) time" (9). Our working definition of the campaign biography must therefore attend to its specific one-hundred-year window (1820s–1920s), a conceptual framework that allows us to address, with firmer footing, a variety of contextual clues: what spurs its birth, how precisely it evolves over a certain period, and what may have caused the literary variants to all but vanish from popular discourse by the Roaring Twenties. Once we have established this concrete timeline, we can survey dominant literary as well as political influences upon the genre, including the gradual rise (and fall) of American realism as well as the incremental rise (and fall) of campaigns infused with chameleonic populist energies. Simply put, to track the campaign biography through its life span enables us to chart the ever-shifting shape of American politics during the century in question.

This book sketches the evolution of major American campaigns – although I must admit, due to the sheer size of the archive under review, that such a sketch can only be a cursory one. In the years prior to the first campaign biography, a period that historians commonly refer to as the "Era of Good Feelings," contemporary readers would barely recognize Presidential campaigns, since the

Commander-in-Chief was selected by a process more closely resembling aristocratic succession than the much messier affairs to follow. In the Era of Good Feelings, the whims of a cabal of party insiders matters far more than a well-executed campaign strategy. Written on behalf of his friend Andrew Jackson for the 1824 contest, and marking a clear departure from the political modus operandi, John Eaton's tract inaugurates the genre of the campaign biography. Many of the formal characteristics of Eaton's contribution appear relatively unchanged in future iterations: an attempt to link the candidate to a proud national lineage; an effort to paint the candidate as a self-made man with humble beginnings; the aim of presenting the candidate as a reluctant participant by harkening back to ancient Roman stories of Cincinnatus, who purportedly forfeits personal power for the good of the republic. The date of 1824 remains in one sense unremarkable because at that point only a very small percentage of the nation's residents could legally vote. On the other hand, Jackson's candidacy fundamentally alters the nature of campaigning in the United States. Jackson departs from his predecessors by fashioning himself a "man of the people," which is to say, the Jacksonian campaigns mark the symbolic end of the Era of Good Feelings by striking fear into the hearts of early American rulers that remain fearful of "the primal Augustan nightmare, discord – which is, institutionalized, faction" (Rogers 101). Politically and aesthetically, then, the campaign biography helps to politicize American life by entering discord and faction, the lifeblood of any democracy, into more general circulation. At the time of Jackson's reelection in 1828, the number of eligible voters nearly triples and, in parallel, states start to relax voter restrictions (Jamieson 4–5). This cultural context of democratization, as well as its resistance, underscores a core impasse in the campaign biography, one that the genre never quite resolves: a desire for formulaic continuity (the republican emphasis upon predictable outcomes) at odds with the drive for change (the constitutive premise of democracy). Born from the fires of Jacksonian populism, the campaign biography reflects an enduring incongruity between the republican and democratic beliefs of a Janus-faced America.

Still, John Garraty persists in arguing that even the more highly regarded campaign biographies "are not significantly superior to the general run" (158). Mere dusty relics destined for oblivion, Garraty insists, these "strange" texts are only ever interesting by accident. They are little more than "simple" byproducts of a marketing scheme meant to appeal to as many voters as possible (359). The outcome is reflective of an unwieldy commercial exercise. As a result, readers of these texts would immediately recognize what Gérard Genette calls the paratextual elements: the campaign biography's cheap binding, the biographer's self-abnegating preface, and so forth. The paratextual elements of the campaign biography ostensibly speak to the innate disposability that characterizes the genre as a whole. Like the rest of the formulaic literature being peddled in the United States, from the dime novel to the mass-market paperback, the campaign biography cannot be completely divorced from its appeal to the so-called lowest common denominator. Can we truly locate meaningful differences between the hawking of "partisan brickbat," like Tippecanoe shaving soap, Harrison letter paper, the "Keep-Cool-with-Coolidge" high ball, or an alcoholic drink minted as "The McKinley" – so cleverly conceived that Teddy Roosevelt likened these trinkets to the sale of "patent medicine" – and the more literary biographies surveyed throughout this book? (Troy 123; Boller 172). The campaign biography regularly seems uninspired and repetitive, at least to modern sensibilities. And I hasten to admit that serious dangers do accompany some of the formulaic enclosures proffered by the campaign biography. These texts can undoubtedly function as *agitprop*. "When someone who can sweep you up in a plot takes a turn into being a partisan hack," Fuller comments, "they can use their powers in the service of very bad political ends" (n.p.)

Of course, the campaign biography exists as just one "gimmick" among many others in a candidate's bag of tricks, and so its impact on voters cannot be considered within a vacuum. We should avoid amplifying the assumed influence of these texts on the outcome of a given campaign because, with an overabundance of materials at their disposal, campaign operatives can never be fully sure of "what will stick" with voters, and so it would be hyperbolic to declare any particular campaign biography as crucial in orchestrating a candidate's ascent. After all, in addition to a number of campaign biographies, William Benjamin Harrison's 1840 campaign – the first in which a candidate visibly stumps for himself – delivers powerful symbols such as the modest log cabin, a mythical birthplace for any successful candidate, including the wealthy Harrison, and the hard cider that crowds ritualistically imbibe as a sacrament to bond farmer to candidate. Harrison's Whigs also roll an infamous giant ball through campaign stops as a sign of the candidate's endurance as well as tenacity. Campaigns throughout the nineteenth century grow increasingly spectacular as candidates are drawn to center stage as more visible avatars for "the people." From Jackson to Harrison to William Jennings Bryan and Theodore Roosevelt, the candidate advances from relative silence during the Era of Good Feelings to adopting a far more active role by inviting voters to his front porch and, ultimately, into his living room (we will return to this pivot at length in the final chapter). So too does the campaign biography progress from extreme compliance within a residual formula to new, "spellbinding" styles, complete with novelistic interior lives meant to stimulate the electorate. But this evolution never moves along a perfectly linear trajectory. Instead, the campaign biography negotiates a precarious position between outright demagoguery and the salvific undercurrent of democratic wrangling.

While certain campaign biographers undoubtedly transform candidates into "figureheads, icons drained of reality and relevance," formulaic men in formulaic positions (see the duller passages of Hawthorne's sometimes plodding biography of Pierce), other biographers embrace a Cult of Personality and capitalize upon excesses to excite the masses (see Riis's genre-busting account of Teddy Roosevelt). With its ongoing instability as an index of American politics, the campaign biography lacks well-defined aesthetic parameters (Troy 59–60). The contours of the genre constantly shift according to the developing narrative of a particular campaign as well as the ever-fluctuating demands of relatively diverse audience members with variegated desires. In turn, the perceived monotony of the prose need not be chalked up exclusively to artistic failure. Although I would not go so far as to defend these one-off documents as canonical literature that should be assigned to every undergraduate student, as legitimate peers of *The House of Seven Gables* or Howells's *Rise of Silas Lapham*, these works are not nearly as monolithic as most critics presume. Nor must we presume that personal reflection trumps public petition, that art should be removed wholesale from social function, or that "men of letters" must maintain a degree of indifference to political punditry. These presumptions are in and of themselves neither universal nor inevitable. To dismiss the campaign biography off-handedly is to overlook its unique context and to hold the genre, its authors, and its imagined audience to the literary and political standards of the present. Why should we condemn the campaign biography in a blanket fashion as intrinsically stagnant, or its readers as always-already dupes? To debunk the pervasive claim that campaign biographies are merely monolithic, we need only gesture at some of the diverse issues on display in two of the most prominent examples, which we shall unpack at length in chapters to come. Hawthorne's campaign biography of Pierce, for one, conveys a sense of artistic as well as political ambivalence – a symptom of Pierce's political conviction to preserve the Union wed to Hawthorne's inability to resolve lingering artistic quandaries within the field of American Romanticism. As I have already suggested, the typically detested ending to *The House of Seven Gables* echoes the generally abhorred politics of Pierce's campaign tract. Similarly, Wallace's 1888 campaign biography for Benjamin Harrison conveys the increasingly pictorial quality of campaigns in the late nineteenth century, influenced by a nascent reliance upon human interest stories, Harrison's swelling stable of publicity consultants, and Wallace's unorthodox marriage of a popular Christian ethos with the demands of the historical Romance. To brand Hawthorne's campaign biography with the scarlet letter of "B" for boring, or to repudiate Wallace's offering as less than meritorious according to rather vague artistic standards, involves discounting the myriad ways in which literary and political contexts inform one another. In other words, by telling a story that includes the campaign biography – rather than marginalizing it – Americanists pursue a richer understanding of American culture during the long nineteenth century.

At their most compelling, campaign biographies are not static accounts of a singular figure, but active stories of a "people" in search of itself. Consider well-known writer Edward S. Ellis's *From Tent to White House: Or, How a Poor Boy Became President*, written for William McKinley's 1900 campaign. While the title suggests a predictable rags-to-riches account of McKinley's life, Ellis's campaign biography has precious little to say about McKinley the man. Instead, it dwells at length upon military campaigns during the Civil War and then the Spanish-American war – stories of conflict designed to "quicken the pulse and thrill the heart" (39). Ellis's text also spends an inordinate amount of time recalling the struggle of political conventions (in chapters IX and X, respectively). It would be a waste of time for readers today to read *From Tent to White House* with the goal of learning untold information about McKinley. It remains far more productive for readers to approach this text as a dynamic document detailing what a democratic community wishes, in concert, to become. Ellis's narrator confesses,

> In giving a biography of President McKinley it is not our purpose to include a history of the war between the United States and Spain, but since the two are so intimately associated our work would be incomplete without an intelligent survey of one of the most important epochs in our history. (156)

Borrowing liberally from trends in boys' literature, Ellis's genre of choice, this campaign biography reveals an acutely jingoistic culture in pursuit of its latest avatar. Campaign biographies thus reflect the untidy process of a populace in the uneven pursuit of its ideal self.

Between the 1820s and 1920s, the plotting of a successful campaign undergoes routine overhaul, and discarded campaign biographies provide a distinctive window into this tumult. In form as well as content, the texts under review reveal a crucial paradox from the century in question: "The President was to be both king and prime minister, a national figurehead and the people's representative," elected but never subservient (Troy 9–10). From its inception, the campaign biography provides "a symbol of the new democracy struggling to be born" (Boller 35). These publications occasionally suppress the voice of "the people" by portraying a fetishized individual to supplant the antagonism at the heart of American democracy. In contrast to the historical biography or the Presidential memoir, though, a contrast to which we will return in the book's first as well as final chapters, the campaign biography cannot exorcise the agonism attendant to its very purpose – that is, it cannot be free of its dependence upon imminent disagreements, political as well as aesthetic. Forged by the pressing electoral decisions at hand, these harried narratives open the debate and, at the same moment, intend to serve as its (im)possible last word. Equal parts pragmatic function and idealistic gesture, unvarnished Truth and rhetorical deception, the campaign biography may be a tardy entry into ongoing discussions of American literature – but its contributions could yet prove to be of considerable value.

Function and Form

Because the campaign biography appears to follow a relatively stable formula across generations, we must take a brief detour into genre theory to be precise in its classification. I do not intend to offer a strict taxonomy. Quite the opposite: by tracing the contours of the campaign biography as a genre, we recognize its permeability as well as its intertextual undercurrents. Akin to the political enterprise that it signifies – the form is once more the content – the genre of the campaign biography can (indeed, must) be granted a definitive shape, much like the candidates that it portrays. But in granting the genre/candidate a definitive shape, its inflexibility as a generic category, the campaign biography, like elected officials themselves, offers a placeholder: a rather flimsy fetish that could never fully encapsulate that which it promises to embody – namely, an imagined communal essence. Far from another rote exercise in categories and catalogs, when we infuse our study of the campaign biography with lessons learned from genre studies, we thicken our comprehension of these oft-neglected artifacts.

Many critics still consider the term genre to be a pejorative one. As we have already established, of the critics that do examine campaign biographies, the majority of them view these works as heavily codified and thus subject to unbending rules that dictate a relatively narrow range of readerly expectations. According to John Frow, a genre maintains four structural components: formal features, themes (*topoi*), a situation of address, and rhetorical function (9–10, 81–83). At the level of form, the campaign biography would have been highly recognizable to nineteenth- and early twentieth-century audiences, due to its cheap binding and its liberal use of excerpts from speeches, personal correspondence, and personal as well as political endorsements. Thematically, the genre orbits around equally common tropes, including the self-made man and a reluctance on the part of the candidate to accept the nomination since American voters as well as party operatives from the period had little appetite for outward displays of ambition. The situation of address varies, certainly – not all politicos approach campaigning in precisely the same fashion – but the overarching situation remains more or less the same: a candidate currying favor with a "people." And although the rhetorical function of the campaign biography is never totally moored in place – candidates like Lincoln attempt to appeal to a pragmatic, "Western" sensibility, while other candidates like Theodore Roosevelt aim to "spellbind" potential voters – the genre of the campaign biography nevertheless appears upon first blush to be rather fixed by its constitution.

Yet, like all generic texts, the campaign biography actually exists on a spectrum, from the extremely formulaic to the generally unpredictable. The texts that this book surveys exist across this spectrum, from Wallace's paint-by-number account of Harrison to Lane's novelistic rendition of Herbert Hoover's life on the frontier. I choose to focus upon these authors due in part to their expressed literary commitments as well as their prominence as influential cultural figures. Unlike the less self-reflexive party operatives behind the countless campaign biographies that have circulated at one time or another, these major writers bring to their task a range of concerns that inform overtly artistic final products. Subsequently, neither these authors nor their biographies should be considered representative of the genre as a whole. Nevertheless, these writers do offer templates with which future critics might cross-reference other campaign biographies across the aforementioned spectrum, ranging from relative sameness to a surprising level of inventiveness.

Nonetheless, when scrutinizing the handful of well-known writers under consideration in the pages to follow, some readers will hesitate to use the term literature because – as Tzvetan Todorov argues – the concept of literature appears to be autotelic, which is to say, it ostensibly requires nothing outside of itself to justify its existence. However, to segregate these works from a romanticized sense of literariness advances the faulty argument that we must treat the designation of literariness as an innate "essence" instead of as a specific mode of reading, with specific guideposts and specific cultural baggage. Once we recognize that the campaign biography, like all genres, fosters relatively diverse readerly expectations, we can strip away the preconceived notion that these tracts cannot be conceptualized as literary. A significant part of this discussion revolves around the issue of heuristics. As E.D. Hirsch, Jr. argues, readers usually approach texts by submitting to assumed laws that govern their engagement – that is, a "system of expectations" (77). The reader approaches the campaign biography with a "preliminary generic conception (that proves to be) constitutive of everything that he subsequently understands" (74). Previous interpreters of the campaign biography remain largely "genre-bound," as they enter into their encounter with these works with a host of preconceived notions that dictate their relationship to the genre. In particular, whereas literature is meant to be read through a literary lens – with an assumed emphasis upon the figurative and the symbolic – biographies are frequently meant to be read through a scientific or historical lens. When addressing campaign biographies, then, the intended mode of reading matters a great deal. Darrel Mansell extrapolates upon this difference in his study of a "Great divide" between biography and narrative fiction: the reader does not typically approach a biography with the intention of deciphering complex metaphors or allegories; rather, she recognizes from the start that such a text should be read literally. Most readers do not read Wallace's tract in order to consider Harrison as a symbol; they read the work to consider Harrison objectively, as a well-defined human being. However, Mansell continues, this "Great divide" is in truth never clearly defined, because both modes of writing and reading resort to similar kinds of aesthetic decisions. The idea of a well-defined border between biography and fictional novel, Joanny Moulin argues, "may well never have had any great relevance" (74). Readers of the campaign biography are encouraged to make sense of a scientific-historical account of a real-life candidate as well as to revel in the stuff of national myth, framed by trappings from popular literary movements of the day. This unsettled quality continues today via campaign autobiographies (the subject of the final chapter).

Indeed, even cultural historians that approach the campaign biography by relying heavily upon strict generic taxonomies occasionally concede that the campaign biography possesses literary dimensions, although these scholars never fully follow through on the premise. Brown, for instance, records that the genre of the campaign biography displays a paradox of "pride in lineage ... (versus) the democratic insistence that a man is evaluated upon the basis of what he himself has achieved." Unfortunately, Brown ultimately folds this thought-provoking aside into his dismissal of the genre as mere "propaganda" designed to serve "a definite and immediate purpose" (17, 141). Casper takes Brown's alluring aside one step further when he suggests that readers should not dismiss these unusual artifacts as "monolithic," but instead interrogate their "mixed messages." He ruminates all too briefly upon how the campaign biography reflects "a cultural ideology that (fuses) republicanism, liberalism, and democracy." But in the last tally Casper downplays the value of investigating this amalgamation because, he claims, campaign biographers themselves do not "probe the contradictions between these values" (11, 94, 105). Assuming that adherence to pattern dramatically reduces the possibility of literary intrigue, disparagers of the campaign biography remain for the most part unwilling to venture into this line of criticism, at least beyond the tantalizing, off-handed remarks cited above.

We will try to overcome a general reluctance among the naysayers of the campaign biography to consider ongoing developments in genre theory (an area of study that remains, admittedly, outside of the disciplinary scope of many cultural historians). Although detractors persist in lambasting the genre – "they are boring," Fuller proclaims, "the good campaign biography ... is a myth" – we must not too quickly endorse this recognizable critique, itself bound to a formula that precedes it (n.p.). For their part, students of genre remind us of the ways in which formulaic fiction's incremental changes assist readers in adapting to sociopolitical upheaval, and so the comforts of formula can be said to play a key role in the development of the campaign biography.[9] Familiarity in politics can be a powerful asset. In an age of soft-spoken, apparently dignified candidates that do not stump for themselves, wouldn't electoral politics appear to be less "exciting" *by design*? The fact that most critics of the campaign biography do not take this ritualistic function seriously indicates a broader bias in the academy against formulaic works, because they are perceived as the fruits of a closed imagination, as well as a lack of appreciation for the openness that actually endures within of these tracts.[10] Although the formulaic quality of the campaign biography allows a society to maintain cultural coherence, and assists in easing difficult transitions between regimes, literary interventions analyzed in the chapters to come never merely confirm "our confidence that in the formulaic world things always work out as we want them to" (Cawelti 16).

In the pages that follow, I employ the term genre instead of formula because, while the two terms are often mistakenly rendered as synonymous, the two terms are not actually identical. John Cawelti demonstrates that while formula and genre are closely related, they are in truth "two phases or aspects of a complex process" (7). Formulas are a first stage, in which creators combine a number of fixed conventions, like a log cabin or a refusal to grovel for public office. Genres then manifest in a second stage, in which audiences come to recognize "a set of artistic limitations and potential." A composition within a genre instigates deviations from the "flat standard" of formula in order "to accomplish some unique individual expression or effect" (7). In other words, genres explore the limits as well as potentialities of formulas that become clearer as they develop over time. I prefer the term genre in this context, then, because genre connotes a degree of self-reflexivity. Counter to Casper's contestation, some campaign biographies do in fact "probe the contradictions." In their heightened, literary moments, campaign biographies by writers like Howells or Riis wrestle with the restraints as well as the capacities of the form itself.

While campaign biographers occasionally uphold the arguably less-appealing aspects of formula, such as complacency and uncritical thought, their periodic self-reflexivity suggests a degree of slipperiness. Jacques Derrida considers the classifications of genre as necessary but false demarcations: "As soon as the word 'genre' is sounded ... a limit is drawn" (56). For Derrida, genres are always-already assemblages fueled by an openness to other genres, through an endless string of differences.[11] "At the very moment that a genre (is) broached," he argues, "At that very moment, degenerescence has begun" (66). And the same thing might be said of a candidate for public office: a limit must be drawn and a sense of closure must be delivered to prevent outright anarchy; at the same time, the eventual holder of the office can only ever be a placeholder, the deferral of a new self-image to come. And mercifully so, for democracy could not endure if the campaign biography served instead as a regurgitation of endless certitude. Ernest Fenollosa once said, "There could be no complete sentence ... save one which would take all time to pronounce" (47). The propensity of a genre to probe its own limits and potentialities parallels the propulsion behind democratic discourse itself; in turn, campaign biographies force us to confront the unfolding of this process in forms literary as well as political.

The campaign biography is a genre, like all other genres, comprised of relatively distinctive elements. There is no unitary "essence" in a genre since it remains made up of free-floating, ever-changing ingredients, altered in perpetuity by "situational requirements, strategic responses, and stylistic choices" (Jamieson and Campbell 20). The campaign biography not only reflects the variegated desires of candidates, parties, and interest groups – it also relies upon Mikhail Bakhtin's *heteroglossia*: a plurality of voices that must be contained within a more or less cohesive text, including letters, speeches, and endorsements. Moreover, as minor myth-makers, campaign biographers grapple with a constant conflict between fiction and fact, and their prose can seem novelistic (Lane), evocatively poetic (Riis), or objectively historiographic (Wallace). The *semantics* of two campaign biographies – that is, their stylized window dressing – can be similar, even if their *syntax* – that is, the agenda or lesson learned – widely diverges. For instance, Riis and Wallace employ similar pictorial language to convey dramatically different candidates. In reverse, the semantics of two campaign biographies can be wildly different yet the texts can still depend upon a similar syntax. Howells and Lane, for example, craft extremely distinctive portraits in order to achieve the same end: the lionization of President-managers, Lincoln and Hoover, with little appetite for democratic input. To complicate the supposedly simplistic formula of the campaign biography a bit further, many of these authors cross-pollinate their works with material from dominant as well as minor literary genres, including the dark Romance, the realist novel, the historical Romance, the male friendship narrative, and the prairie story. On the subject of novelists-turned-biographers, Howells observes: "Some witchery of their invention steals into their narrative, and makes us read the delight of their fiction into their fact" ("Autobiography" 796). In sum, critics that discard the campaign biography as a fixed form with a limited artistic function have yet to account for the complexities of genre studies.[12] The pages that follow aim to rectify this oversight.

By resituating the campaign biography in such a fashion, this book looks to expose crucial aspects of the relationship between American politics and literature. Although fictional genres, like democratic discourse as a whole, may appear destined "to escape" from "divisive and agonistic effects," to be granted a catalog status with finality – and although genres remain ostensibly driven, in Fredric Jameson's estimation, to uncover a utopian kernel – this illusion of closure remains fundamentally (im)possible. Like democracy as a form of political expression, literary genres possess an innate (im)perfection that allows them to adapt. A genre remains "essentially contestable," despite countless efforts to strip it down to its "powerfully essentializing" core (Farrell 613, 601). Democracy and literary genres are both, at the level of their constitution, antagonistic; they exist to be transformed rather than canonized. Characterized by its unstable generic profile, the campaign biography is informed by a persistent struggle between fetishistic drift (authoritarian closure; idolatrous) and the deconstructive impulses of democracy (open; iconoclastic).[13]

In Search of the Real

It is important to recognize that literary interventions in the campaign biography initially pick up steam at a moment of heightened literary significance in the United States. Hawthorne, a dark Romantic and the first towering "man of letters" to compose a campaign biography, passes the figurative baton to William Dean Howells, a writer referred to as the progenitor of American realism, who composes one of the most enduring contributions to the genre with his treatment of Lincoln. When situated within this distinctive historical moment, the campaign biographies of Hawthorne and Howells raise questions about the differences as well as similarities between the two dominant strains of American literature, dovetailing in the second half of the nineteenth century: Romanticism and realism. Each of the authors considered in the chapters to follow could reasonably be classified as a realist with a Romantic streak – or, just as plausibly, a Romantic with a realist streak. Many campaign biographies written by literary figures share an investment in what Warner Berthoff names "the realist impulse," or what Jameson calls, in an effort to broaden the scope a bit, the "narrative impulse": an impulse that proves to be both a dead end and a catalyst for aesthetic as well as political "progress" (Berthoff 43; Jameson 8). Through the campaign biography, readers pursue an ever more Real candidate, a candidate that could more directly capture the essence of "the people." Invariably, though, the campaign biography arrives at an imperfect stand-in, thereby kindling the fire of future candidates and future biographies. Emerging from the unsettled waters of American realism and Romance, the campaign biography advocates endless regime change while concurrently repressing the democratic surges that make it possible as both an aesthetic genre and a political exercise.

Through a wide variety of works, including the campaign biography, American realism instigates reform as well as a sense of comfort to accompany social unrest. Berthoff suggests a crucial overlap that I will argue exists between realists and campaign biographers (they are, in fact, routinely one and the same): "Embracing the cause of realism was much like joining an insurgent campaign in American politics. You committed yourself to a radical attack upon existing offenses, to honesty and a clean sweep, to partisan feelings of evangelistic intensity" (2). In effect, every candidate introduces something new to usher out the old, even if the rhetoric ultimately proves hollow in terms of instigating actual policy initiatives. Most campaigns deconstruct the messaging of the previous administration. As Stephen Skowronek states, successful candidates are eternally driven "to establish order anew on his own terms" (20). In pursuit of authenticity – a candidate that truly speaks for "the people" – the campaign biography harnesses a rejection of fixed ideals that have apparently grown stale (the realist's modus operandi). However, a problem that plagues American realism simultaneously plagues the campaign biography: to refuse the current state of things frequently involves sliding into what Howells denounces as "romanticistic" platitudes. When campaign biographers attempt to excavate the genuine "will of the people," to establish a sense of the Real that defies previous chroniclers, they typically wind up erecting new fetishes that are designed to enchant their ideal reader.[14] "The old and clouded Romantic commandments to originality and sincerity," Berthoff observes, are hardly abolished under realism, but "redefined and restored to use" (43). And so even as Hawthorne or Howells break down the flimsy fetishes maintained by earlier politicians, they unconsciously erect novel but equally (im)possible candidates – as well as represented "people" – that must be deconstructed by campaign biographies still to come. Realism and Romanticism blur together in a ceaseless hunt for a "sincere" symbol to serve as the final word, the ultimate Truth, and so the campaign biography in turn highlights America's "realist impulse" as it stirs and stagnates in a given candidate.

In this sense, the book that follows contributes to a growing body of scholarship concerning aesthetics in the age of realism and reform, including recent works by Laura R. Fisher as well as Russ Castronovo. As these critics have shown, during the period of the campaign biography (1820s–1920s), a number of cultural voices attempt to wrest the role of literature from its presumably sheltered place above and beyond political influence. Whereas the first half of the twentieth century witnesses a general distancing of art from social function – recall, for instance, the hugely influential, and ostensibly detached, Boston Brahmin – the second half witnesses a rejuvenated call for treating literature as an essential tool in the kit of democracy. We encounter once more long-standing debates among "men of letters" concerning the "proper" function of aesthetics in American politics. And so the campaign biography parallels an emerging sensibility that underscores the politically transformative possibilities of literary experience. Simply put, the realist novel and the campaign biography both illustrate a heightened correlation between art and politics that emerges in the second half of the nineteenth century.

Many campaign biographies share with American realism a vested interest in fixtures of the Real – that is, proponents of this mode also habitually pursue a "realer Real." Realists claim to debunk the dewy-eyed idealism of Brahmin like Ralph Waldo Emerson in favor of what they frequently view to be "a positive, democratizing development" (Barrish 10). Given this consistent set of concerns, one might surmise that many literary realists gravitate toward the campaign biography because they too engage in vigorous public campaigns to claim ownership over the Real. They too wish to attract a broad array of people on the street, not merely the genteel upper crust, to their cause (or so the story goes). What curious readers uncover in campaign biographies and realist literature from this era, then, is a "recurrent pattern of similarly structured 'my real is more genuinely material than your real' one-upmanship" (155). Literary and political combatants claim, albeit in somewhat different registers, "privileged access to hard, irreducible realities" (8). Of course, Phillip Barrish adds, this presumed Real remains neither "hard" nor "irreducible," as the illusion of absolute access to a candidate is always-already mediated by a rhetorician.[15] In this way, realism speaks to a need for democratic disruption while maintaining an anti-political posture. Realists might recognize the Real to be an ever-receding horizon, but they nevertheless proclaim themselves to have dominion over a fixed Real – namely, the imagined essence behind an ideal figure or a "people." The text's awareness of this internal paradox may explain why most commentators consider Howells's campaign biography of Lincoln to be the most enduring contribution to the genre to date.[16] Howells's "uncertain middle position" between realism and public myth-making marks him as uniquely in tune with the relatively nuanced negotiations required of an effective campaign biographer (Orvell 109). Said another way, Howells's cultivation of a "middle position" likely affords Howells his positive status within a genre that has been almost universally panned by cultural historians and literary critics alike.

The most vocal proponent of realism in the late nineteenth-century United States, Howells forges a relationship to the campaign biography – he writes two of them in his lifetime – that reflects a widespread ambivalence from the *fin-de-siècle*. Specifically, Howells remains "torn between the sin of art and the socially sanctioned imperatives of worldly, 'masculine' success" (Bell 25). Disparagers of Howells lament his attack upon the lack of genuine social function in literature; their critique of Howells once again implies that literature and politics should not be intimate bedfellows. Michael

Davitt Bell faults Howells for being "too political" in his aggressive advocacy for the cause of realism. But Howells remains well aware of the awkward strain between art and politics – a fact confirmed when one places his realist novels into conversation with his campaign biographies (the task undertaken in Chapter 3). Howells oscillates between pursuit of an unspoken Real – the blameless character of Lincoln – and admission of an (im)perfect articulation of this Real – Lincoln as the stuff of hagiography. As the godfather of American realism, Howells declares as well as deconstructs the national mythology via the story of the log-splitter from Illinois. By so doing, Howells positions himself in a turbulent middle between the two fields of realism and Romance (or, the "romanticistic") – a complicated position that he expresses adroitly in his campaign tracts for Lincoln and, to a lesser extent, for Hayes. Since realism remains for Howells always "part of a popular political struggle," we must not discard his campaign biographies as secondary to, or of lesser merit than, his other works (Bell 32). These essential texts evoke a paramount friction within Howells's corpus as well as the evolving project of American realism.

Following in Howells's wake, a cadre of critically ignored but broadly read realists in the second half of the nineteenth century regards fiction as a forum for political intervention. And in one sense, these literary works certainly are political interventions, at least when compared to the relative indifference of the earlier Concord cohort against which Howells defines himself. Alan Trachtenberg remarks, "The literary battle lines were drawn ... on a distinct political terrain. *Realism represented nothing less than the extension of democracy into the precincts of fiction*" (184, emphasis mine). Wrenching themselves free from the cerebral currents of the American Renaissance, many realists engage with society more directly and, in so doing, bypass the affectation of Transcendentalist intellectuals. From a practical perspective, the political and aesthetic marketplaces of the late nineteenth century demand an ever greater appeal to common readers. Howells recognizes this demand very early in his career when he performs on the front porch of candidate James Garfield. Confronted with a widespread perception of literature as disconnected from social concerns and therefore "unproductive," realists like Howells prove their "social worth" by contributing in concrete ways to larger political causes.

However, Daniel Borus contends, we must remember that this cultural shift never actually leads to a "realer Real"; rather, it tends to restore a delusion of fetishized wholeness that runs counter to its outwardly declared dedication to the dynamism of democratic difference. The resultant one-dimensional "fraternal feeling" – fed by a sense of the "unity and naturalness of social life"; conveyed in the synthesis of an ideal candidate and a "people" – does not support a more open-ended political worldview, which is to say, a worldview that reflects the variegated desires of a populace. In contrast, the impression of the Real often forecloses democratic wrangling in favor of a renewed idealism. As American realists in the Howells mold move away from their initial political agenda to debunk icons, seemingly instigated by the push for "more democracy," they tend to install equally deficient fetishes. For Howells, "resorting to Romance was a tacit admission that to become political the writer needed to abandon realism for another form" (Borus 182). The campaign biography affirms the degree to which democracy and demagoguery continue to push and pull against one another in the popular imaginary. It is not terribly surprising, then, that a loose assemblage of realists feels drawn to the genre of the campaign biography – or, that campaign operatives seek the services of popular realists of the day to amplify their campaign's message in the public square.

At an even more significant level, as we survey the successes as well as the failures of realism via the campaign biography, we concurrently probe into the under-acknowledged role of dissatisfaction in American literature as well as politics. Of the realist movement in literature, Borus argues: "The same protest had to be made again and again" (4). As we have already seen, the essential kernel of American realism cannot be isolated from its political or, more specifically, democratic underpinnings. The drive to protest "again and again," to antagonize the fixed icons and ideals of American life, resurfaces in the campaign biography and consequently interrupts a potential drift into "romanticistic" stasis – and so on, ad infinitum. American democracy and American literature persist in a quilted state of ceaseless unrest. Stitched together by the crossing currents of political contest, the genre of the campaign biography unconsciously aims to put an end to its own impetus: to culminate in one final text, one final candidate. But it cannot. Even as it cultivates in readers a profound sense of certainty ("my chosen group alone can see what is Real"), it sustains a niggling suspicion that any given candidate is only ever a momentary placeholder because, if the Real could be fully articulated, the "realist impulse" would surely cease to be – and American democracy as well as American literature would shapeshift into an authoritarian regime. Jules Abels summarizes, "The displacement of officeholders when a new administration came into power was pleasing to the common man" (95). In dialectical fashion, the campaign biography gives form to an avatar for "the people" by tapping into something "more Real," only to undercut itself by broadcasting the futility behind such an endeavor. Howells oscillates between Lincoln the myth and Lincoln the man, finding both versions to be equally unsatisfactory. If the genre of the campaign biography did not actively destroy itself from within, and undercut its own iconoclastic impulses, it would one day find itself no longer necessary. And democracy, that eternally unfulfilled promise, might well follow suit.

To illustrate the perpetual dissatisfaction of the campaign biography, the chapters that follow rely upon a range of political theorists including Chantal Mouffe, Ernesto Laclau, and Jacques Rancière. Since these theorists enable us to understand better the (im)perfect character of the campaign biography and its role in a mercifully (im)perfect society, we must say a brief word about their mode of inquiry and why it remains so instrumental for this study. In a word, the genre of the campaign biography is endowed at its inception with high levels of democratic potential. In form as well as content, it thrives upon a basic assumption of division, a constitutional antagonism: vote for this figure, not this other figure; pursue that "more perfect union" without succumbing to the allure of utopian sentiment. While its degree of intensity may vary, a democratic impetus infuses the pages of the campaign biography with the energy of an open-ended social order.

Yannis Stavrakakis argues that most political expression focuses upon a fantasy in which essential Truths can be absolutely realized: in the case of the campaign biography, a utopian social order in which no further amendments must be made and all individual desires could be fulfilled by a single winning candidate. Authoritarian-leaning structures of governance in particular posit a harmonious promise of total positivity in which all signs of contestation could be purged and all desires fulfilled. But this illusion of fulfillment represses a fundamental reality, aesthetic as well as political: "Democratic politics – and politics in general – can never eliminate conflict and dislocation, antagonism and division" (112). Without question, run-of-the-mill campaign biographies occasionally stifle this constitutional antagonism to pursue the delusion of a perfect candidate, one that could reign forever and satisfy all the desires of a homogeneous constituency. Yet at the same time, the campaign biography – at least in its more literary variations – cannot erase its *raison d'être*: the democratic drive of a society designed to reimagine itself in perpetuity. Critics of the campaign biography have not yet accounted for these moments of disjuncture.

At a root level, aesthetic as well as political dissatisfaction propels these texts because, as we have seen, "no symbolic social construct can ever claim to master the (im)possible Real." The kernel of (im)possibility, almost entirely extinguished in historical biographies by the likes of Parson Weems or Washington Irving (see Chapter 1), shifts the reader's attention away from issues of posterity and the monuments of "great men" to issues that surround a community's self-actualization – "the people," the candidate, and the process that binds them together. The campaign biography may initially appear to be a failure due to its hagiographic tendencies. However, these perceived "failures" blind most critics to sites of vital interest tied to the campaign biography's generic mutability as well as its dynamic relationship with American realism,. Indeed, the genre's "constitutive (im)possibility" encapsulates an indispensable characteristic of America's political discourse as a whole (Stavrakakis 120).

Alexander Hamilton once cautioned his readers to take care with the fantastic dimensions of the Presidential commission and its occupants: "Attempts so extravagant as these to disfigure, or it might rather be said, to metamorphose the object, render it necessary to take an accurate view of its real nature and form" (452–453). Counter to Hamilton, we must not dismiss campaign biographies as mere hagiography, but confront instead the underlying tension between idols and iconoclasm – the very same tension that greases the machinery of American realism. What Raymond Williams describes as the "living tension" of realism enables us to declare the eminently disposable artifact of the campaign biography to be in many cases much more than easy-to-digest *agitprop* (315). Beyond their basic opposition to "idealization or caricature," realists promote "a relation between individuals and society," that is, they incessantly return to the imagined bond between society and individuals (in this case, the candidate for public office) as "a whole indivisible process" (300, 305–306). Williams adds, "In the highest realism, society is seen in fundamentally personal terms, and persons, through relationships, in fundamentally social terms" (314). Moving in a steady, at times unconscious, rhythm between form and formlessness, the campaign biography choreographs this "indivisible process" by transforming society into a singular figure – and then, in turn, transforming this singular figure back into a society.

While it should by now be quite clear to the reader why I use the term literary in the title of this book, I hope it is also becoming apparaent why I employ the term intervention. An intervention is primarily perceived to be extraneous – and American literature has wrongly been viewed as extraneous to politics, a schism that this book interrogates at length. Furthermore, an intervention occurs between events or points in time, and as we shall see, the campaign biography demarcates a period between the hagiographic Era of Good Feelings and our own era of postmodern electoral spectacles. In effect, the genre of the campaign biography reflects an age in which politics and literature might still maintain a productive, if permanently unsettled, relationship, as opposed to the apolitical detachment that precedes and follows the period under review. Similarly, an intervention serves as a kind of intermediary stage, and the campaign biography – at least, at its most interesting – engages the Real and the fetish in dialectical fashion. Finally, and perhaps most significantly for our purposes, to intervene means to prevent or hinder. I wish to argue that the campaign biography interrupts, in the most useful ways, an increasingly unliterary understanding of the political sphere. That is, a reappraisal of the campaign biography encourages us to halt the current propulsion driving campaigns into becoming simulated events entirely devoid of nuance or self-reflection. The phrase literary intervention therefore sets the stakes for a critical return to this nearly obsolete body of work.

As the intimate relationship between realism and the campaign biography affirms, the Real remains always-already displaced and forever standing just out of reach – although the unyielding nature of this search does not deter ambitious writers and politicians for long. Placing the campaign biography into dialogue with genre studies and America's realist turn, two prominent jurisdictions of literary critics, we begin to recognize how these texts follow a political and aesthetic trend of hunting for the (im)possible Real. Caught up in a futile pursuit, the campaign biography exists within a crucial vector between America's literary and political worlds. And, to forecast the conclusion to this book, a gradual loss of the genre's literariness throughout the twentieth and twenty-first centuries reflects profound and troubling changes in contemporary understandings of democracy itself. If readers today wish to reclaim the ever-elusive spirit of democracy in the face of its imminent demise, literary campaign biographies may offer an ideal site at which to rekindle these pressing conversations.

Notes

1 As we craft a definition of the campaign biography, I must acknowledge that the list of texts that I consider at length is not an exhaustive one, and so a word on the more prominent omissions: Richard Hildreth writes a well-known anti-slavery novel as well as the campaign biography for Martin van Buren in 1840, but today he is regarded as a historian rather than a literary mainstay; Fireside Poet John Greenleaf Whittier contributes to a campaign biography for Henry Clay – but because he does so in concert with George Denison, it remains difficult to know exactly where Whittier's influence begins or ends (the issue of "ghostwriting" continues to be a pressing one, especially in the final chapter); elsewhere, the Ulysses S. Grant campaign of 1868 capitalizes upon material from Harriet Beecher Stowe but Stowe's text was written in a different context, for a different audience (her *Men of Our Times* monograph) and so it cannot be considered a campaign biography in the strictest sense of the term; finally, John Hersey – like Stowe – contributes material to the successful campaign of John F. Kennedy, including his laudatory story of Kennedy's wartime heroism, "Survival" (*The New Yorker*, 1944), but here again we find the campaign recycling material from another context to fashion together its own materials, and so we cannot classify Hersey as a "campaign biographer" without a number of qualifications. These examples, while interesting in their own right and illustrative of an ongoing relationship between American literature and politics, muddy the waters of the genre to such an extent that I must regrettably set them aside for the present.
2 This book extends a broader discussion concerning biography as literature. Paula Backscheider notes, "For both narrative and interpretive strategies, biographers draw heavily on literary devices … all biographers borrow what they can from fiction" (7).
3 For an exhaustive bibliography of the campaign biography, see William Miles's *The Image Makers: A Bibliography of American Presidential Campaign Biographies* (Lanham, MD: Scarecrow Press, 1995).
4 Of note, literary critics have also contributed to the genre of the campaign biography, including G.S. Hillard for George B. McClellan and Eugene Didier for James G. Blaine.
5 William Spengemann observes, "As Americanists commonly use the term 'literature' is merely a nominal category for writings that meet their own retroactively imposed criteria of literariness" (145).
6 Although he incorrectly asserts that the genre was established in 1960, Leonard Bushkoff does make an important plea on behalf of the genre as a whole: "Such books, though destined ultimately for remainder tables of yard sales, should not be ignored" (Bushkoff n.p.).
7 An early observer of this tendency, De Tocqueville comments: "Political parties in the United States are led to rally around an individual in order to acquire a tangible shape in the eyes of the crowd and the name of the candidate for President is put forward as the symbol and personification of themselves" (131).
8 For extended examinations of the Presidential campaign, see Eugene Roseboom's *A History of Presidential Elections* (Macmillan, 1968) and Gil Troy and Arthur Schlesinger Jr.'s *History of American Presidential Elections, 1789–2008* (Facts on File, 2011).
9 John Cawelti argues that formula fiction assists audiences in resolving "tensions and 'ambiguities' in a controlled manner. It enables a society to process changes in values while contributing to a necessary sense of "cultural continuity" (35–36).
10 Carolyn Miller outlines a treatment of genre that runs against the closures of formalism. Genres, she writes, are "an open class, with new members evolving, old ones decaying" (153).
11 Paul Hernadi follows a similar turn in genre studies. Rejecting the bugbears of formalism, a new wave of genre theorists prefers to be "descriptive rather than prescriptive, tentative

rather than dogmatic." When we accept the open-endedness of any genre, when we privilege "adaptable concepts" above "ready-made labels," we can more beyond a purely deterministic vision of what the study of genre can produce (7–9).
12 As Robin Wood argues, genre remains "inherently riddled with hopeless contradictions and unresolvable tensions" (61). Contradiction, he insists, is the very heart of genre.
13 It is worth noting that many of these texts did circulate widely and many of them did shape the audience's attitudes toward a candidate. Lincoln, for instance, became known to American readers "chiefly through campaign biographies" (Peterson 9).
14 In his critique of the late works by Georg Lukács, Theodor Adorno writes: "Does he not simply don the dictatorial mantle of socialist realism in order to expound an immutable doctrine which differs from the one he rightly repudiates only by its greater insensitivity?" (162).
15 Joseph Litvak delimits this aesthetic project as accompanied by an "inexplicit but unmistakable effect of sardonic unmasking, along with the strong, lingering odor of bad faith" (qtd. in Barrish, 10).
16 Jill Lepore commends Howells's campaign biography for Lincoln as "the best example of the genre and a cunning parody of it" (n.p.).

Works Cited

Abels, Jules. *The Degeneration of Our Presidential Election: A History and Analysis of an American Institution in Trouble* (New York: Macmillan, 1968).
Adorno, Theodor. "Reconciliation under Duress," in *Aesthetics and Politics* (London: Verso, 2007), pp. 151–177.
Backsheider, Paula. *Reflections on Biography* (Oxford: Oxford University Press, 2001).
Barrish, Phillip. *American Literary Realism, Critical Theory, and Intellectual Prestige, 1880–1995* (Cambridge: Cambridge University Press, 2001).
Bell, Michael. *The Problem of American Realism: Studies in the Cultural History of a Literary Idea* (Chicago, IL: University of Chicago Press, 1993).
Berthoff, Warner. *The Ferment of Realism: American Literature 1884–1919* (New York: Free Press, 1965).
Boller, Paul F. *Presidential Campaigns: From George Washington to George W. Bush*, revised edn (Oxford: Oxford University Press, 2004).
Borus, Daniel. *Writing Realism: Howells, James, and Norris in the Mass Market* (Chapel Hill, NC: University of North Carolina Press, 1989).
Brown, William Burlie. *The People's Choice: The Presidential Image in the Campaign Biography* (Baton Rouge, LA: Louisiana State University Press, 1960).
Brubaker, B.R. "Spoils Appointments of American Writers." *The New England Quarterly*, vol. 48, no. 4, 1975, pp. 556–564.
Bushkoff, Leonard. "Folksy and Friendly Political Portraits, Campaign Biographies." *The Christian Science Monitor*. March 4, 1988. https://www.csmonitor.com/1988/0304/bleny.html. Accessed February 5, 2021.
Casper, Scott E. *Constructing American Lives: Biography and Culture in Nineteenth-Century America* (Chapel Hill, University of North Carolina Press, 1999).
Castronovo, Russ. *Beautiful Democracy: Aesthetics and Anarchy in a Global Era* (Chicago, IL: University of Chicago Press, 2007).
Castronovo, Russ. *Fathering the Nation: American Genealogies of Slavery and Freedom* (Los Angeles, CA: University of California Press, 1996).
Cawelti, John. *Adventure, Mystery and Romance: Formula Stories as Art and Popular Culture* (Chicago, IL: University of Chicago Press, 1977).

Derrida, Jacques, and Avital Ronell. "The Law of Genre." *Critical Inquiry*, vol. 7, no. 1, 1980, pp. 55–81. *JSTOR*, www.jstor.org/stable/1343176. Accessed February 1, 2021.

De Tocqueville, Alexis. *Democracy in America* (Chicago, IL: University of Chicago Press, 2000).

Ellis, Edward S. *From Tent to White House: Or, How a Poor Boy Became President* (Philadelphia, PA: David McKay, 1901).

Farrell, Joseph. "Classical Genre in Theory and Practice." *New Literary History*, vol. 34, no. 3, 2003, pp. 383–408. *JSTOR*, www.jstor.org/stable/20057790. Accessed February 1, 2021.

Fenollosa, Ernest. *The Chinese Written Character as a Medium for Poetry: A Critical Edition* (Fordham, NY: Fordham University Press, 2011).

Frow, John. *Genre*, 2nd edn (New York: Routledge, 2014).

Fuller, Jaime. "A Brief History of Mostly Terrible Campaign Biographies." *LitHub*, September 12, 2009. https://lithub.com/a-brief-history-of-mostly terrible-campaign-biographies/. Accessed February 1, 2021.

Garraty, John. "*The People's Choice: The Presidential Image in the Campaign Biography*. By William Burlie Brown. (Baton Rouge, LA: Louisiana State University Press, 1960. xiv + 178 pp. Illustrations, notes, list of campaign biographies, bibliographical essay, and index. $4.00.)" *Journal of American History*, vol. 47, no. 2, 1960, pp. 358–359.

Hamilton, A., Madison, J., and Jay, J. *The Federalist*, ed. Jacob E.Cooke. Middletown, CN: Wesleyan University Press, 1961.

Hernadi, Paul. *Beyond Genre: New Directions in Literary Classification* (Ithaca, NY: Cornell University Press, 1971).

Hirsch, E.D. *Validity in Interpretation* (New Haven, CT: Yale University Press, 1967).

Howe, Irving. *Politics and the Novel* (New York: Horizon Press, 1957).

Howells, William Dean. "Autobiography, a New Form of Literature," *Harper's Monthly*, October 1909, pp. 795–798.

Hutchison, Anthony. *Writing the Republic: Liberalism and Morality in American Political Fiction* (New York: Columbia University Press, 2007).

Jameson, Fredric. *The Antinomies of Realism* (London: Verso, 2015).

Jamieson, Kathleen Hall. *Packaging the Presidency: A History and Criticism of Presidential Campaign Advertising*, 3rd edn. (Oxford: Oxford University Press, 1996).

Jamieson, Kathleen Hall, and Kohrs Campbell, Karlyn. "Rhetorical Hybrids: Fusions of Generic Elements." *Quarterly Journal of Speech*, vol. 68, no. 2, 1982, pp. 146–157.

Lee, Hermione. *Biography: A Very Short Introduction* (Oxford: Oxford University Press, 2009).

Lepore, Jill. "Bound for Glory: Writing Campaign Lives." *The New Yorker*, October 20, 2008. https://www.newyorker.com/magazine/2008/10/20/bound-for-glory. Accessed February 5, 2021.

Mansell, Darrel. "Unsettling the Colonel's Hash 'Fact' in Autobiography." *Modern Language Quarterly*, vol. 37, no. 2, 1976, pp. 115–132.

Miles, William. *The Image Makers: A Bibliography of American Presidential Campaign Biographies* (Lanham, MD: Scarecrow Press, 1995).

Miller, Carolyn. "Genre as Social Action." *Quarterly Journal of Speech*, vol. 70, no. 2, 1984, pp. 151–167.

Moulin, Joanny. "The Life Effect: Literature Studies and the Biographical Perspective," in *The Biographical Turn: Lives in History*, ed. Hans Renders et al. (New York: Routledge, 2017), pp. 68–79.

Orvell, Miles. *The Real Thing: Imitation and Authenticity in American Culture, 1880–1940* (Chapel Hill, NC: University of North Carolina Press), 2014.

Peterson, Merrill. *Lincoln in American Memory* (Oxford: Oxford University Press, 1994).
Rogers, Pat. "Swift and Bolingbroke on Faction." *Journal of British Studies*, vol. 9, no. 2, 1970, pp. 71–101. *JSTOR*, www.jstor.org/stable/175156. Accessed March 16, 2021.
Skowronek, Stephen. *The Politics Presidents Make: Leadership from John Adams to Bill Clinton*, 2nd edn (Cambridge, MA: Belknap Press, 1997).
Spengemann, William. *A Mirror for Americanists: Reflections on the Idea of American Literature* (Hanover, NH: Dartmouth College Press, 1989).
Stavrakakis, Yannis, *Lacan and the Political* (New York: Routledge, 1999).
Trachtenberg, Alan. *The Incorporation of America: Culture and Society in the Gilded Age* (New York: Hill and Wang, 2007).
Troy, Gil. *See How They Ran: The Changing Role of the Presidential Candidate*, revised and expanded edn (Cambridge, MA: Harvard University Press, 1996).
Whalen-Bridge, John. *Political Fiction and the American Self* (Champagne, IL: University of Illinois Press, 1998).
Williams, Raymond. *The Long Revolution* (New York: Penguin, 1965).
Wood, Robin. "Ideology, Genre, Auteur: 'Shadow of a Doubt'," in *Hitchcock's Films Revisited* (New York: Columbia University Press, 1989), pp. 288–302.

1
PRESIDENTIAL BIOGRAPHIES AND THE KNICKERBOCKERS

While the two modes of writing share a great deal in common, historical biographies – which are sometimes referred to as national biographies – depart in significant ways from their close cousin, the campaign biography. Both variations of the life story depend upon at least the illusion of "authenticity"; both variations can be didactic when they instruct readers on how to live a "good" civic life; and both variations cover up their own ideological agenda under the guise of complete impartiality. And yet, despite their similarities, historical and campaign biographies part company in meaningful ways, as when the historical biography promotes nationalism through seemingly apolitical, self-enclosed memorialization, while the campaign biography cannot shake its democratic underpinnings. Whereas the historical biography often disavows or represses signs of its connection to social arrangement (and rearrangement) by outwardly declaring itself to hover above the vagaries of political contest, the campaign biography, with its characteristic disposability and innately antagonistic form, remains infused with the open-endedness of American politics – an outcome frequently at odds with the professed aims of the historical biographer. By comparing the works of two writers from the Knickerbocker Group, a loose literary assembly from New York in the early nineteenth century – Washington Irving's historical biography *The Life of George Washington* (published in five volumes from 1853 to 1859) and Epes Sargent's campaign biography *The Life and Public Service of Henry Clay* (1844) – readers can illuminate the unique political dynamism of the latter genre.

To start, nineteenth-century America experiences what Scott E. Casper describes as "Biographical Mania." Writers and readers alike seize upon this mode of writing to bolster a fledgling national history and advocate for certain civic values through the celebration of "great" or, in Ralph Waldo Emerson's terms, "representative" men. Casper comments, "Biography (has) constructive, cultural

DOI: 10.4324/9781003132448-2

purposes" (3). By modeling "proper" behavior, the stories of these so-called exemplary figures successfully stir patriotic sentiment, thus attracting prominent writers like Jared Sparks to the newfound initiative of "biographical nationalism" (4). However, as Casper demonstrates, these biographies do not always follow an identical blueprint. Unlike the many other dalliances in biography throughout the nineteenth century, campaign biographies, due in part to their heightened partisan agendas, promote "a concept of the public sphere that (fuses) earlier republican notions with newer ideas of liberal democracy" (78). In other words, although the campaign biography echoes its historical cousin by routinely romanticizing the candidate and elevating him above the fray, the genre of necessity also reflects the profound impact of democratic wrangling upon the young nation's imaginary. As opposed to Irving's maturation within the Era of Good Feelings, in which "the choice of the President would be two steps removed from the folly of the people," the campaign biography is born alongside the Jacksonian moment of the 1820s, in which "the selection of Presidential electors was shifted from state legislatures to the people, as the belief flowered, enforced by his vote, that the government belonged to the common man" (Abels 79, 216). The genre of the campaign biography correspondingly encourages greater democratic engagement by including, at least in theory, more readers in the electoral process: "Any young man who could read could rise" (Casper 106). Moreover, campaign biographers cannot remove their subject from the tumultuous *demos* to laud them as floating, disembedded individuals because the candidate at the center of the stage must be made to serve as an avatar for "the people." The campaign biography, then, unfolds in acutely relational terms – underscoring connections between a body politic and its chosen representative. William Holland, an early biographer for candidate Martin Van Buren, remarks upon his own goal "to exhibit by the history of an individual, the nature of the relation which that party sustains to its public men" (79–80). Put a bit differently, the campaign biography tracks the dialectical bonds of private and public lives: a sustained negotiation between the always-changing political apparatus, ever-volatile communal ideals, and inner workings of subject formation. Readers encounter in this largely forgotten genre a tenuous link between the relatively fixed façade of political demigods and the forever shifting contours of an evolving "collective consciousness." Through their generic titles alone – such as "*The Life and Public Services* of Henry Clay" – these texts alert readers to the genre's interplay between an individual life and the public sphere.

In contrast, many nineteenth-century biographies do not require such a relational element, at least in ways that go beyond the purely gestural. As the century progresses, there is a growing appetite for historical societies as well as the commemoration of the early republic's major sites. Whereas biographies from the first half of the century tend to privilege moral instruction over scientific authority, the second half of the century inaugurates a much stronger emphasis upon archival materials and the value of "authenticity" (Casper 141). Perhaps not surprisingly, the discipline of American historiography slowly codifies in parallel with shifts in the art of biography. Irving's treatment of George Washington exists in a sort of liminal space between the biographical style of the early republic in which he was raised and the style of a post-Civil War era that is about to dawn. On the one hand, Irving presents the first President through "grand, archetypal virtues" instead of through careful analysis of the man's underlying humanity; on the other hand, Irving proves relentless in his documentation, and he strips away almost all signs of his earlier interest in myth-making in order to provide what he feels to be an honest, unvarnished account of Washington's life (90). *The Life of George Washington* therefore tells us a good deal about conflicting approaches to biography in nineteenth-century America. Straddling the Romantic and scientific modes, Irving creates a starkly different portrait of a President than Sargent and various other campaign biographers by deliberately distancing his hagiographic subject from "the people." Hermione Lee writes, "To set one Great Life centre-stage can be read as … consolidating a hierarchical, anti-egalitarian social structure" (14). In effect, through his reliance upon archetype as well as archive, Irving crafts a stubbornly undemocratic image of the office as well as its holder. When we place his historical biography into dialogue with the campaign biography, we can address some of the most important tensions that characterize early America's literature as well as the fledgling nation's political discourse.

Irving's President Without Politics

Despite his protestations against the designation, Washington Irving must be regarded as a political writer, which is to say, a writer with a clear political agenda that surfaces frequently in his prose. Irving serves as a seasoned diplomat overseas – first as Secretary to Legation in London (1829–1832) and then as Minister to Spain (1842) – and he fights vigorously for issues as diverse as international copyright law and the establishment of the Oregon Territory. In his lifetime, he confers regularly with Presidents including Thomas Jefferson, Andrew Jackson, and his close friend, Martin Van Buren. As we shall see, Irving habitually takes up topics that are expressly political in nature, in his late nonfiction as well as his earlier fantastical stories. It should come as little surprise, then, that when he retires to his New York home, Sunnyside, at the twilight of his career, Irving turns his attention not to strictly literary pursuits, but to a voluminous biography of the country's first President. However, Irving's politics are hardly straightforward. As he ages, Andrew Burstein writes, Irving ostensibly has "less and less to say about national politics" – although he maintains familiar relations with "just about everyone in high office" (319). Despite his status as a well-connected politico, America's first literary celebrity cares surprisingly little for the significant political debates of his day. *The Life of George Washington* ostensibly reflects the later Irving's relative indifference to politics and, more specifically, to the demands of democracy – a stance, we must acknowledge, that remains definitively political in nature. Irving thus practices the evergreen strategy in American politics of appearing to be apolitical in order to achieve certain political ends.

According to Henry Canby, to understand Irving's superficial indifference to the political discourse of his nation is to recognize simultaneously his longstanding Federalism.[1] "Irving," Canby insists, "represent(s) the Federalist spirit in American literature … (an) aristocratic feeling" (77). Raised in New York – the epicenter of Federalism in the early Republic – Irving eyes the concept of democracy with relative distaste. In the first decades of the nation's history, elections are very far from inclusive affairs, since only a very small percentage of the electorate can vote. Notably, George Washington does not ascend to higher office on a wave of popular support (although he was, of course, enormously popular); rather, he serves at the discretion of a cadre of elites. Given the climate of the United States during his evolution as an artist, a so-called Era of Good Feelings in which Presidents are appointed more than elected, it is perhaps obvious why a writer like Irving does not gravitate toward the genre of the campaign biography – and, in turn, why he prefers the genre of historical biography, in which a single, well-informed authority figure curates public memory. Ever the "arch-Federalist," Irving attacks the concept of democracy throughout his career, re-enforcing for literary critics the preconceived notion that he does not "take politics seriously" (79).[2] Yet it is not that he becomes apolitical as he ages – again, there is no such thing as being apolitical; he instead anchors himself ever more securely to his belief in an authoritarian politics with ever fewer public displays of partisanship.

What characterizes a "Federalist style" of literature? For one, Irving appears to be a "stylist," not "a man bursting with ideas" (72). That is, he views literature less as a democratic instrument or a political tool than as a purely aesthetic exercise. Similarly, Irving turns to burlesque comedy in order to avoid conveying concrete convictions, the cost of sharper-edged satire: "Irving had a deep personal revulsion to politics, and he tended to express or exercise his disgust through invective or burlesque comedy" (Roth 63). By making fun of anything and everything, he outwardly evades political engagement. Irving's brand of political writing involves the denunciation of engagement by "the people." Martin Roth points to the target of Irving's *A History of New York*, published under the pseudonym of Diedrich Knickerbocker in 1809: "The overall haranguing nature of American politics with its town meetings, election meetings, holiday speeches, and tavern and street corner arguments" (73). In a word, Irving's Federalist style represses signs of democratic discord by highlighting an all-encompassing sense of absurdity among citizens that maintain, erroneously, that they are entitled to participate in governing their nation.

Donna Hagensick outlines how Irving's antidemocratic approach manifests throughout Irving's fiction. By displaying "a kind of non-thinking attitude toward politics," the Knickerbocker seemingly gestures at political problems without offering solutions (179). It is apparently enough for him to scoff and ridicule the masses. Moreover, his stories suggest a need to protect the rights and property of the wealthy class while degrading "the common people." Hagensick records Irving's acute "fear of the mob achieving political victory when it was ill-equipped to govern" (181). Although it seemingly lacks genuine political convictions, Irving's fiction does sustain at least one major tenet: an active disavowal of the *demos*. According to Hagensick, the author's disinterest allows him, not unlike George Washington himself, "to transcend party considerations in the interests of nationalism" (189). However, a pressing question arises: what is "nationalism" without faith in the populace that comprises a nation? Or, more to the point, what is politics without "party considerations," given the reality that politics without discord is not politics at all? Irving's Federalist style infects his fiction as well as his historical biography of the President, and to examine this mode of writing will enable us to understand better through contrast the unique characteristics of the lesser-known campaign biography.

Let us briefly consider two of Irving's most enduring fictional tales to underscore the utter pervasiveness of the author's "arch-Federalism": "The Legend of Sleepy Hollow" and "Rip Van Winkle," both included in the 1820 collection, *The Sketchbook of Geoffrey Crayon, Gent*. In "The Legend of Sleepy Hollow," a backwards Dutch village mocks the new schoolmaster, Ichabod Crane, a petty tyrant who holds "absolute sway" over his "little empire," as well as his provincial neighbors that do not possess the mental acuity required to imagine "beyond the boundaries" of their own farms (35, 38). On one level, "Legend" mocks both sides of the political spectrum, master and slave alike, as a burlesque tale unwilling (or unable) to establish a direct political message. In a humorous postscript, the storyteller Mr. Knickerbocker admits that the preceding story is "extravagant" but encourages readers to "take a joke as we find it" (55–56).

Importantly, though, "Legend" circles back frequently to undermine the provincial townsfolk without a sustained critique of the ruling class. In the end, Crane proves little more than an imposter; he too believes in foolish superstitions and lacks the cultural refinement to appreciate "sweetness and light." Irving's mock "man of letters" remains nothing but an overhyped simpleton. In the final tally, all of Irving's commoners prove to be greedy, lecherous, violent, and uncouth. The narrative ridicules the notion that any of these bumpkins would ever be a worthy subject of American history or literature – an insult that Irving further accentuates by comparing the village's laughably small-minded affairs with the grandeur of Greek mythology and chivalric quests. "Legend" debunks its initial Romantic overtones by exposing the unflattering reality of a community that inflates its own Revolutionary legacy beyond recognition:

> The British and American line had run near (the village) down the way; it had, therefore, been the scene of marauding, and infested with refugees, cowboys, and all kinds of border chivalry. Just sufficient time has elapsed to enable each story-teller to dress up his tale with a little becoming fiction. (47)

Irving tells of quixotic "knights" doomed to insignificance – "little wooden warriors ... valiantly fighting the wind" – and "vegetating" rubes that refuse, at last, to educate themselves (41, 33). After Crane's mysterious disappearance, Irving's provincial posers allow the schoolhouse to fall into a state of abject disrepair. "Legend" exclusively guffaws at cloddish locals due to their innate ability to advance themselves or their "little society."

In a similar way, although "Rip Van Winkle" ostensibly satirizes the master – in this case, Rip's shrew of a wife – as well as the slave – a henpecked husband that strikes readers as a lazy, unworthy lout – the story ultimately only targets hapless rural residents. The text uses the nearby tavern sign to suggest that nothing ever really changes: society easily swaps the old king (George III) for a new king (George Washington). All such a change requires is a slapdash coat of paint, from red coat to blue, and a bit of creative editing to turn a scepter into a sword. In one sense, even as this tale tracks a dramatic transformation from pre-Revolution to post-Revolution, the general absence of meaningful difference prompts Irving's readers to laugh at the follies of men both powerful and weak. Nonetheless, this apolitical burlesque offers a significant political commentary: Irving's object of ridicule is once more the very notion of democratic engagement. The story takes pains to depict the rabble and its futile political chatter: "How sagely they would deliberate upon political events some months after they had to take place" (5). Irving's readers encounter "a lean, bilious-looking fellow ... haranguing vehemently about rights of citizens – elections – members of congress – liberty – Bunker's Hill ... a perfect Babylonish jargon" (10). When Rip Van Winkle returns to regale his neighbors with the fantastic story of his remarkable slumber, his new neighbors can only think to ask him about whether "he was Federal or Democrat" (11). Unmoved by his astonishing yarn, the quotidian crowd dissolves and launches back into "the more important concerns of the election" (13). If we can classify Rip as a hero, it is because he does not consider himself to be "a politician" and because "the changes of states and empires made but little impression on him" (14). In other words, the only thing to recommend this yokel to Irving's reader is his boredom with political strife, since he alone finds amusement in the face of helplessly pugnacious pundits. It thus remains difficult to interpret "Rip Van Winkle" as anything more than an invitation for "the people" to idle indefinitely and to allow "better" individuals to conduct the important business of running the country. Irving's best-known fictions assume an arch-Federalist posture by diminishing the role of democracy, which is to say, by delegitimizing the notion that citizens ought to govern themselves.

On the surface, Irving's final work *The Life of George Washington* shares precious little with the burlesque tales of his youth. For one, Irving's historical biography of Washington – which can be cataloged beside contemporaneous works by Parson Weems or John Marshall – demands greater sincerity (there is almost none of the metacommentary upon myth-making that Irving's readers find in, say, *The History of New York*) as well as a stronger sense of veracity. As a genre, the historical biography involves a subject sincerely standing in for "a debate about national myths and character" (Lee 107). For some critics, Irving's hagiographic text offers little more than sycophantic idolatry at the feet of a Founding Father. Its privileging of "honesty" lacks the charm that characterizes Irving's earlier, fanciful yarns. The form of the historical biography removes what most readers appreciate about the rest of Irving's oeuvre: "The *Life* does not ... have the charm that characterizes many of Irving's writings. In judging it, the reader must consider the wide difference between this subject and the romantic themes with which the author was most at his ease" (Bryan 105).[3] But the generic distinctions between his early and later publications obscure a unifying thread: namely, the fact that Irving incessantly degrades American democracy. Writing in the genre of the historical biography, Irving simply amplifies his initial critique of "the people" by divorcing the "great man" of Washington from the public that he purportedly serves. On this front, Irving's contribution to the genre is hardly unique; in its idolatrous treatment of a "great man," Irving follows the template of numerous biographies of "exceptional men" from the early Republic. And yet, while many preceding biographies "contrasted American manners and beliefs favorably against English ones," Irving's *Life* does quite the opposite by admiring Europe at the expense of America. Elsewhere, historical biographers aim to "improve" readers, to "stir the reader's own patriotism and hatred of tyranny" (Casper 36, 31). Irving's contribution to the genre departs quite dramatically from this generic pattern. The text does not stir "patriotism" so much as it stirs the actions of a single man, and it longs for a kind of benevolent tyranny. In short, Irving's arch-Federalist style, when fused with the structure of the historical biography, mutates fundamental elements of the genre by isolating a solitary hero (Washington) from his historical context as well as the contemporary community that venerates him. Irving's *Life* erases almost all traces of participatory governance – the impetus behind campaign biographies – in order to present a static, unmoving portrait of the nation's most iconic President.

Irving's Washington rules with an impersonal calculus instead of a political mandate from "the people." The Knickerbocker depicts Washington as a manager that establishes private property lines on the frontier during his first career as a land surveyor. In *Life*, Washington remains fundamentally "unromantic," with "an eye to the profitable rather than the poetical" (9, 14). The frontier provides Irving with an ideal backdrop against which to stress certain aspects of Washington's personality, as when the future Commander-in-Chief "tones up" his mind to discipline "the careless and self-indulgent habitudes of the wilderness" (17). At the same time, Irving evokes nostalgia for the "good old days" in Virginia, when patriarchs oversaw their manors and there existed no "turbulent factions," no "fierce democracy," and no "fermenting populace" (27). Irving's historical biography expresses a degree of fondness for feudal America with its rigid hierarchies. Indeed, his biography rarely expresses any contempt for the British, with a few exceptions, suggesting instead a strongly felt admiration for the colonial mindset.[4] The character of Washington, unimpressed by his own troops, finds delight in watching the "perfect order" of his British opponents: "A well-disciplined European army marching in high confidence" (66–67). Later, the character of Washington explains his sustained friendships with British aristocrats by lauding "the well-bred decorum that seemed to quiet the turbulence of popular excitements" (140). If a majority of American biographies of "great men" from the nineteenth century intend to inculcate patriotic sentiment and a love of nation, Irving's contribution proves to be an anomaly thanks to its refusal to regard most Americans as "patriots." It describes instead a fledgling society that possesses a lone figure to recommend it: Washington.

In Irving's account, what separates Washington from the rest of the rabble remains his remarkable composure. The leader displays a "manly" indifference to "personal indulgences" (59). As an icon of managerial excellence, he "kept his own accounts, posted up his books and balanced them with mercantile exactness" (111). Irving augments admiration for Washington's character through his use of the President's personal journals and correspondences. These first-hand documents play a dual role in *Life*: they both uphold a popular vision of Washington as absolutely honest and forthcoming and, at the same time, they stress the scientific impartiality of historical biography itself: "No greater proof need be given of the rectitude of that heart than the clearness and fullness with which, in these truthful documents, every thought and feeling is laid open" (199). The text gushes: "How precious are those letters! (They are) the outpourings of Washington's heart" (225). That is, as Irving perpetuates the illusion of Washington's blameless life as well as the illusion of Irving's own unprejudiced methodology as a biographer, he further disconnects the "great man" from the expectations of the electorate.

Washington stands out as a father-figure to the young country and a warrior without blemish. For example, he attempts to shield his soldiers from the ever-lingering depravations of camp, and he alone lifts up the troops in times of trouble: "It was a difficult task for Washington to 'keep the life and soul of the army together' ... he had breathed his own spirit of perseverance in his yeoman soldiery" (358, 455). For this American Fabius, to spare the road means spoiling the child – a belief that underscores the undemocratic outlook of the first President. Given its status as hagiography, of course, it comes as no surprise that Irving heaps praise upon his subject; historical biographies of this sort habitually romanticize the individual at the expense of historical veracity. However, Irving's *Life* not only elevates Washington above his peers, an ethically questionable choice in its own right; it does so by bludgeoning the character of "the American public." Irving's readers witness what happens when the general drift of historical biography – into solitary "great men," without tethers to connect them to the rest of humanity – reaches it extreme, fundamentally reducing the depths of history and politics into a one-dimensional caricature.

On a related note, it perhaps strikes the contemporary reader as a bit strange that Irving focuses so much of his attention on stories of treason during the Revolution. He pursues at great length tangential plots involving figures such as Lord Howe and Benedict Arnold. While readers will no doubt recognize the significance of these figures on early American history, why does Irving opt to linger upon stories of treason instead of other possible subplots? Indeed, *Life* can be characterized as a story in which treason lurks behind every corner. The biography describes the troops as being only respectful to commanding officers "of their own choice," and acting as men "strongly imbued with the spirit of insubordination" (173, 184). Irving's reader is meant to appreciate Washington all the more because he runs down a veritable gauntlet of mutineers. Why is it that Irving's reader almost exclusively eyes American soldiers with grave suspicion? Irving writes gloomily, "The touch of a feather might turn them" (626).

Life expresses revulsion at "the common people" that serve in Washington's army, and it does so to such a degree that a full survey of the instances would consume far more pages than this book could accommodate, so a brief overview will have to suffice. On prospective soldiers: "Some may be tempted by love of adventure, but in general they require some prospect of ultimate advantage that may 'better their condition'" (28). Over and over again, Irving dwells upon the selfish impulses of the yeoman soldiery.[5] Captains cannot compel soldiers to do anything without "a shilling sterling a day"; the men will not even assist Washington with his luggage unless they are "paid liberally" (40–41). Rarely in other hagiographic texts concerning the American Revolution do authors attend to the revolutionaries as agents acting on behalf of their own self-interest; Irving does so relentlessly. When the purse strings tighten, soldiers "refused to serve any longer, (and they) disbanded themselves" (46). Washington shakes his head in dismay as soldiers randomly shoot one another due to their gross incompetence.

> The garrison were merely amusing themselves firing at a mark or for wagers. In this way they would waste their ammunition as freely as they did their provisions ... how lively a picture does this give of the militia system at all times when not subjected to strict military law. (91)

While these unflattering portrayals may be historically accurate to some extent, we must wonder why Irving feels compelled to include so much incriminating evidence against native citizens, far more than would be required to establish Washington's exceptionalism as a point of contrast. The famous Knickerbocker depicts the troops as fickle, sensitive, and generally worthless. Appearing to side with the harsh appraisal of the British, Irving declares that the name "Boston Massacre" is in truth "an opprobrious and somewhat extravagant name," because the "massacre" itself was a rather measured response to the "rash and intemperate proceeding of a mob" (135, 137). When left to their own devices, Irving writes, "the provincials ... acted from individual impulse, without much concert" (162). Irving belittles "the people" mercilessly: "Washington made repeated and animated appeals to their patriotism. They were almost unheeded. He caused popular and patriotic songs to be sung about the camp. They passed by like the idle wind" (214). In one sense, this constant attack sets up the biography's concluding message: democracy does not work.

Irving recounts the American people as over-heated throngs that lack all judgment. He paints a picture of a mob zealously tearing down a monument to King George:

> Since kingly rule is at an end, why retain its effigy? ... The status was pulled down amid the shouts of the multitude ... Washington censured it in general orders as having much the appearance of a riot and a want of discipline ... irregularities ... vulgar passions and perturbations. (247)

Life petitions for more effigies, such as the one that it erects on behalf of the first President. And in so doing, Irving's biography makes the case for less input from the masses, since these yokels clearly do not have a clue as to how to govern themselves. Washington must perpetually leave his beloved Virginian home of Mount Vernon to clean up the mess made by ignorant and uncivilized citizens. Against "the lethargy that seemed to deaden the public mind," Washington must return – constantly, until his death – to inspire a better Union (490). But what kind of nationalism has no patience for a citizenry? And what kind of patriotism can endure when only one man truly deserves the title of "patriot"? Simply put, *Life* cultivates a Presidency without politics.

Although in Irving's time readers had already long consumed the analogy of Washington as Cincinnatus – the Roman that gave up his own power to circumvent tyranny – the difference between Washington and his Roman predecessor, at least in Irving's narrative, could not be starker. After all, Irving's version of Washington could not truly wish to cede power to "the people" because he so adamantly distrusts them. The Jefferson/Hamilton feud characterizes the nation's precariousness; only Washington can reconcile the "warring parties" and "overrule any occasional discord" (676, 666). Of note, Irving's plea for "consensus" resonates with his unique political climate: in the buildup to the Civil War, the Knickerbocker advocates for a soothing balm to the public mind's "alarming state of ferment" (682). Yet Irving's politics actively deconstructs itself as the biography's not-so-subtle love of tyranny undercuts the very premise of Revolution and, in turn, the very premise of the political – that is, the constitutive antagonism of individuals with different interests. The great fiction of Irving's historical biography remains its reliance upon a fetish (the Commander-in-Chief) to bypass the part of human nature that cannot be fully managed or put to rest: the openness required of democratic struggle. Against the democratic impulse, historical biography aspires to canonization, to marble halls and gallery walls, to political and literary styles defined by arch-Federalism.

However, despite the text's best efforts to foreclose this innate open-endedness, it inevitably fails to achieve the (im)possible. Even as regulation and rigidity shape the contours of *Life*, unconscious traces still exist of a fundamental incompleteness – an underlying inability to be conceptually closed off. By stressing his own compliance with a broader drive to commemoration, Irving inadvertently makes good on the promise of his earlier metacritiques by alerting his reader to the fact that his own project is unnatural (read: constructed). In effect, *Life* acknowledges the futility of recovering a lost past by tacitly admitting that its biographical aim may be an (im)possible one: "A stone marks the site of the house, and an inscription denotes its being the birthplace of Washington ... the site is only to be traced by fragments of bricks, china and earthenware" (4). The text further accentuates a gap between a retrievable past and its own hopeless mission of preservation by lingering on moments of rot and decay – the "mouldering" of an important historical place; the bones of fallen soldiers, "mementoes of former disasters ... whitening in the sun" (17, 106). Irving' historical biography similarly highlights the effectiveness of propaganda, as when it tells the tale of a French leader that was killed in battle and how, subsequently, "his fate was made the subject of lamentation in prose and verse – *chiefly through political motives*" (35, emphasis mine). *Life* periodically reveals its own "inauthenticity" and deconstructs its own paralyzing edicts of consensus by gesturing at Washington's political acumen. His "soft manner," for instance, appears "calculated to win favor in ladies' eyes" (11). The future President is seen – rather petulantly, given the tenor of the rest of the book – refusing to participate in the war without receiving a higher rank. When he rides through towns, his "personal appearance was ... calculated to captivate the public eye," a preoccupation that implies that Washington can be "goaded" by the electorate instead of standing apart on some higher, disconnected plane (180, 224). Even as Irving flaunts the President's patriotism without payment, he slides however unaware into an occasional, subtle critique of the very mythos that he is making: "Washington found it more necessary than usual ... to assert his superior command from the attempts which were being made to weaken his stand in the public estimation" (446). In these admittedly rare moments, *Life* underscores its own flamboyance by offering a sort of Presidential *memento mori*, one that stresses the limitations of hagiography. It also dwells upon Washington's implicit endorsement of political wrangling via the President's shrewdly calculated performances. In both cases, the incompleteness of democratic politics – indeed, of politics itself – endures in the face of mere stone monuments.

But Irving's *Life* only hints obliquely at these conceptual openings. For the vast majority of his historical biography, Washington exists as a mythical figure, far above public reproach or democratic engagement. When Irving states with finality that Washington's memory "remains a national property," we must inquire: what exactly does this "ownership" look like? Do "the people" have recourse to this public memory? Surely it cannot be surmised in Irving's context that the electorate "owns" Washington (718). It seems much more plausible to conclude that the memory of Washington "owns" the nation since, in arch-Federalist style, the central figure remains an icon to be worshipped by the populace. Washington appears in this text to be a "public character" acting in a "great drama," intimately "connected with the history of his country" (1). By suturing the presumed metaphysics behind Washington's ascent to the metaphysics supposedly guiding the Revolution, Irving diminishes the most significant aspects of the Revolutionary event and Washington's response: its unexpectedness; its ability to disrupt the status quo; the stubborn fact that the Revolution itself stems from acute political differences, not soothing similarities or ill-gotten consensus.[6] In Irving's hands, American history becomes attenuated as it is thoroughly depoliticized.

As we turn to the campaign biography, we might recall that biography at its most potent tracks a "people" *in process*, which is to say, it wrestles with the dynamic intersection of individuals, their societies, and the political ideas that bind or dissolve them. Whereas Irving's historical biography of the President refuses to budge its stationary subject, the campaign biography must engage on some level with a construction of "the people." True, these works can be hagiographic, and they frequently aspire to provide the "final word" on American politics. Nonetheless, the notion of "the people," of democratic contest freed from Federalist indifference, can never be expunged from this genre to the degree that Irving exorcises it from the stony monument that he dedicates to Washington, in its state of fixity, of symbolic rigor mortis. Irving's historical biography dispenses visions of degradation and death while the pulse of the campaign biography continues to race.

Epes Sargent and the Presidency as Public Service

We should not conclude from the preceding section that historical biographies in nineteenth-century America are universally apolitical.[7] Irving's contribution to the genre offers but a single example, relatively exceptional in its arch-Federalist rebuke of democracy. Once more, even Irving's *Life* retains a clear political agenda: to reverse the nation's trajectory into an increasingly likely Civil War by promoting a consensus forged by elites. But it would be equally fallacious to conclude from the preceding section that there is no significant difference between nineteenth-century historical biography and its cousin, the campaign biography. While the historical biography dwells at length upon issues of posterity and "great men," relatively unmoved by the pressures of any given moment, the campaign biography habitually addresses a community's self-actualization – that is, "the people," the candidate, and the process that binds them together. Written around the same time period, and by an author categorized within the same literary group (the Knickerbockers), Epes Sargent's *The Life and Public Service of Henry Clay* illuminates the democratic underpinnings of the campaign biography.[8]

Irving biographer Brian Jay Jones advances a faulty claim that may help us to clarify this distinction between historical and campaign biographies. He writes, "Washington Irving had never set out to write for posterity, as Longfellow might argue. Irving, like Shakespeare, wrote for the masses" (409). Based upon the reading of Irving's work offered in the preceding section, Jones's position promptly proves untenable: Irving's *Life* remains a text saturated with concerns over posterity – for the image of the first President as well as his own image at the twilight of his career. Moreover, the argument that Irving writes "for the masses" cannot be backed up by a sustained analysis of his work. Although his output remains quite popular, to be "popular" is not automatically synonymous with being composed on behalf of, or in significant dialogue with, "the people." Irving's Federalist style, in tandem with his burlesque sensibilities, overtly distances itself from the *demos* by striving to be twice as clever, twice as hallowed, as the so-called common reader. Meanwhile, Sargent better fits the description advanced by Jones: a dedicated Democrat, Sargent spends much of his life advocating for better educational institutions for the populace.[9] Closely aligned with his friend, correspondent, and fellow Democrat, Nathaniel Hawthorne, Sargent proves to be much more "of the moment" during the American Renaissance than Irving, in part because he – like so many of his contemporaries – relies heavily upon Shakespeare as a well-spring of ideas for his poetry, drama, and prose. His campaign biography for the well-known Senator Henry Clay, a friend that he meets while serving as a Washington correspondent with Boston's *Daily Atlas*, affirms Sargent's dialectical engagement with "the masses," an approach that stands in stark contrast to Irving's arch-Federalism. Of note, Sargent's biography is known to have been Clay's personal favorite of his biographies. Admittedly, it would be as much of a mistake to read Sargent as a true "man of the people" as it would be to read Hawthorne as an unconflicted voice for American democracy. Indeed, internal struggle over the issue of how much democracy would be "too much" characterizes their respective bodies of work. Nevertheless, by engaging with Sargent's ignored tract for Clay's Presidential run, we start to understand why writers overtly invested in the concept of democracy in theory as well as praxis, like Hawthorne and Sargent, gravitate toward the genre of the campaign biography, while writers like Irving seem more regularly drawn to historical biography.

Sargent's *Fleetwood; Or, The Stain of Birth: A Novel of American Life* (1845) follows a pair of lovers as they navigate a gauntlet of aristocratic behavior until they at last arrive in each other's arms, at which point the female protagonist, a former orphan named Adelaide, perishes. Thanks to its emphasis on performativity, re-enforced by countless Shakespeare references, *Fleetwood* is written like a play, driven extensively by dialogue and dwelling upon the idea that all of the world remains a stage. Through this focus on performativity, Sargent's text exposes European-style aristocracy to be false, thereby achieving a levelling effect, a sense that human beings are at their core equal, regardless of their financial status. Concerning well-bred protagonist Fleetwood, the narrator wonders:

> Should he, the last of his race, although tracing back his lineage to the best blood of England and France, should he select for the mother of his children one upon whose genealogy charity would always have to drop her veil. (37)

While most of the unsavory social alignments in the novel thinly disguise a profit motive, Sargent's text ultimately gestures at something that it positions as the Real – an "authentic" interconnectivity beneath the surface of a selfish world.

Sargent fills his narrative with charitable actions that illuminate the power of interdependence. For instance, Adelaide receives protection from a family of German immigrants, even though she is "a stranger, an outcast" (160). Adelaide later recalls what it means to be an orphan when she adopts another young orphan in order to ensure the orphan's education and to provide her with future opportunities. Although we must be careful not to overstate the magnitude of the democratic impetus behind *Fleetwood* (for one, the story takes time to reject the utopian socialism of Charles Fourier), when we contrast this novel – characterized by a drive to level "the people" and to promote charitable enterprises for the less fortunate – with Irving's "apolitical" work, stark distinctions emerge.

In addition to a Shakespearean emphasis upon false appearances, Sargent's *Fleetwood* may strike readers as Dickensian when it forges invisible bonds between vulnerable individuals, typically orphans, and the fraternal chains that connect strangers. This elective unity unfolds as the narrative encompasses its well-meaning characters into a vast tapestry: "You shall supply the place of parents, sisters, brothers" (42). Unlike Irving's burlesques, which laugh at anything and everything, Sargent's more democratically-oriented prose attempts to posit a genuine sense of togetherness, a sense that any member of society is as valuable as any other member – a belief that the author wishes to be viewed with earnestness rather than cynicism. Sargent routinely starts his narratives with a traumatic loss that must be confronted and resolved through benevolent (re) union. At the open of *Fleetwood*, a father perishes in a freak accident, and Sargent dedicates the remainder of the novel to finding a suitable replacement. Underscoring the promise of democracy, traditional visual cues of authority or deference are always suspect for Sargent, since anyone could theoretically rise into the position of the father. The power of what is absent or lacking continually reminds Sargent's reader that love and grace, not hierarchy and discipline, ought to orient American life. In a democratic society, feudal ties can be overturned and unexpected subjects – even those of ignoble birth – can be suddenly elevated to a higher rank. His parents, Fleetwood confesses, "attached a little too much importance, I think, to the circumstance of gentle blood" (13). When Adelaide dies at the close of the text, Fleetwood agrees to instruct the orphan; eventually, it appears as though the orphan will take Adelaide's place as Fleetwood's love interest. This rapid ascent underscores something fundamental about American society: namely, within a democratic society, the object of one's devotion is never quite fixed. Rather, one's affections can – indeed, must – be refreshed on a regular basis. Such is the potency of the idea behind American democracy. It empowers anyone to advance into a place of veneration, guided by the invisible wisdom of strangers whose benevolence cannot be denied by the calculated postures of genteel politicians. An ever-present lack in

Sargent's fictional universe usually ruptures the status quo without forewarning, as in *Wealth and Worth: Or, What Makes the Man?* (1842), when a young neighbor unexpectedly drowns and catalyzes a more egalitarian life for the protagonist. These ruptures remind readers that everyone remains vulnerable and, in turn, that everyone can be promoted above his or her station in accordance with "the will of the people."

Sargent's *Wealth* plays similar levelling chords by advocating the value of "low company" – that is, the intrinsic worth of "common people" (63). In terms of social levelling, the novel comments: "In this land of free institutions, there are few frailties more pitiful than that which leads a man to boast of his genealogy" (23). In turn, the novel petitions for greater charity and a willingness to act on behalf of the least fortunate. It points out that wild strawberries taste more flavorful than berries that have been carefully cultivated in an aristocratic sense. Systemically speaking, there are two kinds of investment in Sargent's fiction: financial speculation in a fickle marketplace – always negative – and investment in individuals living a hardscrabble life – always its own reward. In *Wealth*, after the protagonist falls on difficult times, his former butcher loans him money, arguing that such an investment is the very best kind. Unlike Irving's fiction, which critiques "the people" as eternally undeserving, Sargent's fiction advances a far more generous worldview.

The climactic moment of Sargent's *Wealth* occurs in a highly democratic milieu: a public meeting dedicated to the question of shared drinking water, a public event classified by the text as "a meeting for free discussion." The protagonist "rises" in the audience's esteem by speaking on behalf of the masses and, as a result, becoming their ideal representative. The unfolding synthesis of this character and the will of "the people" marks a final ascent: the protagonist's climactic trial and subsequent redemption. A lively dynamic between the protagonist and the crowd demands a significant amount of the reader's attention. The protagonist's speech triggers "three rounds of good, hearty cheers ... by the majority of the audience." The enthusiasm amplifies as the speech unfolds: "'Ay, ay!' exclaimed a thousand voices. It was triumphantly carried, and thus were the objects of the enemies of pure water utterly defeated." Sargent describes an invisible connection between the masses and the man through reference to their "united hearts" (148, 153, 157). Interestingly, in a novel that concerns itself almost exclusively with the fall as well as resurrection of a solitary figure, the most heightened emotional scene takes place at a public forum in which "the will of the people" topples economic control by a select few, not dissimilar from the arch-Federalism championed by Irving. After considering Sargent's fictional preoccupations, it will perhaps not surprise us to learn that his campaign biography for Clay looks quite different from Irving's memorial to Washington.

The Lives and Public Services of Henry Clay speaks to a democratic undercurrent within the genre of the campaign biography. Sargent composes *Lives* on behalf of Clay's 1844 contest with James Polk, an election that Clay eventually loses.

Significantly, Clay runs as a Whig against the Democrat Polk, and additionally, Clay comes from a Southern state (Kentucky), where he owns slaves. The democratic tenor of Sargent's biography must not be mistaken for a genuine barometer of Clay's ideological position. Our analysis concerns itself with neither Clay's private convictions nor Sargent's willingness to suspend his own beliefs to curry political favor. Instead, we are investigating the ways in which the genre of the campaign biography addresses a dynamic relay between "the will of the people" and the candidate put forward as this "people's" avatar.

Like much of his fiction, Sargent's campaign biography bolsters the credibility of the electorate to govern itself, or "the People at work, who are the legitimate owners of the Public Domain" (n.p.). The text incessantly highlights Clay's connection to "the people," as when it declares him to be "THE GREAT COMMONER" or the "MAN OF THE PEOPLE." Sargent's work reconciles the candidate to the populace because, it states, "We should never be tired of appealing to the reason and judgment of the people." That is, unlike Irving's memorial to Washington, which sets the first President apart from a mostly unworthy body politic, Sargent's campaign biography legitimizes the candidate by simultaneously legitimizing the so-called wisdom of the crowd. The Clay on Sargent's wheel does not place demands upon his society; rather, he waits to meet the demands of the *demos*. "The people" bestow the Presidency as a "gift." Sargent insists, "The patriotism of the people has been, hitherto, equal to all emergencies." Irving's "people" – we will recall – never rise to the occasion.

According to Sargent, the relationship between Clay and "the people" suggests an unbreakable bond. Echoing *Wealth*, Clay's candidacy is said to trigger "swelling in the public heart," and it maintains a "heartfelt attachment" between the man and the masses. In contrast, Sargent presents the former Commander-in-Chief, and personal enemy of Clay, Andrew Jackson, as a despot that operates "in spite of the people." Unlike Jackson, Clay will purportedly treat the electorate as "legitimate judges" and thus embody a "truly democratic spirit." Whereas Jackson "the destroyer" remains tyrannical ("HIS WILL WAS THE LAW OF THE LAND"), Clay offers a prominent counterpoint: "THE WILL OF THE MAJORITY, HONESTLY EXPRESSED, SHALL GIVE LAW." Ironically, Sargent uses populist sentiment against Jackson, the first truly populist President in the United States, in order to foster favorable public sentiments for his preferred candidate.

While Irving merges the history of the republic with Washington to demonstrate the citizenry's indebtedness to the metaphysics behind a "great man," Sargent merges the history of the country with Clay's life to illustrate the power and intelligence of voters. Clay's fame, the campaign biography reads, "is incorporate with the history of the Republic. May they both be blended with the highest honor *which a Free People can bestow*." Whereas Washington's perfection shines forth despite a near total lack of polish in the American populace, Clay manifests the latent perfection of "the people." Irving's historical biography is never dialectical because its subject is always-already perfect, long before he enters into the public domain, and he remains unblemished after he exits the public eye – no better nor worse from his engagements with "the people." Sargent's campaign biography, on the other hand, blends the fate of the masses with the fate of its principle subject. The story of Clay does not exclusively memorialize a "great man"; rather, it illuminates a dynamic interplay between a universal will and a particular person. According to Sargent, one cannot be extracted from the other. While not every campaign biography goes to these lengths to chart the democratic process, every campaign biography engages with this interplay on some level. The job of the campaign biographer is not to preserve a man's legacy, after all, but to shape the course of current events during a contested election.

Admittedly, by circumscribing antagonism to make it more palatable and predictable in Dickensian fashion, critics might counter that Sargent ultimately represses genuine democratic openness, and he perhaps does so even more effectively than Irving. Yet we must not overlook how Sargent's campaign biography does not – indeed, could not – erect a memorial to be worshipped, as it must explain to readers how the public and the person deserve one another in that particular place, at that particular time. Furthermore, even as it sculpts a monument out of Clay, Sargent's campaign biography retains traces of iconoclasm by exposing the incompleteness behind previous claims of social wholeness. For example, Sargent continuously gestures at crumbling statues of Jackson. And these glaring absences must remain, for it is the imperfections as well as dissatisfactions that allow democracy to endure, long after the election in question. While Irving's historical biography for Washington attempts to foreclose democracy, Sargent's campaign biography leaves certain imaginative avenues without closure, thereby contributing to the heated, unresolved, and eternally open-ended moment of a democratic election.

Subsequently, the real interest of Sargent's *Life* for contemporary readers lies less in what it manages to say and more in the innate failures that it cannot erase. For instance, Clay's campaign pursues a "harmonious state" on the issue of slavery, and Sargent praises Clay's efforts to preserve the Union: "The dark, portentous cloud, big with civil discord and disunion, which had been hanging over the country, rolled away and was scattered." Later, Sargent describes another moment of unity, when Clay and long-time rival John C. Calhoun embrace with tears in their eyes, magically sweeping away decades of significant political differences. In these examples, and a number of others, Sargent's campaign biography pauses its populist antagonizing – the lifeblood of the campaign biography as a genre – to gesture at halfbaked notions of consensus and reconciliation. In these heightened moments of tension between iconography and iconoclasm, Sargent's account unveils a fundamental paradox within the campaign biography: authoritarian myth in tension with democratic openness; Clay as a fixture and Clay as imminently moldable in the hands of "the people." Even as the campaign biography on occasion shares a desire with historical biographies to terminate ongoing debates and disagreements, unlike its cousin, the campaign biography depends upon constant difference, that is, the need for antagonism proper. Unlike other sorts of nineteenth-century American biography, antagonism remains the *raison d'être* of the campaign biography. In the chapters that follow, we revisit many of these strange texts, as disposable as they are eternal – literary emblems, we might conclude, of a democracy forever in search of itself.

Notes

1 Another way to understand why Irving's *Life* moves away from the playfulness of, say, his earlier *Mahomet and his Successors* (1849) – a text widely recognized as dancing on the line between fiction and biography – is the context of Irving's impending death as he is writing the tome. Brian Jay Jones notes parallels between Irving creating an icon of the first President and becoming an icon himself as America's first "man of letters." The issue of memorialization is ever-present in Irving's mind as he composes *Life*, and so this pressure may explain some of the somberness with which he treats his subject (Jones 388).
2 Irving's personal politics appear chameleonic as he jumps from Federalist to Democrat and finally to Whig. However, these changes are superficial at best. He supports Aaron Burr not because of sincere political disagreements with the Federalists but because he wants to maintain distance from Jeffersonian ideas. He does not care for the populist democracy of Andrew Jackson – he merely wishes to maintain his friendship with Martin Van Buren (Hagensick 185–187). In short, Irving views party affiliation not as a matter of earnest conviction but as a stratagem for personal advancement. For a time, he calls himself a "Democrat" without any sympathy for democratic principles.
3 Andrew Burstein notes that for Irving the writing of *Life* is akin to "driving a mule," and it feels to the aging Knickerbocker that the task will be his undoing (317, 327).
4 In Irving's *Life*, Washington loves England deeply and expresses regret that the Revolution was unavoidable: "How easy it would have been before that era for the mother country to have rallied back the affections of her colonial children" (30). The narrative admits that "the filial feeling still throbbed toward the mother country" (152).
5 As the text summarizes, "The sentiment of honor, the true characteristic of a soldier, has not yet got the better of interest" (Irving *Life*, 203).
6 William Epstein writes, "Biographical recognition has usually treated 'events' as naturally discrete occurrences which are congruent with the space-time configurations of the biographical subject, delimited by the subject's birth and death, and constituent of a 'life'" (37).
7 Daniel Meister argues that "historical biography should alternate its gaze between the subject and their context, exploring the ways in which they interact" (Meister). In contrast, Irving's *Life* offers a one-way trajectory: the "great man" makes history – but never the other way around.
8 Interestingly, then, at least in the case of Irving and Sargent, the campaign biography might prove more useful to historians than traditional historical biographies, especially the cases like Irving's that prove to be hagiographic. After all, "historians are not interested in simply charting the course of individual lives, but in examining those lives in dialectical relationship to the multiple social, political, and cultural worlds they inhabit and give meaning to" (Nasaw 574).
9 In *The Standard Fourth Reader* (1855), a textbook that he produces for just this purpose, Sargent comments "Instead of such aristocratic institutions, public schools and small libraries have been set up in towns and villages all over the United States" (414). Especially when compared with the "decay" of the school house at the close of Irving's

"The Legend of Sleepy Hollow," Sargent's petition on behalf of these non-aristocratic public institutions underlines his ideological position. For more on this advocacy, see Ruth Miller Elson's "American Schoolbooks and 'Culture' in the Nineteenth Century," in *The Mississippi Valley Historical Review*, vol. 46, no. 3 (Dec. 1959), pp. 411–434.

Works Cited

Abels, Jules. *The Degeneration of Our Presidential Election: A History and Analysis of an American Institution in Trouble* (New York: Macmillan, 1968).
Bryan, William Alfred. *George Washington in American Literature, 1775 – 1865* (Westport, CT: Greenwood Press, 1970).
Burstein, Andrew. *The Original Knickerbocker: The Life of Washington Irving* (New York: Basic Books, 2007).
Canby, Henry. *Classic Americans: A Study of Eminent American Writers from Irving to Whitman* (New York: Harcourt, Brace and Co., 1931).
Casper, Scott E. *Constructing American Lives: Biography and Culture in Nineteenth-Century America* (Chapel Hill, NC: University of North Carolina Press, 1999).
Epstein, William. *Recognizing Biography* (Philadelphia, PA: University of Pennsylvania Press, 1988).
Hagensick, Donna. "Irving: A Litterateur in Politics," in *Essays on Washington Irving*, ed. Ralph M. Aderman (Boston, MA: G. K.Hall, 1990), pp. 178–190.
Irving, Washington. "The Legend of Sleepy Hollow," in *The Complete Tales of Washington Irving*, ed. Charles Neider (New York: De Capo, 1998), pp. 31–57.
Irving, Washington. *The Life of George Washington: Abridged Version* (New York: De Capo, 1994).
Irving, Washington. "Rip Van Winkle," in *The Complete Tales of Washington Irving*, ed. Charles Neider (New York: De Capo, 1998), pp. 1–17.
Jones, Brian Jay. *Washington Irving: An American Original* (New York: Arcade Publishing, 2008).
Lee, Hermione. *Biography: A Very Short Introduction* (Oxford: Oxford University Press, 2009).
Meister, Daniel. "The Biographical Turn and the Case for Historical Biography." *History Compass*, 2017, https://www.rug.nl/research/biografie-instituut/meister_the_biographical_turn.pdf. Accessed March 15, 2021.
Nasaw, David. "Introduction." *The American Historical Review*, vol. 114, no. 3, 2009, pp. 573–578, https://doi.org/10.1086/ahr.114.3.573. Accessed February 12, 2021.
Roth, Martin. *Comedy and America: The Lost World of Washington Irving* (New York: Associated Faculty Press, 1976).
Sargent, Epes. *Fleetwood; Or, The Stain Of Birth A Novel Of American Life* (Whitefish, MT: Kessinger Publishing, 2010).
Sargent, Epes. *The Life and Public Services of Henry Clay* (Scotts Valley, CA: CreateSpace Publishing, 2018).
Sargent, Epes. *Wealth And Worth: Or, Which Makes The Man?* (Miami, FL: HardPress, 2017).

2
NATHANIEL HAWTHORNE AND THE (IM)PERFECT PRESIDENT

Published on behalf of the 1852 Presidential campaign of Franklin Pierce, Nathaniel Hawthorne's *The Life of Franklin Pierce* marks a significant turning point in the history of the campaign biography: for the first time since the genre's inception in 1824, an American politician exploits the credentials of a major literary figure to market himself. To produce the idea of Pierce for mass consumption, Hawthorne draws from formulaic elements of the campaign biography as well as his own unique brand of literary intervention. Given the recent "political turn" in Hawthorne studies, and our ongoing concern with the relationship between American politics and American literature, *The Life of Franklin Pierce* serves as an object of renewed interest.

According to many of Hawthorne's critics, *The Life of Franklin Pierce* reveals a fundamental limit, a fixed horizon for the genre of the campaign biography, beyond which even Hawthorne's considerable talents apparently could not reach. And it is not just that Hawthorne finds himself hemmed in by the political as well as formulaic demands placed upon him, although he certainly does bow to these pressures in important ways. His propaganda for Pierce also underscores an impasse within Hawthorne's literary project – indeed, within the broadly-defined project of American Romanticism. Namely, when Hawthorne attempts to craft a persona for Pierce that aims to be all things to all people, he rehearses the enduring ambivalence that serves as a hallmark of his corpus. Pierce himself problematically follows the advice of his friend, Gideon Wells: "Be the candidate of all" (qtd. in Troy, 56). Unable to dedicate itself to progressive or conservative causes, the Hawthornean Romance similarly straddles the proverbial fence. In turn, *Life* unveils not only the failures of the campaign biography as a genre, but evidence as well of an impending standstill in Hawthorne's overall artistic development, crystallized in his 1851 novel, *The House*

DOI: 10.4324/9781003132448-3

of Seven of Gables. And Life's aesthetic deadlock concurrently underscores a deep-seated crisis in America's liberal democracy, one that bubbles to the surface as the nation lurches toward Civil War. To preserve the Union, popular actors like Pierce and Hawthorne lean on the vagueness of compromise as well as the illusion of consensus, and in so doing they forfeit an opportunity for bold political reforms including, most prominently, the abolition of slavery.

Yet, from another perspective that appears to be gathering steam among contemporary Hawthorne scholars, behind the charge of critics like David Reynolds, Hawthorne's work deflates utopian delusion in favor of sustained personal reflection. From this vantage point, Hawthorne manages to project the image of a candidate that is somehow perfect – an emblem of America's grand political lineage – as well as imperfect – a mutable symbol that could only ever fall short of voter-reader expectations. If we place Life in conversation with political theorists like Carl Schmitt or Chantal Mouffe, contemporary readers might wonder if Hawthorne in fact sustains political dissatisfaction: the ceaseless democratic wrangling that tenuously holds together the Union. That is, when he pauses to reject Pierce as a Romantic whole, Hawthorne speaks to the nature of democracy as a never-ending process and he subsequently staves off authoritarian paralysis. When considered in this light, Life fits Jacques Rancière's definition of "effective political art," since it produces

> a double effect: the readability of a political signification and a sensible or perceptual shock caused, conversely, by the uncanny, by that which resists signification ... a negotiation between opposites, between the readability of the message that threatens to destroy the sensible form of art and the radical uncanniness that threatens to destroy all political meaning. (59)

The latent (im)possibility of forming a stable representation of the nation in a single candidate – the "double effect" of Pierce as mythic totality *and* forever incomplete – makes Hawthorne's campaign biography worthy of a second look.[1] His account of Pierce is not exclusively a story of strained transcendence or faux consensus, but a story of the gap between a given candidate and a restless populace that the candidate could never hope to embody fully.

Said another way, Hawthorne's Life can be read as a grim failure as well as a beacon of hope for a nation standing at the brink of dissolution, a sentiment that readers today will find quite recognizable. This campaign biography highlights a series of concerns about the genre that resonate from the time of the Civil War to the present, including Romantic undercurrents that perpetually sound the death knell of America's political experiment while preserving an internal dynamic that ensures the continuance of that very arrangement. Richard Brodhead outlines how Hawthorne's "enigmatic openness" inspires countless "new Hawthornes" in the years that follow his death, including William Dean Howells, the subject of the following chapter (16, 66). With its production of a uniquely (im)perfect candidate, Hawthorne's text allows readers to reconsider the enigmatic openness of campaign biographies, and to reconsider the limits as well as possibilities of ever-evolving rhetorical strategies that surround democratic discourse. Yet perhaps instead of too quickly dismissing *Life* as an abject failure, or too hastily redeeming it as replete with political potential, we ought to consider these competing interpretations as mutually co-constitutive. That is, Hawthorne's formulaic account of Pierce remains deficient and it threatens always to function as mere propaganda; however, I would argue that it succeeds precisely as a result of this failure. Hawthorne depicts Pierce as a composite of democratic and Romantic ideals, torn between a desire for naïve wholeness and the feeling that this fallacious wholeness could never take shape. Echoing an enigmatic openness cultivated in his dark Romances, including *House*, Hawthorne's *Life* compels us to reappraise the complicated Romantic valence of nineteenth-century American politics as well as the complex political valence of the American Romance.

Trans-Patronage

Let us begin our re-reading of *Life* with a provocative image of the bookish Hawthorne, strolling alongside his friend and former President Pierce through the streets of Rome. When Hawthorne's daughter Una falls ill, Pierce – no stranger to such heartbreak, having lost his own son in a freak railroad accident – rushes to stand by his friend's side, to comfort and distract him during his emotional trial. This visual of the two men, walking in such an ancient place, conjures ghosts of patron Caesar Augustus and his client Vergil, who famously wrote *The Aeneid* (19 BCE) as propaganda in support of the emperor's reign. Upon such well-trodden ground, we might be tempted to draw classical parallels as we watch yet another client-patron relationship blossom between a cunning author and a shrewd politician.

Pierce and Hawthorne first meet at Bowdoin College in 1821. As members of the school's Athenean Literary Society, they immediately hit it off, and germinate a friendship that endures throughout their lives. Bred in a political family in New Hampshire, Pierce inherits considerable public clout that he later uses to secure Hawthorne a number of plum political jobs, including work at the Boston and Salem Custom Houses. In return for his assistance, Hawthorne offers to write Pierce's biography ahead of the 1852 election – an offer that Pierce eagerly accepts. This quid pro quo arrangement reveals Hawthorne to be an astute opportunist that understands well the contractual inner workings of New England's unique partisan machinery. But this story is hardly a unidirectional one.[2] It remains difficult to label Pierce the patron and Hawthorne the client. Scott E. Casper describes the tectonic shift that takes place when a figure of Hawthorne's literary stature agrees to compose a document that had been historically churned out at party headquarters in quick (and cheap) order: the relatively unknown Pierce benefits greatly from his friend's status, thereby paving the way for a "new authorial role for the campaign biographer based on his literary fame" (204). This transaction reframes the nature of the campaign biography, as now instead of a writer using a politician exclusively for political gain, a writer could theoretically exploit American politicians in order to sell more books. Early editions of *Life* are replete with advertisements for Hawthorne's fictional works, including *House*. If for no other reason than the associations that such an intermingling likely form in the minds of his readers, the physical proximity between Hawthorne's fiction and his political biography – mere pages apart – encourages us to place *Life* in conversation with Hawthorne's literary endeavors, despite relevant differences in intention, audience reception, and so forth. Several critics have already gestured at the literary crossover between Hawthorne's fantasies and *Life*. For instance, Lee Warner suggests that Hawthorne relies "to a surprising extent on his earlier fiction to construct (Pierce's) character," in particular a sketch of General James Miller (25). The Pierce–Hawthorne professional bond thus sheds light upon the nascent possibility that for-profit cultural production could drive the political narrative rather than the other way around. This pivot will perhaps not surprise readers in the first half of the twenty-first century accustomed to the inundation of political spectacles that keeps the consumer's eyes glued to her mobile device.

Pierce and Hawthorne do, however, share partisan beliefs that simply cannot be ignored in any analysis of *Life*. Most prevalently, the two men waver at the prospect of an impending Civil War. Pierce crafts his image as "a politician who (avoids) having an opinion on the slavery issue"; he supports the Kansas-Nebraska Act, which allows slavery to spread northward; and he backs the Compromise of 1850, which defuses growing hostilities by deferring reform. Although Hawthorne's position is considerably "foggier" than Pierce's – Pierce would later go so far as to denounce Lincoln publicly and be accused of treason as a result – Hawthorne nonetheless shudders at the thought of radical reform, a stance that earns widespread condemnation among his Transcendentalist neighbors in Concord, MA (Cheever 118, 150). In reality, Hawthorne dislikes slavery and privately admits that the U.S. would be better off as two separate nations. But his obstinate support of Pierce continues to mar his image as a man who at the very least appears to lack conviction on the issue of human rights. The two men share a reluctance to fight for the basic dignity of enslaved peoples – an issue to which the following section will return.

Still, the spoils system proves fruitful for both the politician and the noted "man of letters." As a reward for his good work on *Life*, Pierce appoints Hawthorne as a consul in Liverpool (1852–56). This appointment rewards Hawthorne with long-sought financial stability and allows him to travel abroad with his family. Upon his eventual return to the states, Hawthorne once again repays his now-disreputable friend, this time by dedicating to him a collection of essays about his years spent in England, *Our Old Home* (1863). The dedication page causes an immediate uproar in America's literary circles. By most accounts, the gesture costs Hawthorne dearly and exiles him from his contemporaries. In one last act of repayment, Pierce tends to the ailing Hawthorne at the end of his life, promising to take care of his family after his death. When Hawthorne eventually succumbs to illness in 1864, it is none other than Pierce that finds his corpse and alerts his friends as well as colleagues about the passing. In sum, the transpatronage between the two men suggests a relationship far more impactful than the typical bond between candidate and campaign biographer.

At the same time, when one views it as a literary artifact, *Life* calls into question the state of Romanticism at the twilight of the American Renaissance. In fact, Whig opponent Horace Mann rather cheekily describes *Life* as nothing less than Hawthorne's "greatest work of fiction," and even Hawthorne admits: "Although the story is true ... it took a romancer to do it" (qtd. in Lundberg). What are we to make of this turn to politics by "the romancer"? Hawthorne's hybrid creation invites us to interrogate the candidate as a trope, which is to say, as a construct that can be interpreted within the field of literary criticism.[3] For some critics, the manner in which Hawthorne crafts the character of Pierce concurrently exposes the limits of his Romances. Nevertheless, and partially as a result of the "political turn" in Hawthorne studies, we can still position Hawthorne as a provocateur whose Romances have had a lasting impact on the poetic dispensation of American democracy.

The Third Way of American Romance

Pulling no punches, Sacvan Bercovitch encapsulates a common critique of Hawthorne's politics by declaring him to be an Ahab of compromise.[4] If Hawthorne's aesthetic genius resides in his capacity to dance deftly between competing aspects of human existence, the fatal flaw of his fiction remains its willingness to reconcile these dueling aspects, to prefer the illusion of consensus above sustained uncertainty, and to repress or foreclose the contestation of pressing social issues. In a word, Hawthorne's perceived quietude underscores a profound moral weakness in certain quarters of American Romanticism in the years leading up to the Civil War. The genre's characteristic ambivalence becomes increasingly unpalatable as it subscribes to a "both/and" mentality that elevates soporific navel-gazing over political conviction, especially on the subject of slavery. Hawthorne's "both/and" mentality becomes an acute concern when one considers the human rights atrocity that eventually sparks the conflict over the fate of the Union. By opting to craft the character of Pierce within the Romantic tradition, Hawthorne's *Life* has been condemned for reducing Pierce to a figure akin to Melville's white whale: a mutable symbol that could mean anything at all – or nothing.

We might be permitted at this point to gesture at related concerns for readers in the early twenty-first century. After all, Brodhead declares that any study of Hawthorne demands to take on a "new life," to be made relevant to "living concerns and needs" (215). Due to its failings as a Romance, Hawthorne's campaign biography of Pierce informs contemporary concerns regarding what has been described as the "Third Way." Perhaps best embodied in the Democratic presidencies of Bill Clinton and Barack Obama, followers of the Third Way make a plea for moderation – an effort to preserve the value of social safety nets and, concomitantly, to leave untouched the mechanisms of late capitalism.[5] Third Way-ism obscures partisan initiatives under the cloak of apolitical "commonsense." In Hawthornean fashion, the Clinton and Obama administrations sound as if they maintain a "progressive" agenda; at the same time, these administrations erode the legacy of the Left by enacting draconian cuts to the welfare system. Stuart Hall writes:

> The "Third Way" has been hyped as "a new kind of politics." Its central claim is the discovery of a mysterious middle course on every question between all the existing extremes. However, the closer one examines this via media, the more it looks, not like a way through the problems, but a soft-headed way around them. It speaks with forked, or at the very least garbled, tongue. (286)

Hawthorne drafts a blueprint for this Third Way-ism, with its forked or garbled tongue, as he blends "progressive" and "conservative" values in a way that sustains a toxic status quo. From one vantage point, then, Hawthorne's ideal candidate functions as a blurry Romantic symbol to defuse genuine political engagement.

This Third Way-ism materializes when Hawthorne treats Pierce as a perfect synthesis of the dualistic tendencies that run through human existence. For instance, Pierce appears to be a muscular, aggressive fellow, as taciturn as he is powerful and imposing. Hawthorne's deeply problematic assessment of Pierce as a "hero" of the Mexican War displays the would-be President as an embodiment of patriotic vigor as well as judicious restraint. Even after he sustains a serious injury, Pierce reportedly dives headfirst into battle against the wishes of his less-fortified companions. Because Hawthorne greatly exaggerates the heroism of Pierce, the fifth chapter of *Life* – which concerns episodes from the war – remains its most flawed politically as well as its most formulaic aesthetically. Hawthorne's campaign biography falls prey to the jingoistic hyperbole that characterizes many other biographies of the day. Concurrently, however, Hawthorne paints his subject as a gentle and considerate leader, quick to deliver to his fallen comrades "a cup of tea." Pierce supposedly channels "magical kindness" in his ability to soothe the soldiers that surround him. In turn, Hawthorne captures a synthesis of militancy and graciousness with his repeated use of the phrase "chivalrous beauty" to describe his Romantic candidate (55, 43).

Hawthorne accentuates this Third Way-ism by depicting Pierce as a "conservative" as well as a "progressive." On the one hand, Pierce proves the existence of a very long lineage, that is, a constancy of American character. Once more, we find traces of Vergil and his creation of a universal mythology to legitimize the reign of Caesar Augustus. Hawthorne's "conservatism" upholds a sense of continuity between the past and the present and, as a result, Pierce plays the role of preeminent inheritor.[6] When the candidate speaks, he recalls the Revolutionary Congress, or the Long Parliament of England (24). By insisting upon his subject's endowment with "native traits" and "innate characteristics," Hawthorne reassures his reader that precious little will change upon Pierce's election (3, 8). The status quo will mercifully persist. Yet Hawthorne does not depict Pierce as a static object, a marble statue that will not yield its position; instead, he oscillates and transforms Pierce into a malleable ball of clay to be (re)molded from page to page.[7] As a gentle and sweet child, the "progressive" Pierce "does not show the germ of all that was in the man" (5). In the final tally, Pierce proves to be a surprisingly slippery signifier. While he benefits from the "witness" of his father's generation, and from the "drilling" of his ancestors, he also absorbs his character via a more immediate transmission that is more nature than nurture – a patriotic sentiment communicated "from their hearts to his" (7, 11). To his "natural gifts," Pierce adds "whatever was to be attained by laborious study … the faculty, here exercised and improved" (15). In a word, Hawthorne presents Pierce as a balance between two (im)possible demands: the need to sustain established habits in tandem with a push for radical change. He remains bound by "birth" and "youthful training" (3). We therefore locate in *Life* the roots of a profoundly muddied political profile – described by F.O. Matthiesen as obscurantism – that has become quite common at the dawn of the twenty-first century.[8]

Pierce as ambivalent Romantic protagonist finds perhaps its closest literary parallel in Hawthorne's Phoebe from *House*. Interestingly, Hawthorne models Phoebe after his wife, Sophia, whom he nicknames "Phoebe." Given his outspoken adoration of Pierce, then, to compare Phoebe and Pierce is also to compare the two major loves of Hawthorne's life. Phoebe's grace carries over to Hawthorne's depiction of Pierce because she too worries over a world that shifts too quickly: the "dizzying" world of her love interest Holgrave, untethered from any sense of connection to the past (in a particularly pointed example, Holgrave proposes levelling all existing houses to avoid the crisis of inheritance).[9] Yet Phoebe is not exclusively "conservative." Her appearance at the Pyncheon estate also signals something "fresh" and "unconventional" (51). Divorced from aristocratic responsibility, she envisions herself to be a natural salesperson, and so she happily "reduces" herself to the bald commercialism embodied in the family's penny shop – a choice that remains implicitly political, especially given the North/South divide over industrialism versus a plantation-based economy. Moreover, of the novel's characters, Phoebe most unrelentingly recognizes the threat posed by submission to Judge Pyncheon's "terrible idea: that evil is transmitted genetically … a far surer process of transmission than human law." A counterpoint to the story of Pierce as an apex of American achievement, Phoebe – properly, it would seem – fears the "accumulation of ancestry," and at least occasionally posits a legal as well as commercial antithesis to the Judge's outlook (89). To achieve her level of graciousness, Phoebe, like the character of Pierce, must resist radical reform while simultaneously indulging in her youthful, "brisk impulses" (125). She both hesitates at the novel's thresholds, obedient to their call for restraint, and boldly crosses them by reaching out for the utopian resolution that she eventually appears to achieve at novel's end. The Third Way-ism of Phoebe and Pierce emanates a sanctified sense of practicality, a resolution that elevates both characters above the fray. Losing sight of the productive tensions that define them as Romantic actors, Hawthorne ultimately reduces these figures, on one level, to custodians of the existing state of affairs. But as we shall discuss in the final section of the chapter, because this Hawthornean dialectic simultaneously sustains a refusal of resolution, Hawthorne's preferred practicality retains traces of dissatisfaction that allow readers to approach *Life* and *House* as "double events," which is to say, texts that remain eminently political.

By framing his ideal candidate through the most popular literary mode of that period (Romanticism), Hawthorne unwittingly highlights the dead-ends of his fiction as well as his campaign biography. That is, *Life* as a whole suffers from a misguided need to resolve its internal contradictions, and as a result it loses the vitality that defines it as well as the candidate. Henry James famously critiques *House* on precisely these grounds: when Holgrave retreats to the Pyncheon estate and accepts everything against which he previously railed, such as private property and bourgeois stability, Hawthorne imagines an escape from the text's various impasses. But in so doing, he ruins the healthy democratic/aesthetic frictions at the novel's core. A.N. Kaul laments that Hawthorne "does not face" the problem with merging "conservative" and "progressive" positions and, as a result, the author cannot confront the perilous "future of democracy itself" (344). Elsewhere, Amy Schrager Lang confirms a widespread unhappiness with the ending of *House* due to the novel's privileging of "harmonious resolution" over "social revolution" (471). Because the narrative remains unable to sustain its restless democratic spirit, *House* arrives at crude synthesis: the stilling of a disquiet that reflects the fruitful open-endedness of American politics as well as American literature. The function of Phoebe as a Romantic suture translates into *Life* through the character of Pierce, a man ripe with "new qualities" who slips comfortably back into "harmony with those (qualities) heretofore known" (*Life* 28). Never a true avatar for social reform (he only masquerades as such), the figure of Pierce hints at a mutability that would likely evade a more objective biographer. In the end, Hawthorne's Third Way-ism exposes an important point concerning the Third Way-ism common to American politics at large: in its calls for consensus and "peaceful" resolution, the text suppresses any sign of revolutionary fervor and prolongs unjust conditions, thereby further confusing an audience standing at a crossroads, in search of moral clarity and facing imminent social dissolution.

According to critics like Clark Davis, Hawthorne's work can be redeemed from the charge of obscurantism only if it is approached through an ethical, rather than a political, lens. Indeed, in his campaign biography, Hawthorne – who practices "a type of engagement that is based upon disengagement" – straddles an attenuated line between ethics and politics. According to Davis, Hawthorne's ethical approach via his aesthetic decisions remains "open," whereas *Life* appears to be "closed" due to the text's stridently partisan message. For Hawthorne, Davis continues, political arguments are invariably reductive. *Life* consequently falls short for several interrelated reasons, including the general preclusion of self-critique or irony from campaign biographies (in contrast to the self-critique and irony that feels at home in the more "literary" *House*), the absence of a "critical interest" that "genuine" literature makes possible, and the "inevitable thinness of adversarial debate" (91, 99–101). Simply put, Davis argues that Hawthorne's ambivalence stems from a set of ethical preoccupations that result from his supposed suspension above the "distasteful" arena of political discourse. The shortcomings of *Life* are indicative of the shortcomings of American politics in the lead-up to the Civil War. But the field of American politics is never fully "closed," and the Romantic contours of *Life* reveal that critics should not depoliticize Hawthorne's work too readily. We might interpret the Hawthornean "veil" through political theorists of late that attend to the restless remainders of the political. In effect, no matter how hard the text tries to foster an illusion of consensus, or to champion a retreat into a detached sort of individual ethics, Hawthorne's campaign biography of Pierce cannot erase incessant, brutal, and dissatisfying signs of actual antagonism. Even as readers must not overlook the real costs of Hawthorne's urge to compromise or his relative quietude on the subject of slavery, they should not too readily revive his reputation by elevating his aesthetico-ethical principles – presumed to be open – above his declared partisanship – presumed to be closed. Readers cannot ignore the signs of political uncertainty throughout *Life*, made all the more palatable due to their suppression at the hand of Hawthorne. If we account for the sheer openness of the political, as well as the sheer volatility of American democracy, we cannot dismiss Hawthorne's *Life* as limited, reductive, or "thin."

Hawthorne's campaign biography illuminates the best and worst of American Romanticism in artistic and political terms. It aims to unify as well as harmonize the nation's story; at the same time, it welcomes dramatic alterations at a moment's notice. Drawing together Phoebe and Pierce, *Life* conserves tradition even as it breaks down the established order. Hawthorne's campaign biography consequently preserves hope for peaceful overthrow – hope enough to sustain disheartened members of the electorate that invariably desire a different candidate. Hawthorne's Pierce appears, like Phoebe, to be (im)perfect: perfect enough to hold the Union together; imperfect enough to maintain political potentiality. Consequently, Hawthorne's Romantic impulses help to refine dominant tropes associated with the dissensus of American democracy. We might say, then, that Hawthorne's main contribution to the genre of the campaign biography is not the author's resistance to radical reform, as James and other critics might contend, but his evocation of a candidate that could be cohesive as well as incomplete – a precariousness that renders *Life* a more fascinating work than most critics have heretofore considered it to be.

Open and Closed Biographies

Unsurprisingly, Hawthorne extracts Pierce from what he portrays as the swamp of American politics. To do so, he casts his friend as a Cincinnatus figure – a begrudging candidate with precious little patience for the inner workings of government (of note, this image of Cincinnatus remains one of the staples of campaign biographies in the United States). Hawthorne simultaneously portrays himself as "apolitical" by declaring in the preface his own lack of acquaintance with the formula of the campaign biography – a disingenuous statement, given how closely the text tracks with the established roadmap. Hawthorne's rhetorical maneuver is overt: he elevates Pierce's "democracy of good feeling" above the "chill," shrewd calculations of the politician (*Life* 8). But Hawthorne's petition for he and Pierce to be considered "apolitical" hides the fact that both men remain deeply political. As we have seen with Irving in the preceding chapter, and as we continue to see with the Third Way politicians of our contemporary moment, the claim of being "apolitical" rings hollow under any degree of scrutiny.[10] Hawthorne's foray into the world of campaign biographies reveals something fundamental about the politics of American Romanticism as well as the unavoidable two-sidedness of the political. Accordingly, we may shift, as Casper suggests, although he eventually balks at the audacity of his own proposal, from thinking of campaign biographies as mere formula to thinking of them as a genre: a literary mode that affords greater exploration of "aesthetic and authorial possibilities" (Casper 207).

By stressing the tension between formula and genre in Hawthorne's campaign biography, we shift our working analogy between Hawthorne and Vergil, exemplars of patronage and bald propaganda, to a different association for Hawthorne: Vergil's Roman contemporary, Ovid. Gregory Staley demonstrates how thoroughly "Hawthorne's aesthetic is conceptually and terminologically indebted to Ovid" (127).[11] Like Hawthorne, Ovid's *Metamorphoses* (8 CE) blurs a line that supposedly demarcates politician from poet, and reveals in the process how fiction creates its own political realities and, as a result, how poets can morph into powerful patrons instead of obsequious clients. Hawthorne and Ovid each spend periods of their life as political exiles of a sort: Caesar Augustus ejects Ovid from Rome; the Whigs reject Hawthorne from his appointment at the Custom House. Finally, and most importantly for the purposes of this chapter, Ovid stresses the "ambiguity" behind Augustan and anti-Augustan forces – a world "of unstable ephemerality that can only be at odds with ... the foundation of Rome as the center of a stable cosmos" (Feldherr 6, 29). In other words, if we reframe Hawthorne as Ovidian, we can spot the hermeneutical dance that takes place at the center of *Life* – a dance that compels readers to treat Hawthorne's text as open and closed, all at once. If an assumed historical parallel with Vergil diminishes the merits of Hawthorne's campaign biography because it reinforces a tacit correlation between the American writer and mere *agitprop*, a historical parallel with

Ovid yields more dynamic results by inviting us to re-assess the generic playfulness throughout Pierce's biography. In *Life*, unstable ephemerality clashes with the stable American *libertad* that Pierce presumably inherits. The text's Ovidian character, however unconsciously, unveils a fluid border between permanence and eternal change. Hawthorne's Ovidian style speaks to both the American Romantic tradition as well as the undergirding spirit of American democracy.

One of the most outspoken figures behind the recent "political turn" in Hawthorne studies, Larry Reynolds remarks that for Hawthorne "all people and causes (are) irrevocably 'variegated'." As such, politics in its organizational form always reeks of naïve utopianism. Hawthorne considers any revolution, indeed, any significant social reform, to be at its core "morally dubious" (2, 229). As an example, consider Hawthorne's early short story, "My Kinsman, Major Molineux" (1832), in which American revolutionaries show their innate barbarism, or *The Blithedale Romance* (1852), a novel based upon Hawthorne's own disillusionment at Brook Farm, which eyes utopian communities with what it holds to be a healthy degree of skepticism. According to the logic of these texts, since human beings are inherently (im)perfect, no political arrangement could ever hope to please everyone. There will forever be discontents. Hawthorne's distaste for politicians and "the people" that elect them underscores his "rather unusual Christian democratic elitism" (226). We can therefore classify Hawthorne as a political writer that anticipates the looming limitations of the American experiment.

Yet even critics that want to revisit Hawthorne's long-ignored politics regularly cast *Life* as a failure due to the text's inability to inspire political engagement in audiences in terms of activism or the petition for social reform. Once more conjuring a connection to Vergil, many of these detractors summarily dismiss the Pierce biography as little more than foreclosed propaganda. In the final tally, Richard Boyd posits, Hawthorne strives for the "concealment of the reality of social antagonism ... (expelling) from his text all those disturbing elements which might disrupt his utopian sense of social harmony." Consequently, naysayers declare that Hawthorne's *Life* shifts the author from his role as a demystifier of American myth in his dark Romances to "a mythmaker and a concealer of those dark acts of real violence" (345–349). Said another way, due to his multiple retreats from antagonism into the illusion off consensus peddled by his friend Pierce, Hawthorne never manages to institute an effective political program. David S. Reynolds adds that Hawthorne instills an excessively generalized sense of social reform via "benign-subversive texts," in which the author transforms "suggestiveness itself (into) an assertion of value" (134, 257). Hawthorne does not know how to express political dissatisfaction without simultaneously repressing it, or channeling it into texts that are at best "benign-subversive." Nonetheless, we might approach *Life* in a different fashion by reading the text less as a failure and more as a document punctuated by the very inconsistencies that remain the hallmark of American democracy as well as the American Romance. That is to say, we ought to adopt a mode of analysis inspired by the literature of the American Renaissance and dwell not upon his drift into consensus but upon the impasses that define Hawthorne's text. In Hawthorne's hands, the candidate slips constantly between closed composite and open plasticity – a delicate balance that need not be discarded as mere concealment or neutered Third Way because it retains a vital two-sidedness. Hawthorne's figuration of Pierce disappoints some critics due to its delusional wholeness yet it energizes others as a result of its incompleteness. Instead of dismissing this binary as a rigid limit, an ill-advised synthesis, or a misguided conflation of mere suggestiveness with moral value, I wish to read *Life* as a rumination upon the dissatisfying nature of the political: a dissatisfaction that remains the principle impetus behind the campaign biography as a genre.

Once again, *House* offers a useful parallel. In one scene, a barrel-organ show reminds Hawthorne's audience of the dissatisfying undercurrent of American politics. Following a great deal of commotion, "nothing (comes) to pass" in the show. An over-heated lover at last receives a kiss from his beloved but finds himself "none the happier." Hawthorne's novel then promptly pivots from pondering the existential lack at the center of the barrel-organ show to tracking a nearby political processional. Manifested first as a barrel-organ show and then as an absent-minded processional, American politics proves to be little more than a "fool's play." Although from a certain perspective American politics might be oriented around a "vast, homogeneous spirit" – a link that dovetails with the mythic processional that Hawthorne trails behind Pierce – such transcendental sentimentality quickly becomes "petrified," as *House* moves from the apparent fullness of democracy's exuberant display to the utter vacuity of a parade that brings "nothing to pass." Of course, it seems unlikely, but not entirely out of the realm of possibility, that Hawthorne consciously posits that a Pierce administration will leave readers "none the happier" (*House* 116–118). Still, *Life* reveals a significant sense of lack thanks to the near total absence of any record of Pierce's political speeches as well as Hawthorne's intimation that his preferred candidate could still change in ways that voters cannot anticipate. Although restrained by various aesthetic and political conventions, *Life* at times echoes *House* in its presentation of American democracy as inherently (im)perfect.

While *Life* does gesture at a "chilled society of politicians" to inflate, through contrast, democracy's "good feelings," the text also retains traces of necessary political antagonism. For instance, Hawthorne elucidates how his future President "provokes an innate self-confidence" while, at the same time, indicating "the sedulous cultivation, the earnest effort, the toil, the agony, which are the conditions of ultimate success" (13). On the one hand, then, Pierce transcends the ugly realm of electoral contest thanks to the strong ethical character that he "inherits" from his patriotic father; at the same time, he (as well as the reader) remains a work-in-progress, which is to say, a figure that must strive, toil, and fight for temporary success. Hawthorne therefore characterizes Pierce with a pronounced sense of agonism – the basis of any democratic order. In Ovidian fashion, the character of Pierce thrives upon competition, with himself and others, and upon the diligent struggle required of anyone that recognizes her condition to be eternally incomplete. As a result, the two sides of Pierce's Janus face – chilled totality versus sustained agonism – reflect how the genre of the campaign biography frequently evokes consensus alongside an endless evocation of a better social arrangement yet to come.

To understand better how Hawthorne produces Pierce as a Romantic trope, though, we must unpack the term "political." Why should we read Hawthorne's cultivated ambivalence as *political* rather than treating it, in line with a host of Hawthorne scholars, as primarily *aesthetico-ethical*? Chantal Mouffe classifies the political as "the constitutive role of antagonism in social life" (2). Because individuals possess wildly variegated desires, and these desires change from moment to moment, Mouffe argues that the notion that any partisan answer could satisfy everyone's demands remains fundamentally (im)possible. No social arrangement could disarm the ever-present possibility that dissatisfied parties will gather to overthrow the current hegemonic order. Attempts to repress the political through "democratic good feeling" – in Hawthorne's time, or in our own – will inevitably end in failure. On this score, a host of critics read Hawthorne's *Life* as similarly repressive due to the fact that the tract ostensibly bypasses antagonism in favor of flimsy communal consensus or hastily-declared perfection of personal character. Yet, whether conscious of his choice or not, Hawthorne incessantly gives rise to the antithesis of his consensual Pierce in a process that Mouffe would call "the return of the political": "Conflict and antagonism are at the same time (our) condition of possibility and the condition of impossibility of (our) full realization" (8). Hawthorne posits the figure of Pierce as both an emblem of the nation's fullest realization as well as a reminder of the futility of pursuing such total and permanent fulfillment. Hawthorne himself acknowledges on multiple occasions that internal and interpersonal antagonisms can never wholly disappear, because (he reasons) the promise of consensus excludes subjects with divergent interests. Instead of adopting a partisan perspective, Hawthorne – like Mouffe – regularly claims that we are condemned to eternal difference from one another. We are political animals with shifting interests and alliances that force us to undermine any superficial claims of lasting unity. In his campaign biography, Hawthorne reminds the reader of this underlying restlessness. He portrays Pierce as existentially lacking through much of the text: "The boy did not show the germ of all that was in the man" (5). Not only does Pierce, and the nation for which he serves as a stand-in, defer final ascent to that City on the Hill; he does not even show "the germ" of this eventual actualization. In effect, he does not appear to display even the kernel of a utopian vision. Pierce – and America's body politic – appears weirdly devoid of promise, as though they are founded upon a core absence instead of upon the premise of absolute fulfillment. In her study of nineteenth-century biography, Hermione Lee highlights a recognition within these kinds of texts that "the vision that has been constructed is bound to be partial and temporary" (140). Counter to the narrative that the campaign biography is closed off as blatant propaganda, Hawthorne's *Life* dwells upon moments of partiality and incompleteness.

Hawthorne stresses this necessary dissatisfaction in his discussion of Pierce's texts and speeches. As we have already seen, the glimmering promise of "all that was in the man" occasionally reveals itself in Pierce's "noble" visage. But in Hawthorne's hands, these manifestations harbor a distinctive sense of lack. In response to the pages of Pierce's journal, for example, Hawthorne laments that he cannot "gain a very definitive idea" of the candidate's rhetorical prowess. He visibly wrings his hands over the fact that Pierce leaves "few materials" for posterity (32). While critics might account for this commentary as a clever way for Hawthorne to spin an unfortunate reality into a positive, since Pierce was not a very gifted orator, we could also read the void behind Pierce's letters as a correlation between democracy's distinctive demand for dissatisfaction with a Romantic style of writing that was enormously popular at that time thanks, in no small part, to Hawthorne himself. According to Hawthorne, Pierce's journal has "no purpose of displaying" his native strength – that is, the candidate's language, like Hawthorne's, remains insufficient because it cannot hope to capture the comprehensiveness of Pierce's potential or, by proxy, the potential of the American ideal (45). As a result, Hawthorne advances the written figure of the candidate as a placeholder that remains pregnant with possibility but forever falls short of achieving its initial promise. Part of this failure can perhaps be attributed to Pierce as a "silent and passive" candidate, one selected by his party to unify a fractured bloc by offering a blank canvas onto which different voters might project their own values: "Candidates, then, became figureheads, icons drained of reality and relevance" (Troy 56, 59–60). The figure of Pierce cannot completely relinquish the role of representation or it would sink into pure nihilism – a political formlessness that would foreshadow impending anarchy. The germ must bear some kind of fruit. At the same time, though, the figure of Pierce must remain incomplete, not so much because Hawthorne's sketch reflects a particular man who is in reality an unproven entity, but because his sketch refuses – by its very design – to evoke the idea of fulfillment that would theoretically accompany Pierce's election into office. Hawthorne frequently renders the condition of Pierce's "ultimate success" inaccessible to the reader, a threshold that cannot be crossed. Hawthorne's biography of his friend's campaign thus elicits the toil and agony of a dream constituted by the (im)possibility of its own attainment.

Rather than discard Hawthorne's creation as an entirely naïve composite, we must examine moments of rupture in the text in which American mythology exists as a surplus, as that which cannot be contained. When Pierce "proves his faith in the great mind and heart of the country both by what he says and by what he refrains from saying," Hawthorne's reader experiences the two-sidedness of Mouffe's account of the political (*Life* 57). After all, within any democratic order, the political must be articulated as a chosen representative – but only to extend its necessary restlessness, the open-endedness of democratic wrangling yet to come. Put differently, the political cannot be articulated with any conclusiveness because it must preserve the potential of still better formulations in the days ahead, which is to say, the ontological engine behind democratic revisionism. Hawthorne's depiction of Pierce "fails" when it tries to give a form to an American ideal that must remain formless and, in turn, it "succeeds" precisely because of the futility of the biographer's endeavor – because of a Romantic gap between the thing-itself and its (im)perfect articulation. For Hawthorne, Pierce's candidacy is alive with many of the same tensions that percolate within *House* (at least, prior to the novel's ill-advised conclusion).

In closing, we must ask why the slipperiness of *Life* matters for either Hawthorne's audience or readers today. Can a nuanced re-assessment of the political in Hawthorne's *Life* reveal the limitations as well as redemptive qualities of the campaign biography as a genre? Or, like many critics of Hawthorne contend, we must ask if Hawthorne's uncertainty merely signals an author with relatively weak convictions – a writer that wants nothing more than to maintain the status quo at the expense of a horrifically oppressed community in which he has little emotional investment; a figure writing on behalf of a society with a similarly pathetic lack of commitment.

If the political exists as a macabre remainder in Hawthorne's fictional universe, it threatens violence, an omnipresent antagonism that may slide all too easily into mortal combat. Hawthorne would undoubtedly be repulsed by Carl Schmitt's elevation of political contest over the tepid façade of liberal universalism. Given that this sort of repulsion is heightened to an extraordinary degree in the buildup to the Civil War, the specter detailed by Schmitt plagues Hawthorne's textual landscapes in some of the most brutal forms imaginable. To avoid the brutality of revolution or reform, Hawthorne responds by relegating the political to the recesses of his fiction and nonfiction alike, allowing it to interject, to "return," only indirectly. For proponents of American democracy – a social arrangement that, at its most basic level, orbits around the prerequisite of ongoing partisan discord – the barbarism attendant to politics hovers at the margins, always about to burst into frame. Because Hawthorne cannot exorcise the ghost of the political, he attempts to channel it into more productive, and less bloody, ends:

> Instead of shying away from the component of violence and hostility inherent in social relations, the task is to think how to create the conditions under which those aggressive forces can be defused and diverted and a plurality democratic order made possible. (Mouffe 153)[12]

Hawthorne's *Life* defuses and diverts the aggressive forces of the political by treating democratic campaigns as open-ended arrangements that do not bypass dissatisfaction in one bold sweep, but offer instead an elusive signifier – the candidate as temporary placeholder – that allows readers to maintain a delicate balance between illusions of sameness and the intervention of requisite difference.

Critics will undoubtedly argue that the positions outlined in this chapter run the risk of presenting Hawthorne as either too far removed from real-world politics, as ethical mediator or, worse, apolitical escapist, or more politically charged than he actually proves to be. "We should be careful," Casper warns, "not to overemphasize the extent to which Hawthorne was revising biographical conventions" (222). Hawthorne's biography of Pierce undoubtedly remains flawed in ways that we should not ignore: it omits consideration of U.S. atrocities in the Mexican War, for one, and it understands slavery in purely theoretical, as opposed to empathetic, terms. Nonetheless, it is also possible for us to claim that Hawthorne's *Life* marks out new territory for the campaign biography by infusing it with tactics borrowed from his darker Romances. The parentheses in the title of this chapter convey the crux of democracy around which *Life* tarries – while the character of Pierce possesses "innate fitness," he is likewise a "new man" that has plenty of room to grow; subsequently, he must be characterized as (im)perfect, a harbinger of wholeness that simultaneously admits its own futility (75). Although Hawthorne's promise of a Pierce victory conjures mystical unity, it also demands wiggle room with which to account for the unavoidable dissatisfaction felt by a large percentage of voters after each election cycle. "No man," Hawthorne acknowledges, "ever did or ever could possess, in the slightest degree, what we may term a legitimate claim to be elevated to the rulership of a free people" (71). The sharpness of this sentiment recalls Hawthorne's earlier claim that no germ of the man was to be found in Pierce as a boy. Here again Hawthorne does not mince words by accentuating his sentiment with the phrase "in the slightest degree." Although *Life* wants its readers to think that Pierce has a legitimate claim to the Presidency, it periodically registers its own resistance to this very claim. That is, rather than resting exclusively on the notion that Pierce is a candidate well-endowed with Presidential gravitas, Hawthorne's text habitually deconstructs itself by fostering a sense of antagonism – specifically, the toil demanded by a Union that must remain not-yet-perfect, in perpetuity. To do so, *Life* recycles the imaginative tendencies from the more compelling sections of *House*. For example, in lieu of a resolution, Hawthorne closes *Life* by reiterating a liberal democratic principle: "The moral of this little story lies in the stern and continued exercise of self-controlling will" (78). In effect, Hawthorne produces the image of a candidate that can avoid stasis by continuing to exercise his own free will. Hawthorne's candidate, and the nation that he encapsulates, appears to be driven by self-control and individual will – concepts that call into doubt the charges of consensus-building and mindless compromise levelled against Hawthorne. Dissatisfaction thus plays a more pivotal role in *Life* than most critics have allowed.

Analysis of Pierce's (im)perfection aids us in grasping the relationship between Hawthorne's aesthetico-ethical preoccupations and a revived interest in the author's "political turn." Hawthorne pictures a candidate that defies partisanship via a neutral, enclosed Third Way and, at the same time, he manages to hold open opportunities for radical change, in both political and aesthetic terms. By intermingling Romantic ambivalence with the formulaic aspects of the campaign biography, *Life* depicts the downfall – or potential redemption – of an American society spiraling towards its imminent dissolution. As such, the text's subtle but persistent openness renders Hawthorne's biography of Pierce germane to contemporary discussions of the connection between American literature and extant threats to the nation's democratic experiment.

Notes

1 William Burlie Brown notes that the candidate at the center of these biographies is frequently "at once a changing and a static figure." Brown, however, quickly sets aside this pregnant observation, and – a mere two pages later – contradicts the complexity of his earlier statement, saying of the candidate's treatment in campaign biographies over the last century: "Basically he has remained the same" (143–145). It proves fruitful to return to Brown's initial statement and explore the tension of change and stasis in Hawthorne's portrayal of Pierce.
2 According to Lee Warner, "The biography certainly put Pierce in Hawthorne's debt" (22).
3 To consider the role of the President as a trope is not, however, to reduce it entirely to the realm of literary figuration. I wish to maintain a healthy dynamic between the President's political role – accompanied by substantial real-world consequences – and our rhetorical understanding of this role.
4 See Sacvan Bercovitch's "Hawthorne's A-Morality of Compromise." *Representations*, no. 24, 1988, pp. 1–27. *JSTOR*, www.jstor.org/stable/2928474. Accessed February 12, 2021.
5 Former British prime Minister Tony Blair articulates this double movement: "It is about traditional values in a changing world … rights *and* responsibilities… reforming central government to give it greater strategic capacity *and* devolving power to bring it closer to the people" (1, 7 author's emphasis).
6 Michael Tumolo writes that Hawthorne treats Pierce as a "composite of his past accomplishments" (499).
7 Van Wyck Brooks points to Hawthorne's pronounced wariness of New England's long lineage – a lineage that he himself shuns, changing his own name to erase what he perceived to be a corrosive family line: "In its moss-grown, many-gabled houses, paneled with worm-eaten wood and hung with half-obliterated portraits, dwelt at least the remnants of a race that retained the mental traits of a faraway past … morbid family pride" (211).
8 See F.O. Matthiessen's *American Renaissance: Art and Expression in the Age of Emerson and Whitman* (Oxford: Oxford University Press, 1941).
9 Holgrave laments, "We read in Dead Men's books! We laugh at Dead Men's jokes, and we cry at Dead Men's pathos!" To which Phoebe responds, "It makes me dizzy to think of such a shifting world" (130–131).
10 Brenda Wineapple highlights the tension: "If Louisa (Hawthorne's) disdain represented the family's view – politics paved the way to hell, not glory – small wonder that Hawthorne kept his worldly aspirations to himself" (260).
11 Gregory Staley doubts Hawthorne's ability to link Ovidian aesthetics to "historical and cultural processes"; therefore, for Hawthorne, an Ovidian agenda ultimately proves "too challenging" (142). In other words, because Hawthorne ostensibly resists political engagement, he cannot quite measure up to the standards set by his Roman predecessor as a thorn in the side of the Emperor.
12 Mouffe expands upon this concept by distinguishing between enemy and adversary, displaying a preference to the latter: "An adversary's… existence is legitimate and must be tolerated." In order to avoid treating opponents as enemies to be destroyed, a

condition that inevitably leads to Civil War, democrats must recognize the nature of the political as it actually exists (4–6).

Works Cited

Blair, Tony. *The Third Way: New Politics for the New Century* (London: Fabian Society, 1998).
Boyd, Richard. "The Politics of Exclusion: Hawthorne's *Life of Franklin Pierce*." *American Transcendental Quarterly*, vol. 3, no. 4, 1989, pp. 337–351.
Brodhead, Richard. *The School of Hawthorne* (Oxford: Oxford University Press, 1986).
Brooks, Van Wyck. *The Flowering of New England, 1815–1865; Emerson, Thoreau, Hawthorne and the Beginnings of American literature* (New York: Houghton Mifflin, 1981).
Brown, William Burlie. *The People's Choice: The Presidential Image in the Campaign Biography* (Baton Rouge, LA: Louisiana State University Press, 1960).
Casper, Scott E. *Constructing American Lives; Biography and Culture in Nineteenth-Century America* (Chapel Hill, NC: University of North Carolina Press, 1999).
Cheever, Susan. *American Bloomsbury: Louisa May Alcott, Ralph Waldo Emerson, Margaret Fuller, Nathaniel Hawthorne, and Henry David Thoreau: Their Lives, Their Loves, Their Work* (New York: Simon & Schuster, 2006).
Davis, Clark. *Hawthorne's Shyness: Ethics, Politics, and the Question of Engagement* (Baltimore, MD: Johns Hopkins University Press, 2005).
Feldherr, Andrew. *Playing Gods: Ovid's "Metamorphoses" and the Politics of Fiction* (Princeton, NJ: Princeton University Press, 2010).
Hall, Stuart. "The great moving nowhere show," in *Selected Political Writings: The Great Moving Right Show and Other Essays*, ed. Sally Davison *et al.* (Durham, NC: Duke University Press, 1998), pp. 283–301.
Hawthorne, Nathaniel. *The House of Seven Gables: Norton Critical Edition* (New York: W. W. Norton & Co., 2005).
Hawthorne, Nathaniel. *Life of Franklin Pierce* (New York: Clean Bright Classics, 2017).
Kaul, A.N. *The American Vision: Actual and Ideal Society in Nineteenth-Century Fiction* (Oxford: Oxford University Press, 2002).
Lang, Amy Schrager. "From Home, in the Better Sense: The Model Woman, the Middle Class, and the Harmony of Interests," in *The House of the Seven Gables: The Norton Critical Edition*, ed. Robert S. Levine (New York: W.W. Norton & Co., 2006), pp. 460–472. Print.
Lundberg, James. "Nathaniel Hawthorne, Party Hack," *Slate.com*, September 14, 2012. https://slate.com/news-and-politics/2012/09/nathaniel-hawthornes-biography-of-fra nklin-pierce-whyd-he-write-it.html. Accessed February 10, 2021.
Mouffe, Chantal. *The Return of the Political* (London: Verso, 1993).
Rancière, Jacques. *The Politics of Aesthetics* (New York: Bloomsbury, 2004).
Reynolds, David. *Beneath the American Renaissance: The Subversive Imagination in the Age of Emerson and Melville* (Oxford: Oxford University Press, 2011).
Reynolds, Lloyd. *Devils and Rebels: The Making of Hawthorne's Damned Politics* (Ann Arbor, MI: University of Michigan Press, 2010).
Staley, Gregory. "Hawthorne's Ovidian Transformations." *Classical Receptions Journal*, vol. 5, 2012, pp. 126–143.
Troy, Gil. *See How They Ran: The Changing Role of the Presidential Candidate*, Revised and expanded edn (Cambridge, MA: Harvard University Press, 1996).

Tumolo, Michael. "Nathaniel Hawthorne's Greatest Fiction: The Epideictic Function in Pierce's Presidential Campaign," in *The Functions of Argument in Context*, ed. Dennis S. Gouran (Washington, D.C.: The National Communication Associate, 2010), pp. 499–505.
Warner, Lee. *Nathaniel Hawthorne and the Making of the President, 1852* (Concord, NH: New Hampshire Historical Society, 1973).
Wineapple, Brenda. *Hawthorne: A Life* (New York: Random House, 2004).

3
WILLIAM DEAN HOWELLS AND THE REAL AMERICAN PRESIDENT

Besides Nathaniel Hawthorne and his portrayal of Franklin Pierce, there is perhaps no Presidential biographer better known than William Dean Howells. Howells, one of the leading literary voices in America at the twilight of the nineteenth century, is commissioned to write the biography of not one, but two aspiring Presidential candidates: Abraham Lincoln and Rutherford B. Hayes. Although the Lincoln book remains one of the least excoriated in the canon of campaign biographies, few critics have analyzed Howells' contributions in any detail, instead offering it only the faintest of praise. Howells scholar Edwin Cady, for one, describes the book on Lincoln as "not hackwork" (80). More recently, Jaime Fuller bashes the campaign biography as a genre, but she describes Howells' contribution as an exception to the rule – a "charming" piece atop a sea of rubbish (n.p.). This chapter takes the campaign biographies of Howells more seriously than most critics and fills a gap in existing scholarship by analyzing the literary dimensions of *Life of Abraham Lincoln* (1860) and *Sketch of the Life and Character of Rutherford B. Hayes* (1876), two works that idle – like so much of Howells' output – at the intersection of Romance and realism. Of other confused writers standing at this intersection, Howells observes: "Certain of them called themselves realists, certain romanticists; but none of them seemed to know what realism was, or what (R)omanticism" (*Hazard* 266). By projecting the American President as a mythological whole ("romanticistic") as well as a source of common ground (realism), Howells posits a transcendent figure that exists always and everywhere beyond the narrow limits of language; concurrently, because he never loses sight of the fissure between the mythological whole and his own inadequate textual representations, Howells retains important traces of incompleteness. If we re-read these biographies within their greater literary context – in this case, at the hinge between American Romance and realism – we discover a democratic undercurrent in American letters

DOI: 10.4324/9781003132448-4

that remains both absolute and impossible – an evocation that reminds us in its more pregnant moments that no system of thought, no government or its chronicle, could ever provide the final word.[1]

Critics of the campaign biography tend to isolate the genre from the literary output of its most prominent authors. Scott E. Casper acknowledges that these biographies inculcate "morality and patriotism" and, in turn, he assesses them as "not good literature" (10). I too would be reluctant to confuse the two styles in haste, since Howells certainly has a different set of intentions in mind when he writes *Life of Abraham Lincoln* than when he writes say, *The Rise of Silas Lapham* (1885). Nevertheless, we need not foreclose consideration of Howells' political preoccupations in dialogue with his more overtly "literary" concerns. Why not attend to the ways in which these different kinds of texts inform one another, aesthetically as well as politically? Indeed, Casper evokes this sort of dialogue by turning, a bit ironically, to Howells' commentary upon biography in *Lapham* in order to highlight the inherent limitations of campaign biographers: "In Howells's hands the subject emerged as a rounded, multi-faceted character with whom readers could sympathize – not a whitewashed exemplar of virtue, not a formulaic self-made man." Interestingly, Casper concedes that Howells' "realist novel offered the most insightful look at contemporary biographical forms and approaches" (318, 316). But given the fact that Howells himself also composes these biographies, would it not be more productive to create a conversation between these two sides of the realist's output rather than to categorize them as entirely oppositional to one another? After all, as Jill Lepore comments, Howells' campaign biography of Lincoln proves to be at once "the best example of the genre and a cunning parody of it" (n.p.).

Howells launches his career as a journalist with clear political leanings, zealously covering state and local politics on behalf of the Republican Party. In the lead-up to the election of 1860, Howells' publisher Follett, Foster, and Company predicts great profits from an Abraham Lincoln campaign biography, particularly on the heels of their successful Lincoln/Douglas *Debates*.[2] They are hardly alone in their pursuit: "Within a day of Lincoln's nomination on May 18 at least six publishers announced forthcoming campaign biographies"; when the dust eventually settles, Lincoln is the subject of nearly as many campaign biographies as his three opponents combined (Horrocks 45–46). Because of his partisan position, Follett, Foster, and Company ask Howells to write the biography for his fellow Midwesterner. The 23-year-old reporter does not see much in Lincoln at first, and he completes his assignment, with the help of a young law student as his research assistant as well as existing campaign biographies, in a little under a week, without ever meeting the Illinois native in person – a missed opportunity that Howells later regrets.[3] Even though it wins him a prominent position as consul in Venice, Italy, Howells never publicly celebrates his Lincoln biography. He initially downplays his effort due to what he sees as the unlikelihood of Lincoln winning, and later due to his much ballyhooed shift into a supposedly "apolitical" style of writing: "(Howells') self-concept after middle life dictate(s) that his early political activities must be minimized or ignored" (Cady 82).[4] Nevertheless, *Life of Abraham Lincoln* offers a glimpse into Howells' personal evolution as a writer as well as much larger literary tensions between Romanticism, now starting to fade from favor with American audiences, and realism, a movement in the nascent stages of its development. Not only are these biographies relatively complicated and open-ended texts, written in a complicated period, thereby meeting one of the central criteria used to determine "literariness" they also enable readers to recognize a latent `political dynamism within the genre.

On this front, Howells never moves far afield from one of his literary heroes, Hawthorne (the subject of the preceding chapter). Both men seek to move away from a fixed sense of utopia and characters that appear to be inherently perfect. In place of this misguided aim, Howells and Hawthorne each look to capture – albeit in distinctive ways – the beauty of America's unwieldy democratic framework, via what Alan Trachtenberg calls "fictions of the (R)eal" (192). At the same time, because neither writer seems willing to accept the restlessness of a fundamentally antagonist social arrangement, that is, American democracy, they often couch their calls for greater dissatisfaction, or an acceptance of humanity's imperfection, within an orderly, almost positivist literary structure. In other words, even as they present Pierce, Lincoln, and Hayes as temporary placeholders that embody a struggle that should never end – by definition, in a democracy, anyone could theoretically rise to power – they paradoxically associate these candidates with an untouchable American essence. Romantics (or at least, "romanticists") and realists share an ambition to convey something Real that never changes by simultaneously admitting that literature could never capture such an indeterminate notion. The presentations of Pierce, Lincoln, and Hayes thus tarry with the Real, a Truth that lingers beyond our meager faculties to comprehend it. For example, Pierce suggests a timeless lineage and a kernel of utopian ambition, while Lincoln and Hayes evoke a universal bond between all men. However, Hawthorne and Howells still stress their own ineptitude as biographers and acknowledge that their mortal talents could never convey the Real – a characteristic of Romantics and realists alike. In short, to locate the Real in American politics, each writer gestures at an indefinable ideal while concomitantly preserving the impossibility of laying claim to it. Herein lies a shared focus of American Romance and realism.[5] In turn, this chapter operates under the assumption that a stubborn belief in what can never be fulfilled remains the primary catalyst of democracy as well as nineteenth-century American literature – a stubborn, unfulfilled belief that is perhaps nowhere displayed more visibly than in the campaign biography.[6] Said another way, if Pierce, Lincoln, or Hayes ever proved to be the "last word" of American democracy, they would immediately turn into their opposite: an authoritarian's dream, unblemished and utterly oppressive.

It should not surprise us, then, that Howells articulates his unique brand of realism through references to another Presidential biography. "The Personal Memoirs of U.S. Grant," he explains, is

> written as simply and straightforwardly as his battles were fought, couched in the most unpretentious phrase, with never a touch of grandiosity or attitudinizing, familiar, homely in style (and it forms) a great piece of literature, because great literature is nothing more nor less than the clear expression of minds that have something great in them. (*Criticism* 45)

The concept of the American Presidency proves highly useful for Howells in articulating his vision for American realism. Since Howells uses Presidential biography to clarify in concrete details his artistic vision, and critics like Casper reference Howells' artistic vision to make sense of Presidential biographies, it is only logical that we too should engage these texts in relationship to one another. Through the figure of Grant and his other Executive subjects, Howells signals a "romanticistic" *consensus* concerning "greatness" – a vast, permanent state of things in the United States – as well as a stable *character* that needs nothing outside of itself – that is, the well-spring of Howells' bourgeois mindset. At the same time, as Howells demonstrates, the "greatness" of Grant and his fellow Presidents can never be conveyed in words, and so their literary treatment only ever diminishes their illusion of timelessness, their presumed lack of pretense, and their supposed sense of homeliness. Howells' uneven constructions of America's Chief Magistrates therefore do not serve as mere footnotes in his career, but as crucial entries that assist readers in illuminating the political potency behind his eclectic blend of Romance and realism, an eclectic blend that in fact characterizes the broader cultural shifts of post-1860s America.

Romance and Realism

We might start by defining the type of realism espoused by Howells, especially in the final years of his life. Importantly, his brand of realism remains in its very infancy in 1860, and so we must be careful not to retrofit his later aesthetic theories back onto his earlier biography of Lincoln. Moreover, we should not be too quick to set Howells against the Romance because, in actuality, he appreciates the Romance in its proper context, wishing only to reject what he derides as the "romanticistic." What I object to, he states, is "the (R)omantic thing which asks to be accepted with all its fantasticality on the ground of reality" (qtd. in Budd, 36). *Life* displays Howells' keen eye for the Romance stripped of its sentimentality – an eye that he cultivates through long hours poring over Longfellow, Cooper, and Irving. According to Howells, realism need not renounce Romance, at least Romance of the Hawthorne variety; in fact, both artistic modes tap into what cannot be given adequate form because to give the Truth a form always reduces, pollutes, and dilutes it. *The Life of Abraham Lincoln* provides an opportunity to recall how, for Howells, Romance and realism are always entwined with one another, and to consider the political implications of this conjunction. Howells' realism involves two steps: first, evoking common ground for every human being, and second, admitting that this common ground cannot be conveyed by mere words due to the innate limitations of language.[7]

Howells' two-step exercise recalls Hawthorne's *The House of Seven Gables*, written at about the same time as the Lincoln biography, in that both Howells and Hawthorne rail against the chaotic and chameleonic character of American consumerism in order to evoke universal tenets of "being human" that never change, what both Howells and Hawthorne see as existential constants. Trachtenberg observes, "Howells (resorts) often to 'romance' to preserve the moral assurances of his 'realism'" (192). In the words of Henry Nash Smith, the kind of American realism espoused by Howells ultimately espouses a very rigid social order: "Ordinary men and women going about their commonplace affairs (conveys) moral truth to the reader because moral principles are immanent in all experience, are indeed structural features of the actual world" (88). At the same time, though, the texts of Hawthorne and Howells stress the inaccessibility of the essence behind things: existential thresholds through which readers must not pass. Said another way, realism mirrors Romance in the tension that it fosters between faith in a higher ideal and cynicism about the unrealities on display in much of American prose.

Raised on a steady diet of Swedenborg, Howells expresses a crucial ambivalence in his campaign biographies by holding "the deeply imbedded belief that there is a supernatural order, together with a pragmatic willingness to let the unknowable and incommunicable stay unknown and uncommunicated" (Carter 27). In other words, he acts like a Romantic when he searches for the secrets of an invisible yet abiding world beneath the quotidian, but he remains a dark Romantic, intent on undercutting sentimentalism and blatant pandering through incisive truth-seeking. The trouble with this particular ethos, Harold Kolb notes, "is that (definitions of realism) depend on a small, often-repeated group of singularly evasive words – 'truth', 'actuality', 'accuracy', 'reality', 'objectivity'. These words often raise more problems than they solve" (26).

Amy Kaplan unpacks the strange amalgamation on display in Howells' realism. On the one hand, she explores how Howells projects "a vision of a common humanity" (21). Uneasy with the open-endedness of democracy, the author wishes to forge bonds between otherwise antagonistic social classes by professing a sort of "common sense … a communal consensus about the way things are" (23). That is, although Howells ostensibly espouses a more "democratic" experience, in which men come to know one another "as they really are," in actuality he elevates an illusion of consensus above and beyond the muck of political tumult. This prominent thread links Hawthorne's Romance to Howells' realism: the positing of a kernel of the Real that might bring greater order to mercurial modern moods – an appeal to "the common denominator of the ordinary ... a social whole" (25). For Hawthorne and Howells, this sense of wholeness is routinely associated with the anchor of a liberal subject to an unassailable personal character, or an (im)possible impression of consensus between the subject and the rest of humanity.[8] In American Romance as well as realism, "character" and "consensus" frequently serve as conceptual stop-gap measures with which to react against the threat of an ever-changing America.

To illustrate this stress upon consensus and character, let us turn to several of Howells' mature works that follow *The Life of Abraham Lincoln*. Specifically, Howells presents the Real as consensus through his depiction of ideal marriages. Whereas love letters are of fleeting significance, lacking "explicit intention," a genuine marriage involves harmony and equilibrium (*Modern* 25). In Howells' fictional universe, the bedrock of society can be found in the securities of a legal union through which individuals discover their shared imperfections. Consider for instance the Laphams from *The Rise of Silas Lapham*: despite the turmoil that surrounds the husband's fluctuating fortunes in business, it is their marriage that saves them in the end because it grounds them in a uniform human condition. Perhaps the most fully realized vision of this consensus in Howells' corpus remains the Marches from *Hazard of New Fortunes* (1889).[9] The novel argues that, in marriage, "people supplement each other and form a pretty fair sort of human being together" (*Hazard* 34). The bond of the Marches underscores what remains permanent and Real, that which Howells depicts as "authentic" versus the supposed impermanence of contemporary life: "In the high effect (Mrs. March) realized (her husband); she did him justice" (332). Unsettled by the mutability of city life, Howells' unique brand of realism projects an adhesive social animus beneath the surface of daily existence to hold society together, effectively making Two into One.

From here, Howells extends his Romantic/realist notion from the married couple to the body politic in its entirety. *Hazard* moves the reader from the tasteless habitations of the poor, to the idiotically gilded abodes of the wealthy, to his preferred room, where "the family can come together and feel the sweetness of being a family" (58). Beneath the frenzied façade of Manhattan, then, Howells locates a kernel of the Real, a totality that transcends the limited scope of any singular perspective: "I like to think that there is one soul uncontaminated by the sense of money in this big, brutal, sordid city" (207). *Hazard* tells the tale of a common ground that somehow survives the onslaught of urban swell. Howells means for his reader to take comfort in the underlying consensus concerning what is "right" – an uncontaminated soul that is universal, immoveable, and Real. In sum, although Howells' realism outwardly resists the allure of naïve utopia, it habitually circles back to a utopian center through a plea for the reader to grasp what is eternal, unyielding, and True for all people.

In addition to its drift toward the illusion of consensus, Howells' mature works find a moral anchor in the issue of personal character. March embodies the man of principle as he invariably finds his way to an a priori sense of what is "right and just." When his hyper-capitalist boss asks him to fire a war veteran for expressing socialist sentiments, March refuses to do so, thereby putting his principles into action. His wife remarks, upon learning of her husband's valiant stand, "The great thing ... is to be right" (312). The novel declares of another man of principle: "You are good, and you are just!" (367). *Hazard* best articulates Howells' Romantic/realist focus upon character in its final pages when March shares a look with another principled character and, without uttering a word, both individuals glimpse "the peace that passeth understanding" (431). In his late novels, Howells never manages to move entirely away from this authoritative vision because, even when he admits that this vision can exist at best at the outermost periphery of our gaze, he believes in its existence as a beacon of hope and, more important still, as a source of stronger social stability.

Howells' Real exists in an apolitical ether, unpolluted by the *demos*. According to Howells, we encounter the Real only by first decoupling ourselves from society, acting alone and without input from others. March starts to "feel like (the) populace," and in response he must struggle to regain the "character of philosophical observer" (360). When another character witnesses systemic injustice – policemen kill a group of protesters, including the socialist war veteran – she retreats into introspection instead of political activism: "I don't blame the policeman ... I am only trying to find out how much I am to blame myself" (375). Put a bit differently, when Howells stresses the value of a priori personal character, he presents individuals that are disembedded from their community, and by so doing, he removes the idea of "good character" from public debate or accountability. In his construction of the Real, Howells relies upon the Kantian, clinical coldness of liberalism – a notion of what is "just" that never truly changes, regardless of the social context. Charles F. Richardson views this approach as potentially harmful: "(Realism) stands without, not within; (it) gives no evidence of personal sympathy" (431). In Howells' body of work, the apolitical Real becomes at times codified, fixed like some north star to guide us. As Thomas Horrocks describes it, the Real inspires "lives worth emulating – lives devoted to the common good and rising above the boisterous and sometimes undignified world of politics" (41). The authoritarian underpinnings are difficult to miss.

Yet what are we to do with the look exchanged between Howells' principled actors? Are we to trust in this unspoken absence, the (im)possible understanding that passes between them? Despite the unrest that breaks out across Manhattan? Despite a growing schism between chaotic city life and the increasingly implausible ideals of consensus or character? Since Howells recognizes that no language could adequately convey his a priori sense of "right" – being, as he is at heart, a Romantic as well as a realist – his texts cannot entirely foreclose their initial open-endedness. "In spite of himself, (Howells') fictions of the (R)eal disclose the unresolved gaps and rifts within the traditional world view he wishes to maintain, to correct and discipline" (Trachtenberg 192). As a result, the incompleteness of his "fictions of the Real" preserves a number of political possibilities. Many critics of *Life* overlook this vital aspect of the text, as when William Burlie Brown argues: "The sure political instinct which makes (campaign biographers) such adroit propagandists has led them deliberately to ignore the (R)eal and to continue the old ideal" (35). In truth, it is the *tension* between the Real and the ideal that makes *Life* so compelling. The passing glance between March and his companion retains traces of cynicism, of a darker Romance and more brooding realism. These figures cannot actually understand one another – one of them has transformed from a socialite to a nun, after all – and, moreover, as they are transformed by the raging torrent of upheaval that encroaches upon their bourgeois lives, they could never hope to keep track of the ever-mutable sense of what is "right." Instead of holding strong to an unspoken understanding, to that fixed north star, Howells invites his reader to acknowledge an omnipresent lack of understanding. Where words fail and readers must linger at the threshold, it remains possible for them to invent, to change, or to generate something truly different for their community. The One might be made Two again.

For all of its attempts to formulate an authoritative consensus or character to "silence" the unruly reader, Howells' fiction never forgets the omnipresent absence at the center of its project, an anxiety that characterizes many of Hawthorne's Romances as well. Even as his "culture of character (presumes) the existence of an inner core of an essential self," part of the enduring appeal of Howells' realism stems from its stress upon dissatisfaction its recognition that people and their social arrangements will be forever subject to unforeseeable alterations (Kaplan 24). The incomplete nature of Howells' prose leaves open a doorway to democratic differences. Because these differences cannot be foreclosed, his hybrid Romance/realism reveals what is crucial in the unsettling promise of American democracy. Its doomed desire for wholeness, for that City on the Hill, remains perpetually at odds with its drive toward dissolution. Howells' best works prove instructive in their adroit handling of this internal friction.

In *A Modern Instance* (1882), for example, Howells reveals a drive to dissolution through his character's constant disenchantment with modern conventions. The novel's anti-hero, Bartley Hubbard, never tells the Truth, although he assumes the posture of an "authentic" person. Instead of being honest, he manipulates everyone with whom he comes into contact, thus serving as the living embodiment of the sensational journalism that he peddles to the masses. *Modern* is a text about the gradual unraveling of a marriage. Against the supposed utopia of its early days (Bartley comments of a sentimental carriage ride that he shares with his fiancée on his engagement day: "I should like this ride to last forever!"), it turns out that none of this feigned contentment is Real (*Modern* 55). Rather, Howells' entire cast of characters remains caught in a cycle of self-sabotage, since they prefer to return to a state of incompleteness instead of languishing under the yoke of consensus or character. "Why do we try to talk? ... The more we say the more we leave unsaid" (47).

Even though he has achieved everything that he initially sets out to achieve in his career, Bartley eventually undermines his own "happiness" by sinking into reckless financial speculation. For Bartley, the Real mercifully disrupts his superficial gamesmanship to remind him – and Howells' reader – that the "reality" that he has created for himself is only ever a false front, and so he remains alive, free to desire something different instead of becoming fossilized as a caricature of himself. In turn, we need not read Bartley's eventual ruin as a predetermined fate that he must endure, but as "the ruin he had chosen" (348). Said another way, Bartley undoes his own "domestic bliss" because the absence of such fulfillment allows him to continue to desire something else, and not to fall into a stupor. "I can afford anything," he realizes, "When I'm hungry" (136). The running question of *Modern* remains: why do people undermine their own "happiness" by preferring to break down their personal narratives of success? "They chose misery for themselves – we make our own hell" (477). Just why is it that these characters undermine their own happy endings? Unlike marriage as a form of consensus in *Hazard*, marriage in *Modern* appears to be rooted in the absence of unity. For Bartley's wife, Bartley becomes a "fetish" – a static stand-in for an (im)perfect man. By canonizing him, she ensures her own dissatisfaction and defers any address of the Real – that is, the fact that no man could ever fulfill her or make her whole. Unlike the overstated union of the Marches, Howells founds the Hubbard marriage upon the promise of divorce. Divorce, "the guilty hope of escape," signals a Real that cannot be solidified as consensus because, by definition, it promises only to unsettle the Hubbards and deny them final satisfaction. And this promise keeps them from sinking into a sluggish status quo. Indeed, Bartley's wife realizes that the ever-present idea of divorce allows her to deny any irreversible arrangement with her miscreant husband, and to preserve in the process the threshold between them as a meaningful barrier. Even after her divorce, she cannot rest easy, as she and Bartley learn that the Real threatens to overturn any imposed plot, marital or otherwise.

Modern compromises the concept of personal character as a marker that counters the restlessness of contemporary existence. Howells' text calls the concept of character into question through Ben Halleck, a hyper-religious man that secretly covets Bartley's wronged wife. Ben's "love" for her is of the chivalrous variety and so his affections depend upon the premise that this "love" remains eternally unrealized. As the novel makes very clear, if she were ever to return Ben's affections, she would be "spoiled" and her supposed perfection would be destroyed for him. Like Howells' other characters, Ben's desires thinly disguise a drive to remain incomplete. His incompleteness is precisely what saves him from realizing his dreams and then having nothing left to do, no idyllic queen left to woo. Moreover, when everyone lauds Ben for his "gentlemanly" conduct in regards to the Hubbards, he is enraged that no one sees his wickedness. He longs to expose his wickedness to refute the stultifying label of "saint" that has come to define him among the Boston upper crust. He undercuts kindly words used to describe his character because only by preserving a gap between himself as an ideal and himself as not-yet-satisfied can he continue to exist with any sense of movement or purpose. "No more principles," he insists. "There's nothing for me but to *run*, and that's what I'm going to do" (365, author's emphasis). In this way, Howells paints parallel tracks for his two main characters – one a sinner and one a saint – that share the initials B.H., Bartley Hubbard and Ben Halleck While one achieves marriage without love (Bartley), and the other achieves love without marriage (Ben), both men preserve their own incompleteness in order to refuse the creature comforts of consensus or chivalrous character. This is Howells' Real – the ongoing absence of perfection that, in line with American democracy, sustains opportunities to erase bad arrangements and go back to the drawing board.

Even as Eric Sundquist records how, in Howells' fiction, "(R)omance ... remain(s) the visceral, spiritual essence of the (R)eal," neither Hawthorne nor Howells totally strips the Real of its innate political dynamism. Rather, the Real haunts the works of Hawthorne and Howells and leaves them always unfinished, always lingering at the threshold, always open to something different. It is a surplus that no fiction can claim to encompass: the unspeakable mutability that gives bipartisan stewards heart palpitations due to its correlation with prolonged antagonism. After all, if human beings and their respective governments are eternally works-in-progress, attempts to counteract this tumult with an authoritative Truth are invariably destined to fail. And where better to understand the political implications of this unrest than in *The Life of Abraham Lincoln*, a text that funnels Howells' Romantic and realist impulses through an acutely political aperture?

Having surveyed his later works for relevant insights, we are now well situated to return to Howells' campaign biographies with a new appreciation for their generic as well as political qualities, and their important role at a crossroads in Howells' career. Chantal Mouffe writes of the political: "Things could always be otherwise and therefore every order is predicated on the exclusion of other possibilities" (*On the Political* 18). The enduring antagonism between wholeness and incompleteness that defines American Romance as well as American realism also reflects the radicality of American democracy – a shared sensibility that compels us to take greater stock of the complexities behind campaign biographies written by the likes of Howells. Although he encourages his readers to seek refuge with an ontic "conventional politics," he simultaneously encourages them to be discomforted by the uncertainties of political contest: "Antagonisms can take many forms and it is illusory to believe that they could ever be eradicated" (30). In a word, although he employs character and consensus to capture a Real that transcends everyday experience, these meager codes can put a period on the sentence of neither American literature nor politics. Even in their more anxious moments, authors like Hawthorne and Howells cannot erase "the contingent character of the hegemonic politico-economic articulations ... precarious and pragmatic constructions which can be disarticulated and transformed" (33). That is, at the intersection of American Romance and realism, we recognize the importance of a missing link like *The Life of Abraham Lincoln*. This otherwise disposable tract reveals crucial parallels between the aesthetic tensions of Howells' corpus and the ongoing (re)articulations of American democracy.

"Honest Abe"

Howells incessantly employs "picturesque touches" to foster a very specific kind of reception by his imagined reader (*Modern* 169). In Burkean terms, the picturesque exists between the sublime and the beautiful, and so the term invokes many of the same tensions outlined in the previous section. On the one hand, the beautiful puts the mind at ease due to its comprehensive totality – a Real to transcend the fickle worlds of fashion and fiction, what we described in the previous section as consensus or character. On the other hand, the sublime reveals how the mind cannot fully comprehend the enormity of the Real and reminds us of the lacuna behind any fixed representation. When he employs the term picturesque, Howells gestures at the intermediary stage between the sublime and the beautiful: a dynamic phase that reveals the dual impulses behind his hybrid of American Romance and realism. Howells capitalizes upon the figure of Lincoln to convey a Real that exists as a utopian whole beyond the commonplace as well as a Real that sustains the incompleteness of any political arrangement by refusing to resign readers to a blind ideal.

Let us re-read Howells' campaign biography, then, by first attending to its underlying sense of utopian wholeness. Again, this utopian wholeness cannot be exclusively reduced to a naïve, or genteel, aspect of the "romanticistic" – although it can certainly be described this way as well; rather, Howells' notion of utopian wholeness remains associated with American Romanticism and realism, a transcendental concept that exists above reproach and requires confirmation from neither artist nor politician. In Howells' hands, Lincoln's story becomes the larger-than-life myth that circulates widely in the years after his assassination. Of course, the figure of Lincoln is not simply a fable, or it would slip readily under the exclusive purview of the sentimental writer. In contrast, the Lincoln mythos exposes a common thread between Romance and realism. As we have already seen, Romance and realism appeal to a Truth that lies beneath the turbulent surface of American life, which is to say, these twin literary modes reach for a stable Real to resonate beyond the capriciousness of contemporary existence. Celebrated champion of the Union, Lincoln serves as a convenient avatar for a supposedly fixed essence.

The figure of Lincoln signifies an illusion of wholeness through Howells' static depiction of the candidate's "good character." Howells anchors his depiction of Lincoln to hard work, wisdom, and humility because the figure of Lincoln signifies a priori values and makes them appear to be unchanging as well as unpolluted by an otherwise restless populace. In a word, Howells' Lincoln offers a rigid reference point against which the reader might chart her own course. Regardless of the actual biography of the flesh-and-blood Lincoln, Howells imagines a character, in the most abstract sense, that cannot be influenced by the rise and fall of the nation's barometer. He exploits the name "Lincoln" as a placeholder to sustain a thoroughly apolitical set of beliefs and values – beliefs and values that ostensibly depend upon neither political wrangling nor demand to be upheld by the electorate. Herein lies the apolitical message frequently conveyed by American writers like Hawthorne and Howells. Lincoln's elite character appears to float high above the fracas.

To capture this concept, Howells ties Lincoln's underlying character, which supposedly exists outside of the political realm, to the merits of industriousness. Lincoln represents "untiring industry," a Protestant work ethic that stands out as "good" in-and-of-itself (30). According to *Life*, the de facto world to which Lincoln returns when the political arena strikes him as inhospitable is the world of business, where the plain ax only ever does "its work" (27). Lincoln the rail-splitting candidate therefore exists as window dressing for a far more dependable undercarriage. His closed character remains in effect an emblem of efficiency, tireless effort, and the latent rewards of industriousness. Howells draws Lincoln the man as akin to a tool, like an ax, that embodies an inert compliance with the ethos of American business. If left to his own devices, Lincoln would simply "do his work" without question or concern.[10]

Lincoln's inert character serves as a veritable repository of a priori values that, the logic of the biography goes, take shape with little input from the *demos*. In a particularly effusive passage, Howells' biography describes Lincoln as "a pure, candid, and upright man, unblemished by those vices which so often disfigure greatness utterly incapable of falsehood, and without one base or sordid trait" (48). Although Howells' later genteel characters like Mr. March do not appear so overtly fettered to a Romantic ideal, it is worth noting that Mr. March is also tethered to a sense of character that varies only in a superficial sense, and so the utter rigidity of Lincoln's character can be considered indicative of a much larger trend in Howells' corpus. Elaine Hedges concludes, "Howells' (moral) code was itself imbued with a more flagrant species of 'romanticism' than any of which his characters stand accused" (136).[11] The candidate from Illinois embodies solid, universal virtues that undergird human existence. Unlike his fellow politicians, Lincoln does not ride the fence, or "mince matters" with his opponents – which is another way of declaring his apolitical nature, as though he could somehow serve as a "politician" without antagonizing others (Howells *Life*, 57). Stripped of political garb, Lincoln the candidate elicits an "admirable simplicity of diction" and "singular good sense" (62). In contemporary parlance, American politicians habitually resort to questions of "authenticity" in order to appear more Real than their alternates – a tendency that can be traced back at least as far as Howells' campaign biography. Although the candidate's essentialized and inert character may strike careful readers as a hodge-podge of thinly-sketched values such as "industriousness" or "honesty," Howells stresses Lincoln as a singularity. He sketches a sense of character as comprehensive as it is cohesive: a pre-existing constellation of traits that every human being can admire in the most general terms.

Howells' Lincoln (im)possibly precedes the communities to which he belongs. According to Howells, dignity is not a social value that exists prior to Lincoln's arrival on the scene, but Lincoln – by choosing to do certain things – "confers a dignity upon them" (50). Put a bit differently, one does not measure Lincoln by already existing definitions of dignity; instead, one defines dignity through the standards set by Lincoln. During his legal career, for instance, Lincoln's "known (T)ruth" transcends the mere arguments that he constructs, as the jury – with neither evidence nor legal precedent – arrives always at "the belief that Lincoln is *right*" (52, author's emphasis). Above and beyond the candidate, there exist what Howells refers to as "Lincoln's principles," principles that remain absolutely vital to Western civilization. In fact, Howells goes so far as to write: "The advancement of (Lincoln) might impede the advancement of his principles" (73). Like the inert ax that merely does its "work," the weight of Lincoln's character, his "principles," clearly surpasses the weight of the flesh-and-blood candidate. His a priori values separate the figure of Lincoln from any sign of indebtedness to the world around him. He owes "no man anything" (52). Once more, given the commentary upon the inevitability of debt in *The Rise of Silas Lapham*, we might be tempted to reject as naïve Howells' earlier treatment of Lincoln as a man without debts. However, even Silas occasionally models a debt-free existence, as he seems tethered to the consensus that he shares with his wife as well as the character that he preserves as a pragmatic Vermonter. Lincoln too models transcendental ideals removed from any social context, and as a result his neighbors love Lincoln not for his political postures, but as a "logical result" of his stock-still character (43).

Consequently, in Howells' hands, the ideal democratic candidate serves as a cause, rather than an effect, of the nation's "greatness." The winning candidate stands out as neither the symptom of a "wise" society nor the fortunate occupant of an aspirational post meant to lift up the person that occupies it. Howells instead presents shows how Lincoln's strong character precedes his political ascent. The biography directly states: "It is the Presidency, not a great man, that would be elevated" by Lincoln's election (51). In turn, by framing Lincoln's "good character" as a fixed standard, *Life* reminds us of the limited political potential of the genteel American traditions of Romanticism and realism alike.

In sum, *Life* presents Lincoln as the immobile stuff of American myth: a stiff avatar for the spirit of the place as well as its people. Howells captures a consensus that feels quite political but in truth, allows for precious little reflection or revision among Howells' readers. Howells asks that voters/readers rally behind "the man who was the first to utter that great (T)ruth, which all men felt" (88). Again, the Real associated with Howells' Lincoln – an imagined consensus among all Truthful people – anticipates his rise to power; instead of being born from the collective will of a community, the sense of consensus associated with the candidate exists above and beyond public scrutiny (a thoroughly undemocratic sentiment).[12] To gesture at this rigid Real, Howells rejects even himself as an agent of change, and he dismisses almost entirely the political function of American literature: "(I) prefer to leave the future of Lincoln to Providence and to the people, who often make history without the slightest respect to the arrangements of sagacious writers" (94). Whenever Lincoln speaks, "the jubilant responses of the people" are automatic, and Howells' readers are meant to assume that the candidate reflects a static *vox populi*, one that stands out due to its common-sensical overtones (89). Howells constructs Lincoln as an ideal worthy of emulation by positioning the Illinois politician as a placeholder for a Real that exists at the outermost edge of the author's horizons.

Yet precisely because of the gap that exists between the Real and the limits of language, Howells at times concedes that Lincoln acts as a placeholder instead of a marker of perpetual principles. Literature, Howells notes, always involves a degree of conjecture, and such conjecture invariably proves to be "idle and impertinent." Consequently, the hapless biographer attends to Lincoln's "earnest struggle" with the "accidents of ignorance and poverty," opting to focus upon the candidate's ignoble background as a source of uncertainty instead of comfort – that is, as a source of happy accidents, not predetermined "greatness" (20). Simply put, Howells constructs the Lincoln myth even as he deconstructs it. He posits Lincoln's inherent wholeness, like a dutiful dark Romantic or brooding realist, only to alert readers to the incomplete nature of the candidate's exercise.

To maintain this sense of incompleteness, *Life* parallels many of the other campaign biographies in circulation in 1860, as the author actively distances himself from the text that he produces in order to highlight the "authenticity" of the account, which is to say, he deliberately highlights the fictive nature of his own work in order to gesture at what lies beyond it. Howells' recurring withdrawal reminds us that the American President is frequently a figure that resists its own figuration, a democratic symbol that evades its permanent place in the annals of history. Howells foregrounds his inadequacy as a biographer: "If the time had not been wanting one could have made (the biography) a great deal better." Just why is it that so many of these campaign biographies instinctively reject their own claims of legitimacy? According to Howells, *Life*

> will not be numbered with these immortal books which survive the year of their publication. It does not challenge criticism; it fulfills the end of its being if it presents facts and incidents in a manner not altogether barren of interest. (xi)

Howells renders Lincoln "great" because there are no words that could adequately convey the Illinois politician's private journey. Romantics and realists of the stature of Hawthorne and Howells gesture at the inevitable failure of literature to capture ideals that are far more powerful than any given text. In this manner, Howells weakens the candidate's illusion of wholeness, the fixed essence of character and consensus, to preserve Lincoln as a concept that can elude the ability of written expression to memorialize it. In effect, the power of Lincoln's image endures as a result of, not in spite of, his campaign biography being so unyieldingly mediocre.

Howells stresses the decoupling of the name "Lincoln" from a rigid Real with his chronicle of the candidate's dubious family history. Howells writes, "Further back than a grandfather few can go with satisfaction. Everything lies wrapt in colonial obscurity and confusion ... an extremely embarrassing uncertainty as to the fact of great-grandparents." Unlike Hawthorne's depiction of Pierce as a man with a long and important legacy, Howells depicts Lincoln as a man that lacks a substantial genealogical context: "The noble science of heraldry," he asserts, "is almost obsolete in this country" (17). By lifting Lincoln up and away from his family tree in this way, Howells embraces an underlying obscurity, confusion, and – most important for our purposes – uncertainty. Indeed, the "anterior" of Lincoln's grandfather is "incertitude, and absolute darkness of names and dates" (18). Howells' stress upon incertitude momentarily posits Lincoln as a form without content, a signifier without a clear signified. In these instances, Lincoln resonates not because of his mythological status, but because he remains free to mean something else, and so he can be said to gesture at the potential of an always-already (im)perfect democracy. Despite its bourgeois baggage in terms of character and consensus, the notion of Lincoln remains politically charged due to its incompleteness as well as its inability to define American society with any finality.

As a result of this active tension, *Life* follows a sort of dialectical pattern. Howells asserts Lincoln's wholeness only to retract it in favor of what is not being said (and so on, ad infinitum). In one moment, Lincoln represents the frontier, the "forest primeval" that remains a blank canvas, a "wilderness" on which to write the nation's future; in the very next moment, however, he represents "common" trials that are "so often repeated"; and then, mere moments later, Howells undercuts his own portrayal of national consensus with a reminder that the Real cannot be encapsulated in such an elementary fashion: Lincoln's farm life cannot be romanticized, he insists, and so it remains "difficult to perceive how (his farming) has affected his career" (21, 24). In this oscillating manner, Howells' biography operates along a fault line between American Romance and realism, recognizing Lincoln as one of the precious few possible subjects worthy of being read and an (im)possible topic that cannot be conveyed via the ordinary channels of America's political discourse. Howells' biography instills in its readers

> a double effect: the readability of a political signification and a sensible or perceptual shock caused, conversely, by the uncanny, by that which resists signification ... a negotiation between opposites, between the readability of the message that threatens to destroy the sensible form of art and the radical uncanniness that threatens to destroy all political meaning. (Rancière *Politics*, 59)

"Unconscious Even in its Consciousness"

Life was not to be Howells' last attempt at writing a Presidential campaign biography. In 1876, Hayes' campaign asks him to write the biography for Rutherford B. Hayes in his fight against Democrat Samuel Tilden. Hayes, the cousin of Howell's wife Elinor, is a widely respected Republican and Howells goes into his second attempt at the campaign biography with greater zeal than he did in his prior effort for the lesser-known Lincoln. Although the final product *Life and Character of Rutherford B. Hayes* ultimately underwhelms, selling only two thousand copies, because the election itself would be one of the most disputed in American history, every minor bit of assistance for the candidate proves to be vital. Hayes himself finds the work so agreeable to his tastes that he later invites Howells to the White House for six days so that Howells can lobby for literary friends like James Russell Lowell to receive plum political appointments.

Today, critical reception of the Hayes' biography remains divided. Earlier critics such as Louis Budd describe it as "much more convincing than his similar treatment of Lincoln"; in comparison to a rival bibliography of Hayes, Lyon N. Richardson likewise lauds the Howells text for its lack of clichés as well as its unwillingness to be "entirely perfunctory" (Budd 144; L. Richardson 119). Contemporary critics more commonly declare the Hayes' book to be less interesting than the Lincoln book. For Susan Goodman and Carl Dawson, Howells' treatment of Hayes "overlooks any detail harmful to the saintly candidate," and the biography remains, in their estimation, both "overstated" as well as "underwritten" (196). From a historical perspective, *Sketch of the Life and Character of Rutherford B. Hayes* marks a crucial turn in Howells' career because it signals the close of his blatantly political life. From 1876 onward, Howells claims to write novels that are more "metapolitical" in orientation (197). With this unique context in mind, we might ask what Howells' campaign biography of Hayes reveals about ongoing tensions between Romance, realism, and American politics.

As he does with Lincoln, Howells once again projects the candidate's character as a priori and immovable. He tracks Hayes' moral growth along a steady trajectory upward, as the candidate's "progress" remains ostensibly "constant and in the right direction" (*Sketch* 155). Like Lincoln, Hayes' character appears to exist above all reproach. It is so transcendent, in fact, that the word "character" shares billing on the book's marquee with the candidate's "life." Howells elevates Hayes' unimpeachable character by reversing what we might expect to be the typical causal chain: "(Hayes) did not seek promotion," Howells points out, because "promotion was seeking him" (76). Recalling Lincoln's *Life*, the Hayes biography removes its primary subject from the society to which he belongs and transforms his supposedly pure character into a standard with which to measure the merits of American government. Hayes can be elevated neither by the esteem of his fellow countrymen nor by the wisdom of his community's legal system; instead, his unimpeachable character elevates these things by forcing everyone else to rise above their lot to meet his standard. Hayes remains, in the final tally, "simply great" (114). To supplement this message, Howells – for reasons practical as well as stylistic – employs even more primary material from the candidate in *Sketch* than he does in *Life*, and as a result the second biography wants to be read as an unadulterated glimpse at Hayes' inner values: "Let him speak … for himself" (193).[13]

The illusion of an authentic Real extends to Howells' depiction of Hayes as a signifier of consensus. Howells lauds his candidate's refusal to run for office as well as his reluctance to enter the political fray; he uses this rhetorical tactic with Lincoln as well, just as Hawthorne employs it in his biography of Pierce. Indeed, this reluctance characterizes many campaign biographies. Hayes' apparent reluctance to enter American politics empowers him to serve as "the people's unprompted choice" (19). The notion of an "unprompted choice" appears to establish a consensus that exists prior to public deliberation. Howells prompts his reader to discover "a sense of justice and of self-respect in the popular heart which would finally respond to (Hayes') own" (133). Beyond contending that the strong character of the nation is preceded by the strong character of Hayes,' this line also alerts readers to an (im)possible consensus in which the entire citizenry could agree upon all questions of justice. As a composite "popular heart," Hayes maintains "perfect confidence in the people" (148). Howells intends this sense of poetic harmony to be both transcendent and "more Real than reality" – deeper and Truer than the rhetorical trickery of other politicians or artists.

But in playing with the gap between the Real and mere rhetoric, Howells perhaps inadvertently emphasizes the incompleteness of any candidate or campaign chronicle. By stressing his own literariness as well as the unliterariness of his political subject, Howells retains a trace of the Real that can never be finalized in writing – or through formal election, for that matter. On Hayes' diary of the Mexican–American War, for one, Howells writes that Hayes "sees with Dickens-like quickness, but paints as if merely to secure his own sense of it, and not for any literary effect" (31). Hayes doubles as an ideal realist, then, because he subverts his own lofty perceptions of the world's grand plot and, against visions of the war as "a rapture of patriotism," he never loses sight of the ugliness "beneath the smiling mask" (54, 58). The candidate strikes us as apolitical and therefore lacking in rhetorical training, which is to say, he stands "nobly free from the arts of the rhetorician and the clap-trap of the politician" (143). Undoubtedly, Howells partially highlights this shortcoming to account for Hayes' less than electrifying speeches and to underscore once again the candidate's extraordinary personal character: Hayes takes a "purer delight" in literature than "the professional litterateur"; he reads texts in a manner unlike any other reader, "from an unliterary point" (34–35). Partly as an over-compensation for Hayes' inarticulate mannerisms, Howells artfully distances *Sketch* from the Real. His campaign biography for Hayes is in the final tally a "Sketch," not "a Life," since his political treatise conveys Howells' evolving sense of realism by isolating "vulgar sentimentalists" from what we are meant to see as a more "genuine" reflection of the human condition (148). The effect of Howells' distancing of the literary from the Real doubles as a haunting reminder of the political: a reminder that a candidate, like any text, can only ever be a temporary stand-in for an arrangement that can always be otherwise. This trace of difference cannot be expunged from public record. Hayes' primary documents "convey but a fragmentary impression," while Howells' secondary portrayal remains equally "imperfect" (164, 195). Howells' confessed inability to capture the Real endows *Sketch* – like Lincoln's *Life* – with a vitality that cannot be completely stifled by the biography's authoritative fixity of character and consensus.

Readers are therefore left with two candidates that Howells describes as "charmingly picturesque" – a modifier that reveals a good deal about the internal tensions of the campaign biography as a genre as well as the internal struggles of American democracy (10). To reiterate, the picturesque brings the beautiful, what the mind contentedly grasps in its totality, into conversation with the sublime, before which the mind stands in awe. This ambivalence manifests in American Romance as well as realism: a struggle to achieve settled politics without simultaneously sacrificing the contemplative possibilities latent within the nation's democratic order. For example, Hayes is "just touched and not more than touched with poetry," meaning, he conveys a beautiful symmetry with "the people" yet he refuses to become a static, "romanticistic" icon (171). His "proportions are heroic" yet his figure "is not larger than life" (194). He "inherits" his character yet he can only achieve his character through "sturdy" training (47). Hayes strikes the reader as picturesque because of the beauty of the candidate's synergy with America's universal character and his reflection of a universal consensus alongside his evocations of a sublime essence that exists "beyond the scope and limits" of a mere "Sketch" (4).[14] This instability interests us not only because it helps us to understand better the intersection of Romance and realism in Howells' canon, but because it speaks to how these tensions continue to infuse our electoral discourse.

Anticipating the modern moment, Howells' picturesque campaign biographies confuse the appeal of anti-political sentiments with the active pursuit of political ends. For instance, in less than ten pages, Howells admires how Hayes' knows "the whole country politically" as well as how he keeps meticulous track of his opponent's "political turns and windings" – before the biographer states, with no apparent hint of irony, that "how to come to power never gave (Hayes') an hour's unrest" (163, 171). Whereas Lincoln and Hayes ostensibly exist outside of pedestrian politics, their biographies preserve a feeling of political restlessness, an open-endedness, and a sense of innate antagonism that – for Howells, at least – defines American democracy. Perhaps the most pregnant summation of this phenomenon surfaces in Hayes' account of his own life. Howells marvels at how the candidate provides "a frank, simple, generous record, *unconscious even in its consciousness*" (17–18, emphasis mine). Howells depicts his candidate as picturesque due to an ongoing friction between the Real – the unconscious Truth that defies any attempt to pin it down in writing – and a conscious articulation of the man's "greatness." These candidates are whole and incomplete, all at once. In a word, Howells' campaign biographies prove to be "unconscious even in their consciousness," moved in equal measure by the allure of the "romanticistic" and the rhythm of the realist. And mercifully so, because if we were ever to become completely enchanted by the eternal promise of character or consensus, or exclusively enticed by the absence of any such figuration, we might find ourselves under the thumb of a fascist, or in the throes of anarchy.[15]

Notes

1 Lionel Trilling labels this phenomenon as "the chronic American belief that there exists an opposition between reality and mind" (10).
2 Lincoln himself saw the urgent need for good campaign biographers: "More than most politicians of his day, Abraham Lincoln deeply appreciated and understood the influence and the power of print" (Horrocks 5).
3 Howells faces the task of composing Lincoln's *Life* with "casualness" and "less direct interest" than he expresses for his usual assignments. Robert Price notes that "young men of twenty-three do not usually have long sights on great issues," a fact that results in Howells' "perfunctory patchwork" of coverage (234–235, 245).
4 The text itself remains historically significant – indeed, the most famous of the 13 biographies written around Lincoln's election – because Lincoln himself comments upon it extensively. Readers can consider Lincoln's marginalia in later editions of the book; furthermore, the President has a copy of it on loan from the Library of Congress at the time of his assassination.
5 Howells recognizes this shared intent: "Romanticism then sought, as realism seeks now, to widen the bounds of sympathy, to level every barrier against aesthetic freedom, to escape from the paralysis of tradition" ("Criticism" 15).
6 These campaign biographies enact an "uneasy vacillation between the fixed code of the privileged and the potentialities of the outsider" (Becker 284).
7 "It was the play of cognitions, of sensations, formlessly tending to the effect which can only be very clumsily interpreted in language" (Howells *Modern*, 405).
8 Kaplan points to "character, the foundation of the realistic edifice" (35).
9 For a fuller treatment of the Marches, see Clara M. Kirk's "Reality and Actuality in the March Family Narratives of W.D. Howells," *PMLA*, vol. 74, no. 1 (March 1959), pp. 137–152.
10 For some critics, Howells' fixed, rigid ideal reveals an innate elitism. As Arthur Boardman argues, Howells romanticizes "the upper level ... (by) contradicting the egalitarian theme" upon which he dwells (42). Just why is it, Boardman continues, that Howells should "think of himself as having a unique relation to 'Real Life'?" (45–46). Henry Gifford agrees with this critique, dwelling upon the inert "safeness" of Howells' moral conservatism: "Howells ... maintains absolute control of his story ... (he) seems to come down to us rather as a man than as an artist ... Howells unquestionably has character ... but he lacked vision" (133). Lincoln's aloofness from mortal man suggests an anti-democratic streak that runs throughout Howells' body of work.
11 This assessment may call to mind Herman Melville's (in)famous description of Hawthorne as lacking "plump sphericity."
12 In this shift from public input to the disembedded individual, Howells drifts into sentimentalism, and falls short of his own established criteria for realism. Kenneth Warren observes that, in realist fiction, "the redemption of the individual lay within the social

world," but in sentimental works, "the redemption of the social world lay with the individual" (75–76).
13 Scott E. Casper notes, "Biographers offered copious extracts from candidates' speeches and writings to demonstrate their fidelity to partisan values and doctrines" (97).
14 Within only the first ten pages of the campaign biography, Howells both scolds the "too zealous genealogist" for focusing upon matters of "small importance" related to Hayes' family lineage *and* thoroughly romanticizes Hayes' grandmother, Chloe Smith, for her "strong and resolute character… of insurpassable rightness and strength" (*Sketch*, 1–2, 6–9). Howells later jokes that he wishes he could have written an entire biography of Chloe. In sum, Howells conjoins wholeness and incompleteness in a picturesque manner.
15 Jacques Rancière describes this phenomenon as "a promise that has to be kept even though – and precisely because – it can never be fulfilled. It is a democracy that can never 'reach itself', catch up with itself, because it involves an infinite openness to that which comes" (*Dissensus* 59).

Works Cited

Becker, George J. "William Dean Howells: The Awakening of Conscience." *College English*, vol. 19, no. 7, 1958, pp. 283–291. *JSTOR*, www.jstor.org/stable/371630. Accessed February 19, 2021.

Boardman, Arthur. "Social Point of View in the Novels of William Dean Howells."*American Literature*, vol.39, no. 1, 1967, pp. 42–59. *JSTOR*, www.jstor.org/stable/2923048 . Accessed February 19, 2021.

Brown, William Burlie. *The People's Choice: The Presidential Image in the Campaign Biography* (Baton Rouge, LA: Louisiana State University Press, 1960).

Budd, Louis J. "W. D. Howells' Defense of the Romance." *PMLA*, vol. 67, no. 2, 1952, pp. 32–42. *JSTOR*, www.jstor.org/stable/460085. Accessed February 17, 2021.

Cady, Edwin. *The Road to Realism: The Early Years, 1837–1885, of William Dean Howells* (Syracuse, NY: Syracuse University Press, 1956).

Carter, Everett. *Howells and the Age of Realism* (Philadelphia, PA: J. B. Lippincott, 1954).

Casper, Scott E. *Constructing American Lives: Biography and Culture in Nineteenth-Century America* (Chapel Hill, NC: University of North Carolina Press, 1999).

Fuller, Jaime. "A Brief History of Mostly Terrible Campaign Biographies," *LitHub*, September 12, 2009. https://lithub.com/a-brief-history-of-mostly terrible-campaign-biographies/. Accessed February 1, 2021.

Gifford, Henry. "WDH: His Moral Conservatism." *Kenyon Review*, vol. 20 (Winter1958), pp. 124–133.

Goodman, Susan and Carl Dawson. *William Dean Howells: A Writer's Life* (Los Angeles, CA: University of California Press, 2005).

Hedges, Elaine. "Howells on a Hawthornesque Theme." *Texas Studies in Literature and Language*, vol. 3, no. 1, 1961, pp. 129–143. *JSTOR*, www.jstor.org/stable/40753715. Accessed February 18, 2021.

Horrocks, Tony. *Lincoln's Campaign Biographies* (Carbondale, IL: Southern Illinois University Press, 2014).

Howells, William Dean. *Criticism and Fiction, and Other Essays* (New York: New York University Press, 1959).

Howells, William Dean. *A Hazard of New Fortunes* (New York: Penguin Classics, 2001).

Howells, William Dean. *Life of Abraham Lincoln* (New York: Library Reprints, 1960).

Howells, William Dean. *A Modern Instance* (New York: Penguins Classics, 1984).
Howells, William Dean. *The Rise of Silas Lapham* (New York: Penguin Classics, 1983).
Howells, William Dean. *Sketch of the Life and Character of Rutherford B. Hayes* (Ann Arbor, MI: University of Michigan Press, 2009).
Kaplan, Amy. *The Social Construction of American Realism* (Chicago, IL: University of Chicago Press, 1992).
Kolb, Harold H. "In Search of Definition: American Literary Realism and the Clichés." *American Literary Realism, 1870–1910*, vol. 2, no. 2, 1969, pp. 165–173. JSTOR, www.jstor.org/stable/27747649. Accessed February 17, 2021.
Lepore, Jill. "Bound for Glory: Writing Campaign Lives," *The New Yorker*, October 202008. https://www.newyorker.com/magazine/2008/10/20/bound-for-glory. Accessed February 5, 2021.
Mouffe, Chantal. *On the Political* (New York: Routledge, 2005).
Price, Robert. "Young Howells Drafts a 'Life' for Lincoln." *Ohio History*, 76 (1976), pp. 232–246.
Rancière, Jacques. *Dissensus: On Politics and Aesthetics*, trans. Steve Corcoran (New York: Bloomsbury, 2010).
Rancière, Jacques. *The Politics of Aesthetics* (New York: Bloomsbury, 2004).
Richardson, Charles. *American Literature, 1607–1885* (New York: G.P. Putnam and Sons, 1889).
Richardson, Lyon N. "Men of Letters and the Hayes Administration." *The New England Quarterly*, vol. 15, no. 1, 1942, pp. 110–141. JSTOR, www.jstor.org/stable/360236. Accessed February 18, 2021.
Smith, Henry Nash. *Democracy and the Novel: Popular Resistance to Classic American Writers* (Oxford: Oxford University Press, 1981).
Sundquist, Eric. *American Realism: New Essays* (Baltimore, MD: Johns Hopkins University Press, 1982).
Trachtenberg, Alan. *The Incorporation of America: Culture and Society in the Gilded Age* (New York: Hill and Wang, 1982).
Trilling, Lionel. *The Liberal Imagination: Essays on Literature and Society* (New York: Scribner, 1976).
Warren, Kenneth. *Black and White Strangers: Race and American Literary Realism* (Chicago, IL: University of Chicago Press, 1995).

4
INTERLUDE
Wolcott Balestier and the Candidate's Secret

Charles Balestier – best known by his middle name Wolcott – reveals through both his literary and business-related works how American Romanticism as well as realism come to bear upon the campaign biography. *James G. Blaine: A Sketch of His Life* (1884) encapsulates many of the same strains as earlier texts of this sort composed by the likes of Nathaniel Hawthorne and William Dean Howells, considered at length in previous chapters.[1] Like works by these influential figures, the Blaine tract reflects major literary and political concerns of the late nineteenth century. Specifically, the sketch of Blaine's life indicates a commonality between Romance and realism: the futile search for a Real American essence beneath a less than satisfying status quo. As such, Balestier's campaign biography serves as a bridge between the worlds of Hawthorne and Howells and the worlds of Lew Wallace, Jacob Riis, and Rose Lane (subjects of the remaining chapters). His fiction as well as nonfiction gestures at a rapidly changing literary landscape informed by evolving attitudes toward the publishing industry and the hyper-visible presence of the American West. In a word, to examine Balestier's campaign biography is to track prominent patterns in American life at the twilight of the nineteenth century, and to gain a clearer sense of the dynamic interplay between America's literary preoccupations and its broader democratic sensibilities.

Because Balestier is born into an affluent family of former French colonizers from Martinique, he shares a great deal with Blaine, a politician with an imposing pedigree. Their elitist upbringings help to explain why, in the early pages of Blaine's biography, Balestier goes out of his way to dismiss the rags-to-riches formula that remains prevalent in campaign biographies, since it would be impossible to position Blaine – at least, with any degree of plausibility – in the proverbial log cabin that housed so many of the previous Presidents in the American imaginary. Not unlike Blaine, the young author straddles a line in his

DOI: 10.4324/9781003132448-5

personal life and his prose between aristocratic breeding and a yearning for alternatives to his ostentatious origins. This yearning also explains why the young Balestier decides to travel westward to Colorado on a hunt for self-made wealth. While he completes several novels and short stories of note during his lifetime, texts that this interlude will place into conversation with the Blaine sketch, his contemporaries know Balestier better as a literary agent. A close friend and collaborator with the likes of literary giants Edmund Gosse, Rudyard Kipling, and Henry James, Balestier displays seeds of genius that may have grown to greater heights had he not died just shy of his thirtieth birthday. By contemplating *James G. Blaine: A Sketch* in tandem with the rest of his diverse output, we further sharpen our focus on the sociological as well as aesthetic underpinnings of the campaign biography as a genre, especially in the second half of the nineteenth century.

Balestier's career marks a historical transition from the loose patronage sought by Hawthorne under his friend, Franklin Pierce, and Howells under Abraham Lincoln as well as his relative, Rutherford B. Hayes, to the rise of the professional writer as an active member of democratic society that wishes to decouple himself from the sort of patronage that would diminish his artistic independence. Let us make no mistake: like Hawthorne and Howells, Balestier is an opportunist that composes his campaign biography with the goal of securing a cushy government post in Europe. And yet, unlike Hawthorne, he simultaneously resists these "fragmentary patronage systems" by cultivating an identity as a talented businessman. On this front, it may be said that he outpaces even his literary idol, Howells. In so doing, Balestier subscribes to what Christopher Wilson details as the era's "cult of professional expertise and democratic activism," in which writers claim independence by at least hypothetically casting aside the spoils system cultivated by their forebears (7, 3). Balestier thus transitions from the legacy of authorship during the American Renaissance – characterized by writers within client–patron relationships that operate at a degree of removal from the wider audience – into the mold of clear-eyed, self-made men (or so the story goes). Foreshadowing the zeitgeist of the Progressive Era, Balestier longs to participate on the public stage because it is by cultivating a connection with the mass audience instead of isolating as an aloof genius that new literary figures can avoid the apparent humiliations of patronage and instead "make their own way." Balestier derives his unsettled style from a host of successful writers from the age, including the triumvirate of Mark Twain, James, and, most deliberately, the late Howells. A failed prospector, Balestier attempts to maximize personal profit with his Western stories, his own "literary gold" (Benfey 49).[2] Meanwhile, he regularly corresponds with Howells, he aids James in launching an unsuccessful career as a playwright, and he guides Kipling into an opportunity to publish novels and short stories for an international market. Balestier eventually perishes from a bout with typhoid fever because he overtaxes himself by travelling to sell James's works in England (61). The field of literature, critics notes, starts to have a distinctly industrial feel. In his obituary for Balestier, Gosse remarks:

He had, in the first place, a business capacity which in its degree may not be very rare, if we regard the whole industrial field, but which as directed to the profession of publication was, I am afraid to say, unique. (220)

One quickly recognizes in Balestier's creative output an "industrial imagination," which is to say, a tendency to forego "literariness" in order to sell more books. Of course, all writers must negotiate these conflicting aims to some extent, as we have already seen with Hawthorne; still, the Progressive Era dramatically augments this paradigm. In short, as his campaign biography keenly illustrates, Balestier exists in a liminal space at the center of our story: he needs political patronage from the likes of Blaine in order to flourish and yet, at the same time, he crafts a highly individualized, professional persona that ostensibly rejects the Romance of American politics.

At an even deeper level, Balestier's "industrial imagination" compliments the drive of American realism by allowing the young man to deliver a supposedly accurate, authentic account of the Real – that which he presents as being hidden or disguised by the artificial plumage of a Gilded Age. Partially removed from the ideological demands of a patron, he becomes presumably free "to tell the Truth." Self-fashioned as a scientific journalist instead of an aesthete with an overabundance of leisure time, Balestier claims the capacity "to explain the root cause of American problems" (Wilson 14). His career exemplifies the so-called Progressive turn by offering a snapshot of its functional outlook: "A truly democratic and mass literature ... an active role (for authors) in national life and politics" (5). In this way, Balestier's campaign biography for Blaine conveys two interrelated shifts in American literature as well as American politics – a drive to democratize, at least conceptually, alongside a rush to be "realer-than-thou."

Balestier passionately cares about the democratic process. According to Balestier, as it is for Hawthorne (at times) and Howells (more frequently), American literature should actively usher readers into greater democratic engagement. From his perspective, the appeal of becoming a prominent literary voice remains intimately tied to the expansion of democratic sentiment. Balestier, Gosse points out in his eulogy, occupies himself habitually with "the picturesque procession of the democratic life" (223). However, just as he must still grovel before a would-be President to ascend into the upper ranks, Balestier never fully solves the struggles of the writers that precede him – that is, he never fully rejects the genteel attitudes that undergird the work of Washington Irving, Hawthorne, or Howells: their mutual distrust of the populace to govern itself; their wariness of a truly levelled social order. Balestier's campaign biography, then, unveils a man – and an audience – at a crossroads. Americans are increasingly eager to strip away pretense by tapping democratically into a national essence and, at the same time, to preserve a fixed cultural code of conduct regulated by cultural gatekeepers. Informed by his professional development as well as the literary legacies that he inherits, Balestier's sketch of Blaine's candidacy is shaped by the tensions between, and within, Romance and realism.

Idolatry

Part Romantic and part realist, Balestier intends to cut through the falsity of everyday life in America and penetrate into the very core of things – that is, into what we have been calling the Real. As we have seen in previous chapters, Romantics and realists alike tend to conceptualize the Real in rather rigid terms, as a permanent metaphysical presence rather than a gaping void. This presumed thing-in-itself endures as a constant: for example, Hawthorne's sense of spiritual and material equilibrium, or Howells's sense of bourgeois character as well as consensus. Balestier's vision of an ideal democratic candidate follows suit by creating a fetish to signify an ostensibly unbroken, perfect, and absolutely satisfied social order. It is not that Balestier's work is guilty of being excessively Romantic or, as Howells would say, "romanticistic"; such a dismissal would be too easy. After all, in spite of his reputation as the godfather of realism in the United States, a writer that roundly rejects metaphysics, Howells and the majority of his followers still generate an invisible *terra firma* upon which to base realistic stories – a *terra firma* that proves to be comprised of facile trappings from a genteel tradition. And Hawthorne, although frequently classified as a seminal Romantic, does not always come to rest upon this *terra firma*, as his dark Romances instead negate fetish after fetish while declaring, in thunder, "No!" In other words, Balestier's campaign biography reflects overlapping, blurred tendencies in Romanticism as well as realism, and we can therefore regard Balestier as a custodian of the ambivalent legacy of nineteenth-century American literature. As we shall see, this ambivalence also aids us in making sense of strained tensions within American democracy.

Said another way, Balestier's fiction repeatedly returns to an idealistic substratum: the presumed essence of America itself. When the author recalls travelling westward, and feeling "the desire to write earnestly seize him," Balestier's reader might assume that this place of "earnestness" has an actual name, or a recognizable shape (Gosse 217). Beneath layers of social nicety, beneath an abundance of punctilios and rhetorical suasion, lies a yet-unearthed American "earnestness" that can only be brought to the surface by the realist. Balestier locates his Real, a wholeness that supposedly waits to be excavated, just below the nation's gilded surfaces. Like many other writers during his era, Balestier locates the Real in the mythical American West. Balestier spends a good of his short life in the Western states, especially Colorado, and he finds Western sensibilities to have a rejuvenating effect on his constitution. He sets his novel *Benefits Forgot* (1893), a text about a father, James Deed, and his two sons, Philip and Jaspar, against the backdrop of the untamed West. While Jaspar embodies the Eastern character – shrewd, business-minded, cold – Philip embodies the Western character – generous, authentic, warm. The novel therefore echoes Twain's well-known story, "The Celebrated Jumping Frog of Calaveras County" (1865), in which Twain juxtaposes so-called Western and Eastern modes of storytelling: the penetrating gaze of the Eastern detective versus the far-fetched fables of the West. Twain's fables lure the cynical Easterner further and further from his comfort zone and into a trap meant to expose the folly of an overly-suspicious Eastern reading style. Exploring this internal divide, Balestier's *Benefits Forgot* choreographs a familial squabble over inheritance, paternal authority, and familial bonds. More broadly, it celebrates the revivifying qualities of Westernization by tracking characters that come to appreciate the Real of this unfamiliar place: its unvarnished Truth, which looks at first – to skeptical Eastern eyes, at least – uncultured as well as uncouth. The last name of the novel's family suggests an ongoing search for authenticity. While a deed is quite literally a legal document designed to preserve private property and an acutely transactional worldview, a deed is also, and in this case more significantly, an action – e.g., whereas the calloused Jaspar wrangles to maintain his dominion over the family mine, Philip proves himself to be a man of action that recognizes the "right" or "just" cause and then swiftly acts upon it. In this way, Balestier projects into the imagined West a "heavenly unconsciousness of innocence," an unspoken understanding that remains foreign to the distrustful calculus of Eastern financiers like Jaspar. "The understanding eye" of Westerners reveals to readers "the open secret of the no-secret" (5). The phrase "open secret of the no-secret" underscores a dual movement in *Benefits Forgot*, indeed, in most of Balestier's writing: while the conniving Easterner assumes that everything is shrouded in secrecy and utilizes his own secrets to con others, the heroic Westerner embraces utter 2Similarly, Balestier's fiction romanticizes its female characters as being inherently pure and unpolluted. Philip's love interest Dorothy displays "the simple and loving heart which no system of cultivation could have educated out of her" (31). In contrast to the Eastern ladies that declare the West to be undesirable – caricatures of shrews and school marms, in the conventional terms of the day – Dorothy, like countless female characters transformed through their experience on the frontier, recovers an innate lack of pretense, a "divine unconstraint," the longer that she lives in the West (92). Importantly, Dorothy's "open secret of the no-secret" is not a byproduct of a Western lifestyle; rather, it is always-already there, waiting to be unearthed like a priceless jewel. On the verge of suicide from his corrosive upbringing back East, the elder Deed excavates his admirable character, which has been long buried beneath layers of Eastern excess. Once "in his element," the Westernized father realizes his full potential – "so straightforward, so simple and direct, he had no attitude, he never got himself up" (195). For Philip, too, "the West was teaching him something ... he could see his affectations dropping away from him one by one" (344). Conditioned by an imagined feminine grace as well as a heavily-constructed Western ethos, Balestier's male protagonists invariably recover an unmoving moral anchor.

This "romanticistic" core provides *Benefits Forgot* with an overriding sense of stability and security, despite the rhetorical gamesmanship cultivated by an Eastern habitus. Philip learns that he must always be "fair" even if it means losing his competition with Jaspar, and he postulates that, while characters like Jaspar might equivocate or gaslight others into second-guessing their ethical choices, being "a man" means accepting what is universally "right." Dorothy states unequivocally, "Right and wrong remain – surely they are the same in all worlds" (398). Balestier's novel announces, "There are laws of character, you know, and a planetary orbit is wobbly to them" (206). This unmoving "law of character," another variant of the "open secret of the no-secret," requires the institution of marriage to come to fruition. When the elder Deed finally marries his second wife, the text comments: "Their happiness was the quiet, full-bodied content of the long-married" (303). Marriage, according to Balestier, provides a "natural" state of equilibrium, bringing out the very best of both parties. On this point, he sounds a good deal like his literary idol, Howells, channeling in particular Howells's recurrent characters, the Marches. Howells likewise promotes the bourgeois marriage as a bedrock of society – a "romanticistic" nucleus, albeit dressed in the garb of realism. By the close of *Benefits Forgot*, Balestier's reader realizes what is Real as Balestier melts away the falsities of Eastern habit and his characters submit to a stationary fetish: "The purity, the instinctive morality, the pitiless, colorless sense of right ... a nobility beyond praise ... the right is dearer for being difficult ... the truth is better ... the splendid, generous, heroic right" (341, 378). Balestier's treatment of the "open secret of the no-secret," with its effusive dedication to what is "right," "true," and "pure," may not strike contemporary readers as all that realistic. Indeed, *Benefits Forgot* drifts steadily into the sort of genteel revelry that Howells denounces, but ultimately conforms to, as "romanticistic."

Yet in "romanticistic" terms, *Benefits Forgot* never quite reaches the heights of Balestier's earlier effort, *A Victorious Defeat: A Romance* (1886), in which readers are led to believe in the Christ-like perfection of the preacher, Mr. Keator. The narrative orbits around Keator's "perfect manliness"; even when he falters, he preserves the reader's faith in "absolute truth" by displaying personal character of an "uncounterfeitable quality" (73–74, 99). That is, Balestier conveys the Real as the focal point for everything that transpires in his text. He unabashedly idolizes Keator by positioning him as a moral fixture that guides the other characters in the text in spite of, or precisely because of, his own fallibility. *A Victorious Defeat* concurrently tells the tale of a young woman named Constance – her name further amplifies the novel's "romanticistic" undercurrent – who must choose between her fraternal Moravian village via her marriage to Mr. Keator and the secular world, embodied by the English immigrant (another Mr. March). She ultimately chooses March, but only because her feelings toward Keator prove to be idolatrous. She recognizes that Keator alone can overcome his worldly desires to achieve transcendence. His "clear vision distinguish(es) Right through whatever fog of Wrong," and so Constance never truly stops worshipping him: "Constance admires (Keator) – that was it – admires distantly as she would a work of art" (69, 386). Keator's innate perfection endows *A Victorious Defeat* with its assumed "essence": beneath the fallenness of humanity, Balestier encourages readers to glimpse a grand metaphysical Truth.

Balestier's title gives away the novel's metaphysics by underscoring its Christian subtext. Like Christ, Keator emerges victorious by allowing himself to be defeated on behalf of others – in this case, by allowing the marriage of Constance and March. And at novel's end, Keator sacrifices his own life in order to serve an ungrateful member of his congregation:

> (Keator's) unconscious, habitual charity and self-denial seemed always to point the way … ideals upon which I could always draw. The certainty of that cheers me even now … a great happiness to know that somewhere there is such a man. (348)

Recalling Hawthorne, Balestier presents an abiding ambivalence that points always to Christian reconciliation. The long "March" of progress eventually harmonizes with the "Constance" of faith. Keator and Constance thus read like Hawthornean figures, weary of their broken world yet conscious of a higher Truth that exists behind the veil. The Real may not be accessible in this life, but one may nonetheless take comfort in its fixed position at the outermost edge of experience.

With a stronger sense of the fetishized Real within Balestier's fiction, let us now turn to his campaign biography for Blaine. Balestier's campaign biography similarly gestures at "the open secret of the no-secret" by portraying its candidate as a larger-than-life figure that fully embodies the essence of the nation: "(Blaine's) career is part of the national history" (32). As he does in his novels, Balestier generates a moral anchor in distinctly gendered terms: Blaine proves "manly and straightforward" because he acts with "manly simplicity" (149, 188). He exemplifies a "virile Americanism" (112). Stripped of rhetorical genius or political savviness, Balestier's Blaine ascends to a position above and beyond the commons; as an idol, he conjures powerful feelings of wholeness. Like many representative men, Blaine exists as a symbol of America itself, and so he deserves "a *permanent* sentiment in his favor among the people" (161, emphasis mine). A compelling fetish for the Real, Balestier's candidate remains "as self-possessed as the portrait on the wall," thereby inviting citizens to submit to his excellence, which is always-already their own, simply waiting to be reclaimed (195).

Balestier paints Blaine with the same brush that he paints Philip in *Benefits Forgot* as well as Keator in *A Victorious Defeat*. Balestier even recycles many of the same phrases to identify his political idol. Blaine, like Balestier's fictional heroes, receives "the most genuine and spontaneous liking"; he does not need to win over voters because he can supposedly tap into the innermost kernel of their being without political design (221). Precisely like Keator, Blaine maintains "that touch of genuineness – uncounterfeitable" (238). In other words, the candidate's personal story presumably conveys the congenital qualities of the American populace – its assumed wholeness; its unbroken base. "Such unanimity and such harmony, such concentrations of sentiment … signs of the heartiness of Republican preference for the foremost American." Blaine ostensibly stands "dear to the popular heart, grounded securely in the liking of the masses," and he therefore provides readers with a "firm foundation" (227–228).

However, as an idol, Blaine's kernel of the Real remains just out of the reader's view, which is to say, he evokes a fantastic "essence" without giving it direct expression. Ever suggestive, Balestier is never more Hawthornean than when he gestures at an oblique, ethereal Real that exists beyond the borders of the mortal world. In his campaign biography, Balestier comes at the question of Blaine's charisma from an indirect angle. Of Blaine's charisma, Balestier writes:

> It may be doubted if any process would make it known at last. The current explanation, we believe, is 'personal magnetism', but that is very weak ... there is no adequate word, and our borrowings from the language of the most mysterious of natural forces are themselves only attempts at the expression of the inexpressible. (35).

Here Balestier once more illuminates the Janus face of American Romanticism as well as realism by demonstrating how both modes frequently confront the (im)possibility of capturing the Real – an (im)possibility that threatens to undermine the perceived stability of the idol itself. Although often classified in different terms, Hawthorne and Howells each return in their own ways to "the inexpressible," since they are unable to rid themselves of a potent void that lingers beneath their otherwise secure footing. By repeatedly acknowledging that no words exist to convey adequately the "greatness" of Blaine, Balestier's campaign biography sustains the *negative* impulses of the Romantic as well as the realist. For all of its comforts, the fetish reminds readers on some level that the fantasy object is only ever a partial stand-in for something that cannot be given a final form. An illusion of American wholeness – its character; its consensus – remains a powerful, perhaps even necessary, illusion. But it is an illusion nevertheless.

Blaine's "indescribable element" recalls the more poignant moments of Balestier's fiction (243). Specifically, this ineffable quality manifests in the literal and figurative middle of *A Victorious Defeat* as a dark hole at the center of a Moravian church. The congregants sing "without self-consciousness" to achieve a metaphysical sense of connectedness through ancient hymns (42). In this pregnant passage, Balestier's novel focuses upon "the mystery of the centre of the church which the illumination fail(s) to reach" (98). This "mysterious centre" calls to mind the church at the apex of Henry James's later novella, *The Turn of the Screw* (1898), in which the Real manifests as a realm that the governess circles around, endlessly, but into which she never enters. An inexpressible core defines Balestier's characters without exposing itself – to borrow James's phrase from *Turn* – in "any vulgar way." Balestier's "open secret of no-secret," then, remains at a fundamental level a secret. After all, we might ask, why does the author retain the word "secret" in this phrase, since the term is seemingly blown apart by the qualifier of "openness" and the negation of "no"? I would argue that Balestier's readers are meant to come to know his candidate, paradoxically, through a preserved sense of secrecy – that is, through a reliance upon indirect communication, upon a Truth that can only be True because it has not yet been illuminated for the prying eyes of others. Hawthornean thresholds remain uncrossed. The Real is only made whole through Balestier's partial descriptions because the depiction could never fully encompass what the author intends. In a word, the idol always falls short of the thing-in-itself because it can only ever provide a pale substitution for something far more dynamic. In sum, American Romanticism and realism tarry around a Real that ultimately cannot be brought to light, at least, not in any vulgar fashion, and Balestier's campaign biography similarly augments the power of its chosen candidate – and, more generally, of democracy as an aesthetic expression – by inviting readers to ruminate upon the paradoxes of an "open secret."

Iconoclasm

When he blurs the line between "the romanticistic" and reality, Balestier demonstrates his indebtedness to Howells, a writer that walks a similar tightrope between uncovering the Real and settling for flimsy, unconvincing substitutes – namely, the stuff of a genteel tradition. As we saw in the preceding chapter, this tension manifests throughout Howells' fiction as well as his two campaign biographies. To make meaning out of *James G. Blaine: A Sketch of His Life* requires that readers possess at least a passing familiarity with the works of Howells. In his biographical treatment of Balestier, James – a close friend of Howells as well as Balestier – writes that Balestier endlessly lauds "the novel of observation, the undiscourageable study of the actual; he professe(s) an intense relish for the works of Mr. Howells" (qtd. in Balestier, *Average* xix). In multiple ways, Balestier derives his fiction as well as his campaign biography from Howells, specifically with his "realer-than-thou" impetus. But we must also acknowledge the Jamesian quality of Balestier's prose, with its paralyzing punctilios and its psychological undertones. Simply put, Balestier's campaign biography is deeply informed by realists who obsess over divulging as well as defending secrets.

    Critics can classify Balestier's novels, Gosse asserts in his eulogy for the author, as "good imitations" of Howells' output (223). For instance, in *Victorious Defeat*, when a relative passes away, the narrator observes that the world continues relatively unmoved: "Things went on as usual" (139). Likewise, Howells notes how matters of supreme importance for singular characters, even matters of life and death, prove to be insignificant in the grand scheme of things. Balestier's heroine learns never to get caught up in the frenzies or passions of the moment, but to have a "second look" in Howellsian fashion: "To sit down in the midst of the remains of her past life, and take that general account, that large view, impossible while she was still living it" (156). Given the unadulterated pragmatism of

Balestier's vision, it comes as little surprise that his protagonist fails to establish the utopian commune for which he pines. Moreover, Constance's love of March echoes the view of love routinely expressed by Howells: love, according to Balestier, is not idolatry but the non-judgmental acceptance of imperfect human beings. Unlike the love on display in other sentimental novels, the love of Balestier's Howellsian universe remains humble, under-stated, and oriented around the fallenness of the subjects involved. In *Benefits Forgot*, Philip's love interest initially errs by taking him

> on the ground of the fellow she's dreamed, and he has to live up not only to the man she thinks him, but to the kind of man she thinks all good men ... you're punished not on the basis of what you are, but on the basis of what she's all along been thinking you. (419)

Far from an idealized vision, *Benefits Forgot* admits that most characters are, in fact, "a muddle of right and wrong" (356). The text draws upon Howells's classic work, *The Rise of Silas Lapham* specifically when it expounds upon the virtue of certain kinds of indebtedness and when it laments, in line with Lapham, that novels rarely allow individuals to be prove their innate goodness. In Balestier's *Benefits Forgot*, Philip bemoans how his brother Jaspar as well as his love interest pre-judge him and treat him as though he were nothing more than a stock character in a poorly written novel: "You think you know me. You say I'm this and that ... It's like you to be the innocent one, isn't it, and mighty like me to be in the wrong" (239–240). Finally, in perhaps the most Howellsian moment in all of Balestier's fiction, *Benefits Forgot* tracks a self-righteous character in pursuit of heroism, only to acknowledge at the close that heroism never resonates like it does in "romanticistic" tales: "Nothing seems very right, let alone very heroic, when you are doing it," the novel states. "She was doing a fine thing; and there ought to have been some very good music by a concealed orchestra, scenery by the best artists, and electric lights" (164). A survey of Balestier's fiction thus reveals the extent to which Howells influences the young author.

And this influence carries over into Balestier's campaign biography of Blaine as well. In a rare admission for a campaign biographer, Balestier announces Howells' influence overtly when he gushes in his preface to the Blaine tract that Howells' biography for Rutherford B. Hayes is singularly "admirable" (iv). In this brief but exceptional moment, we recognize how influential Howells's entries in the genre of the campaign biography truly are among fellow practitioners. This admission demonstrates how certain biographers in the tradition reference works that came before them – in particular, the "literary" examples. Like *Lapham*, Balestier's campaign biography deliberately plays with the rags-to-riches formula that dominates texts at the close of the nineteenth century. In *Lapham*, the titular character "rises" in an unexpected way, moving from riches-to-rags yet ascending in terms of his moral standing; likewise, in *James G. Blaine: A Sketch of His Life*, Balestier's candidate does not follow the expected path, since he begins his life in a prosperous family, far from the proverbial log cabin. "If that is a shameful fact," Balestier comments, "The truth must nevertheless be told" (5). In other words, the campaign biography of Blaine overtly mocks the rags-to-riches narrative by satirically asking if, by contrasting the wealthy young James with his even more affluent ancestors, the biographer could still declare his candidate to be "reasonably Presidential" (5). Like Howells, Balestier reverses the formula of the campaign biography in order to quilt a layer of virtue into the text.

Much of *James G. Blaine: A Sketch of His Life* reflects the tenets of Howellsian literary realism. At its open, the campaign biography undercuts the manner in which newspapers romanticize the life of important figures. In truth, the biography ruminates, a birth is only ever an open-ended event that lacks glamor because any person's social importance remains "as likely to dwindle as to grow" (1). According to Balestier, a writer tasked with highlighting his assigned candidate's qualifications for higher office, the "highest moment" of Blaine's life is when the candidate expresses a "few adequate words" at the funeral of President James Garfield (192). When Balestier treats the brevity of Blaine's "sincere" speech as the supreme height of his personal achievement, his readers recognize the author's significant investment in the basic principles of American realism: direct and honest language instead of manipulative rhetorical strategies. As a former newspaperman – a role privileged by Howells and Balestier alike, given that both writers labored visibly in the field of journalism during their respective lifetimes – Balestier contends that Blaine benefits from the journalist's "habit of concise and direct statement" (200).

Balestier's campaign biography perhaps echoes Howells most blatantly in Chapter XVIII, a section in which Balestier reviews Blaine's *Twenty Years of Congress*, another text published in support of Blaine's 1884 campaign. Balestier complains that Blaine's account lacks "a certain juridical tone," which is to say, because it is neither a history nor a genuine retrospective, Blaine's book occasionally wanders into the exaggeratory – a negative attribute, at least from the perspective of a dogmatic Howellsian realist. Yet Balestier ultimately redeems Blaine's book by commenting upon its unique "vividness," its ability to leave "the reader much obliged to it for not being history, since it brings him so much nearer the event" (199). Blaine's tract purportedly cuts through a tendency among hackneyed American writers to resort to clinical indifference, or "romanticistic" mythology, in the quest for greater authenticity. Balestier ruminates extensively upon the Blaine text in order to make his case for Howellsian realism. I quote Balestier at length:

> (Blaine) makes his point squarely and enforces it fully, but he does not enforce it too far; the finger is laid upon the spring with a firm touch, is held a moment, and at the delicate instant, which is neither too soon nor too late, is withdrawn. This modest quality of style, which is neither brilliant nor

engaging, and takes no eye because the essence of its being is retirement, makes above all its imposing sister qualities, easy reading ... the style of the volume is, however, something more than easy to read. It can be stately upon occasion. But the occasions are sparingly chosen, and in the midst of its fluency it seldom fails of a kind of dignity. (201)

By including a superfluous tangent on Blaine's book in order to express support for the literary realists of the period, Balestier confirms how strongly the young author shares Howells' aesthetic convictions.

Balestier's tract for Blaine exemplifies an undercurrent of iconoclasm that characterizes the works of Howells and James. If readers contemplate the dissatisfaction at the heart of Balestier's fiction, they are better prepared to grasp some of the more interesting moments of his campaign biography – indeed, some of the more interesting moments of the campaign biography as a genre. According to realists like James, when a character refuses to disclose his innermost secrets, he manages to retain his desirability for other characters as well as the reader. For example, in *Victorious Defeat*, Constant "isn't a girl who keeps her mental doors open," March notes. And "that is what I admired in her from the first" (205). He begs her: "No, dearest, don't expose yourself in that way" (230). Balestier undermines the illusion of wholeness that enwraps the fetishized object when he insists that some things are better left unsaid and, therefore, partial as well as dissatisfying. Constance appears to be driven to reticence in order to maintain her usefulness, her attractiveness, and her connection to divinity. Church elders inflicts wounds when they scold her for what they assume to be her breach of decorum with March: "There is no corner of my heart into which the world has not the right to pry" (108). Balestier himself, like his fictional characters, remains a man of "excessive reticence" – a "young man possessed of so many secrets," with a tendency to "put up the screen" (Gosse 925). Although his writing occasionally makes an idolatrous, "romanticistic" claim for authenticity, Balestier's idols more often serve as obligatory screens to evoke the Real – that is, to sustain the Real by allowing readers to approach it only indirectly.

Along these lines, *Benefits Forgot* chastises and champions the reticence of well-cultured subjects, particularly women. Even as the novel recommends uncouth frankness on display in the imaginary West, it concurrently undermines this impression of total access by advocating for greater discretion. As a result, the two female protagonists of the novel figuratively dance around one another, exchanging "many confidences short of the real ones" (146). An existential impasse that exists between all human beings thwarts the supposed easiness of the "romanticistic." Said another way, by acknowledging that subjects cannot, and should not, know one another's secrets, Balestier approaches the Real like his literary mentors, including James: "The best sympathy, (Deed) knew, would be powerless to guess deeper than the outer envelope of his feeling ... she must be enough like him to understand him and he did not understand himself" (158). The Real functions as a vital gap sustained by the silence of "chivalric reserve" and the "restraint" of personal dignity (211). Balestier's characters communicate with one another by comprehending what must exist between the lines, a form of communication superior, it would seem, to the bluntness of Western dialogue. In one pregnant scene, Philip teaches his lover to use a typewriter and the reader begins to see how indirect communication can be far more profound than unvarnished rhetoric: "I don't think I could write it," his lover tells him, thereby withholding her innermost secret. When she does eventually type out her secret, Philip refuses to look at it. His lover consequently frets over the indiscreet threat of the symbolic order: "I thought … or the typewriter thought, – it wasn't I – it escaped me" (202). Over the course of this scene, Balestier stresses what is lacking in language: the words that his characters type are always flirting with the Real; they dally with telling the Truth, with the allure of removing the screen. But mere words on a page ultimately fail to create a genuine connection. And mercifully so because language actually offers a "proper fence," one that allows the writing subject to retain her secrets and, therefore, to salvage her desirability to the other party, which is to say, the reader (274).[3] A fully exposed Real would be the final utterance as there would be nothing left for anyone to say. Although this reticence characterizes realist novels by Howells and James, it also appears in certain examples of the American Romance; Balestier's withdrawn, highly discreet heroes and heroines resemble the Puritan caste of Hawthorne's New England. As we have seen in the preceding chapters, a longing to access the Real, in tension with the recognition that the Real must remain inaccessible, occupies the attention of American Romantics and realists alike.

In an Orientalist novel co-authored with Rudyard Kipling, *The Naulahka: A Story of West and East* (1891), Balestier further explicates a connection between the Real and the secrets lingering in political fetishes. In order to secure wealth for the hometown coffers from an expanding railroad company, protagonist Tarvin travels to India in pursuit of a legendary necklace of untold value, the Naulahka. The Naulahka, an Indian man reports, is *"the* state jewel – the jewel of the state. It is a holy thing" (172, author's emphasis). Balestier's text makes the case that every state has its jewel – a partial object that stands in for the whole of the town, for its supposed essence. Importantly, Tarvin's hometown is named Topaz, Colorado after a precious mineral resource. This "jewel" frequently manifests in the form of an elected official. The novel opens with Tarvin's campaign to become a political representative of Topaz. In its presentation of the savvy campaigner, the book lingers upon the power of democracy: "the prostrate body of the Democratic party," held enthralled by a charismatic candidate. In effect, Tarvin-as-candidate serves as a jewel to spellbind audiences ("spellbind" being a new word from the era, used to describe the effect of populist politicians on over-eager listeners). Yet while *The Naulahka* does contemplate the necessity of fetishized representatives like Tarvin, by turning the reader's attention to India and its paralyzed political system, the text ultimately means to disabuse its reader of this initial enchantment. By the novel's close, Tarvin forsakes the precious

Indian jewel by sealing it up in a box and refusing to allow it to work its mystical powers upon him. Balestier's narrative thus resigns itself to a state of dissatisfaction fueled by innately iconoclastic impulses, since democracy cannot rest upon any "holy" jewel. *Democracy must remain constitutionally open-ended and never fulfill the promises, the secrets, that it hides.* The text implies that Topaz – indeed, any democratic society – will be infinitely better off without the gilded illusion of "completion." The necklace, Tarvin realizes, offers "a myth, a word, a proverb ... but he need(s) the consolation of persistent search. And the search was always in vain" (205). Upon giving away the precious stone at the novel's dénouement, he sings to himself: "It is not wealth, nor rank, nor state/ but get-up-and-get that makes men great" (376). *The Naulahka* advocates for sustained dissatisfaction because to attain the jewel, the "holy" thing-in-itself, would be to end the hunt and so terminate one's purpose. The limitless frontier must remain unfinished to compel its ambitious cow-punchers over that next horizon. If Indian feudalism relies upon a jewel that promotes sloth as well as indifference, Tarvin's rejection of such a jewel re-awakens what Ernesto Laclau calls "the possibility of politics" (*New* 69).[4] Similarly, Blaine the candidate signifies unspeakable value – a precious stone, as it were; a perfect idol; a national essence – but he actually serves the electorate better when he remains hidden underground, waiting indefinitely to be mined by the masses, than he does when he stands exposed in all of his superficial glory. Balestier actively cloaks – more than he exposes – his ideal candidate.

In a word, Balestier's campaign biography suggests that the candidate must retain secrets if he is to remain desirable to the voting public – a realization that may strike contemporary readers as a bit difficult to accept, given the extent to which politicians are currently over-exposed. Moreover, through its preservation of secrets, *James G. Blaine: A Sketch of His Life* leaves democracy intentionally incomplete. Rather than create the impression of an idol that could satisfy every unique individual, Balestier's tract for Blaine deconstructs itself, and implies that any depiction of the candidate will, in the final tally, prove to be inadequate. Although the candidate remains one of "the most completely public" images in American life, there nonetheless lingers in Blaine a "mysterious and intangible quality of individuality" (236). After Balestier heaps hyperbolic praise onto his subject, he steps back and laments, "It does not complete his portrait" (239). He walks back much of his praise by insisting that "the whole is not said ... it is still very weakly told" (241). Modeled after the creations of Howells and James, Blaine – like the elusive state jewel in *The Naulahka* – is better off living relatively out of sight, if only to lure the spellbound audience into digging ever deeper and with ever growing enthusiasm.

To study Balestier's campaign biography of Blaine, then, is to learn a good deal about the blurred lines that separate America's earlier "man of letters," with his outmoded forms of patronage and his "romanticistic" impulses, from the later realist, with his acutely democratic agenda as well as his enhanced investment in

American literature's function within the public square. Balestier keeps one foot firmly planted in each realm. His all-too-brief career demonstrates how the evolution of realism in the United States bleeds over into democratic discourse. Through his numerous debts to Hawthorne, Howells, Twain, and James, Balestier borrows liberally from America's evolving literary trends to craft an image of his chosen candidate that aims – albeit in ways that are frequently contradictory – to be always "realer-than-thou." He presents his candidate as both a "romanticistic" icon that transcends the falsities of the Gilded Age as well as an opportunity to engage in iconoclasm by negating delusions of wholeness and sustaining the unspeakable secret. This oscillation says something significant about American literature in the nineteenth century as well as the nation's political imagination. In a related sense, to excavate Blaine's campaign biography in these terms allows us to recognize something significant about how we discuss candidates today, as over-recognize fetishes. Balestier's text sounds a cautionary note and tells us that we may be losing sight of a necessary gap: the very incompleteness that keeps our fragile democratic machinery in motion.

Notes

1   Blaine goes on to lose the election of 1884 to Grover Cleveland due in part to his prior association with the heavily tainted Grant administration and the pivotal role of the "mugwumps" (Republicans that switch to the Democratic Party in order to secure the election for Cleveland).
2   According to Christopher Benfey, Balestier stands out as "one of the first to see the literary marketplace as an arena for speculation like any other" (51).
3   Balestier's novel *A Fair Device* (1884) stresses this point by tracking a love affair that only works because it is entirely epistolary and anonymous. The first paragraph of the text states: "There were untellable vistas beyond such an opening" (7). The most satisfying tryst, the story suggests, is one that is driven by what is *not* said: "I would never meet him if I could help it … can't you see how we should tarnish and spoil it all by meeting?" (19).
4   On the interplay between the state as a jewel and the state as open-ended, Laclau continues: "The social always exceeds the limits of the attempts to constitute society … if the suture it attempts is ultimately impossible, it is nevertheless possible to proceed to a relative fixation of the social through the institution of nodal points" (*New* 91).

Works Cited

Balestier, Charles Wolcott. *Average Woman* (Sydney, Australia: Wentworth Press, 2019).
Balestier, Charles Wolcott. *Benefits Forgot: A Novel* (London: William Heinemann, 1893).
Balestier, Charles Wolcott. *A Fair Device* (New York: John W. Lovell Co., 1884).
Balestier, Charles Wolcott. *James G. Blaine: A Sketch of His Life, With a Brief Record of the Life of John A. Logan* (London: Forgotten Books, 2017).
Balestier, Charles Wolcott. *A Victorious Defeat: A Romance* (New York: Harper & Brothers, 1886).
Balestier, Charles Wolcott, and Kipling, Rudyard. *The Naulahka: A Story of West and East* (New York: Doubleday & McClure, 1899).

Benfey, Christopher. *If: The Untold Story of Kipling's American Years* (New York: Penguin, 2019).

Gosse, Edmund. "Wolcott Balestier," in *The Collected Essays of Edmund Gosse* (Hong Kong: Hesperides Press, 2008), pp. 213–227.

James, Henry. *The Turn of the Screw: Critical Edition* (New York: W. W. Norton & Co., 1999).

Laclau, Ernesto. *New Reflections on the Revolution of Our Time* (London: Verso, 1999).

Wilson, Christopher. *The Labor of Words: Literary Professionalism in the Progressive Era* (Athens, GA: University of Georgia Press, 2010).

5
LEW WALLACE, BENJAMIN HARRISON, AND THE HISTORICAL ROMANCE

As one of the bestselling authors of the nineteenth century, Lew Wallace was an obvious choice to write the 1888 campaign biography for Benjamin Harrison. However, critics have not yet considered the relationship between Wallace's Harrison biography and his other hugely popular works, such as *The Fair God; Or, the Last of the 'Tzins: A Tale of the Conquest of Mexico* (1873) or, more popular still, *Ben-Hur: A Tale of the Christ* (1880). Rather than segregate the campaign biography, an overtly "political" text, from Wallace's more "literary" pursuits, we might instead foster a dialogue between these works, and in so doing examine the literariness of *The Life of Benjamin Harrison* as well as the political valence of his bestsellers. This intersection marks a significant moment in which a variety of generic materials become entangled, including electoral discourse, evolving Christian aesthetics, and the complexities of the enormously popular historical novel.[1] Wallace' campaign biography reveals how a long-standing hunt for the Real, prevalent in both American literature and democracy, leads – by the close of the nineteenth century – to a plethora of passive audiences and fixed fetishes.

To understand better how this rich interplay could result in the ineffective iconographies produced by Wallace, let us begin by outlining the "technological, religious, economic, legal, political and social factors" that surround the publication of Wallace's *Life* (Gutjahr 54). Phillip Barrish highlights the many convergences that occur during this era between literary realism and other disciplines, urging readers to pay attention to "overlapping assumptions, methodologies and goals" (1–2). In the final decades of the century, American readers navigate a difficult border between modernity and traditional religious expression, which is to say, between the secular and the sacred.[2] A growing number of pastoral voices want the Bible to feel more "real" to a mass

DOI: 10.4324/9781003132448-6

audience while, paradoxically, many secular voices seek to tap into an unseen Real in order to cater to a considerable appetite for realism. Through the corpus of figures like Wallace, Protestant readers warm up to the oft-castigated realm of popular fiction; meanwhile, readers that prefer scientific methodologies discover in Wallace's prose what they believe to be an authentic, ethnographic Real – one that provides escapism without launching the reader into undesirable flights of fancy. In short, Wallace's historical Romances are enormously influential in part because they curate a sense of the Real that speaks to a significant swath of late nineteenth-century American readers, from Christians to scientists (and occasionally both at once). This widespread desire for an unmediated Real free of rhetorical manipulation directly informs Wallace's campaign biography as well.[3]

Indeed, this longing to leap across the barriers of history and encounter the Real in ancient societies underscores an emerging form of literary consumerism at the *fin-de-siècle*. Wallace's novels lead virtual tours into places and periods previously beyond the scope of the average reader's perceptions. Moving into the Gilded Age, Wallace addresses newly empowered "globetrotters" who are eager to view the Holy Land, pristine and precisely as it once was, through proto-cinematic visuals.[4] Although enticing, the resultant texts in fact "articulate the triumph of reification" (Foley 145). That is, even as Wallace's literary tours into the ancient world promise to expand the "epistemological horizons of nineteenth century discourse," they do so by dramatically limiting these horizons. Because the author transforms complex historical phenomenon into brightly colored fetishes to be consumed at one's leisure, Wallace's reader sees much more than previous generations ever saw, Barbara Foley contends, but the reader also sees much less due to the one-dimensionality of the images produced. While it may be quite striking to picture Jerusalem in all of its ancient glory, or the fields of battle during the Civil War, these feelings – heightened by the apparent immediacy of visual immersion – do not translate effortlessly into a more meaningful reading experience. At the hands of writers like Wallace, unearthed icons from the past tend to "lapse into positivism, and totalization threatens to become self-evidence" (146). Thanks to the penchant for flattened ethnographic surveys among writers working in this genre, and their eagerness to turn dynamic historical moments into consumable icons, naysayers critique the historical Romance for bypassing historical understanding in favor of easy-to-digest substitutes.[5] As we shall see, the reduction of history into a series of fetishes similarly manifests in Wallace's account of Harrison as a candidate for the Presidency.

Although some critics praise the historical Romance for offering an objective, neutral perspective on the past, many historical Romances only feign "unmediated transposition" of the past, which is to say, these texts actually remain embedded "in various political premises" (153–154). Despite its fetishism of the Real and its "empiricist rubber-stamping," Wallace's works evoke a particular political program: namely, the self-governance privileged by liberal democracies during the Gilded Age. Via literary tourism, the study of history becomes what the reader makes of it – not merely a spectacle for placid observers, but a participatory sport. In her seminal analysis, Foley explores how writers like Wallace couple a growing sense of autonomy in readers – one frequently channeled into a new appreciation for active, self-guided tourism – to an emerging, proto-cinematic mode of consumption that renders readers passive. In response, the following chapter explores how this tension between reification and self-utterance manifests in Wallace's campaign biography for Harrison.

Before moving forward, though, we ought to define the term historical Romance, since it remains Wallace's primary genre of choice. In a technical sense, Wallace's novels are historical Romances in that they transport lustful trysts – boys meeting girls – into compelling alternative moments in history. In effect, these works deploy unique historical settings as a background for supposedly universal values like genteel love. However, I do not mean to reduce the term historical Romance to tales of lovers set in far-flung corners of world history; I wish to be a bit narrower in my use of the term. Historical Romances are comprised of two related parts: history – or, the objective study of historical events, conveyed through ostensibly accurate, and distinctively visual, imagery – and the Romance – or, the highly subjective engagement with a world of one's own design (we might recall at this juncture Percy Shelley's poet-as-creator or Walt Whitman's uber-individualist poet). On the one hand, Wallace submits his reader to a proto-cinematic Real that requires little critical engagement; on the other hand, he invites the reader to question the process of "making history" by drawing her into the construction of a "useable past," to borrow Karl Popper's well-worn phrase. Neither fully a historian, at least, of the strictly ethnographic variety, nor a Romantic – at least, of the Hawthornean variety– Wallace reveals the paradox of the historical Romance, which remains as dependent upon iconography as it is upon iconoclasm.

To comprehend Wallace's composite of different generic materials, we must also attend to the complicated role of Christianity within his corpus. Gregory S. Jackson places the homiletic novel, a novel that approximates the religious sermon, in conversation with a propensity for realism in late nineteenth-century American literature. According to Jackson, the homiletic novel attempts to capture the emotional stakes of realism – a Real that apparently transcends the quotidian world – without losing the empiricist's illusion of mastery, an illusion that she also maintains by evoking a Real that transcends the quotidian world, albeit in a different register. "American homiletic realism," Jackson asserts, "mediates between the spiritual and the empirical" (*Word* 6). Some mainline Protestants coopt the language of empiricism to remain socially relevant, under monikers including the Social Gospel and Practical Christianity. The goal of these groups is to renew the New Testament "with fresh relevance for daily living" (211). Although Wallace's fiction may not be considered strictly homiletic under the technical definition offered by Jackson, his historical Romances and the homiletic novel certainly share contiguous borders. For example, *Ben-Hur* and *The Fair God* aim to create pictures of an ancient world that could hold a congregant's attention and infuse "dusty" traditions with supposedly unmediated visuals, and to provoke a specific sort of individual autonomy that could reconcile Christianity with American-style consumerism at the height of the Gilded Age. As a result, the inconsistencies on display in Wallace's works, especially the tension between iconography and iconoclasm, reflect inconsistencies that span a variety of conceptual frameworks from late nineteenth-century America, from religious fiction to historical Romance to the campaign biography. Designed to please ethnographers armed with the scientific method, in tandem with pastors that want the Gospels to strike readers as "more Real," Wallace's texts promote blind obedience as well as radical self-governance: a strange amalgamation that conveys the uneasiness of the times.

With these core tensions in mind, we might turn to *The Life of Benjamin Harrison* and contemplate where Wallace's tale of a democratic candidacy fits within this wider constellation of cultural forces. A long-time friend of the Harrison family, Wallace cannot easily decline the invitation to try his hand at a campaign biography. In fact Wallace maintains a number of significant Presidential connections: he serves under Ulysses S. Grant in the Civil War, and he sustains a lifelong friendship with the future President; Rutherford B. Hayes, whose campaign biography by William Dean Howells is the subject of an earlier chapter, appoints Wallace to serve as governor of the New Mexico territory in 1878, a landscape that provides an ideal backdrop for finishing *Ben-Hur*; and after reading *Ben-Hur*, an impressed James Garfield appoints Wallace to serve as Minister to the Ottoman Empire in yet another example of politicos appointing "men of letters" to prominent posts. Consequently, the ways in which Wallace positions his readers to encounter religious and historical fictions parallels the way in which he wants his readers to conceptualize Harrison.

A concrete political agenda undergirds Wallace's religious and historical iconographies: namely, the advancement of an American liberal democracy that remains equal parts blind devotion and active self-governance. Interestingly, Wallace does not become a Christian until researching *Ben-Hur*. He acknowledges that he only uses Christian themes to sell more copies of his books; in the years immediately preceding the composition of Harrison's biography, Wallace is "not even a lay member of any church" (McKee 164). He appears to employ a Christian ethos, then, as a savvy method for manipulating popular opinion and, of course, selling more copies. I do not include this fact to undermine the Christian character of Wallace's body of work, or to mock the nineteenth-century Christian reader as a dupe. Instead, I underline the issue in order to argue that the political valence of his texts, which has to this point received far less critical attention than the religious dimensions, remains instrumental for any satisfactory understanding of Wallace's output. This chapter moves *The Life of Benjamin Harrison* from the margins of Wallace's career and treats it instead as a sort of guidepost for reading the rest of his corpus.

The first section of the chapter analyzes how Wallace's hyper-visual iconography limits critical thought by preaching the mantra that "seeing is believing," in terms of scientific observation as well as religious experience. In dialectical fashion, the second section highlights how Wallace champions Protestant ideals of self-formation and so paradoxically engages in iconoclasm to undercut his initial Cult of the Image by proposing that true belief, in fact, requires the absence of sight. And finally, the closing section examines how Wallace attempts to reconcile these dueling impulse, icon with iconoclasm, and thereby chart a universal pattern – one that is never as open-ended as it seems. Although Wallace's *Life* partially sustains the fruitful tensions on display in the earlier campaign biographies of Hawthorne, Howells, and Balestier, Wallace's text ultimately forfeits this internal dynamism in favor of an imaginary metaphysical essence: a forfeiture that underscores the confused state of American literature and democracy at the twilight of the nineteenth century.

The Cult of the Candidate's Image

To begin, one of the reasons that *Ben-Hur* translates so well to the silver screen is that Wallace's novels are uniquely cinematic. Wallace prioritizes vision above all other senses because – oddly enough, for a book focused on Christianity – he advocates the inverse of the Christian truism: in his books, seeing is believing. In truth, although "popular history has often labored under the notion that Protestants (are) dyed-in-the-wool iconoclasts: image breakers," Protestants at the close of the nineteenth century very much depend upon "religious tableaux ... unmediated access to the inexpungible reality of the divine" (Jackson *Word* 27, 32). Said another way, there is an increased push in late nineteenth-century Christian discourse to "secularize sin and salvation" by moving these concepts away from "the doubtful realm of metaphysics" and anchoring them "in perceivable reality" (Reynolds *Faith*, 211). This shift helps to explain Wallace's acute scopophilia – that is, his love of visuality as an exclusive means for comprehending historical events. In order to portray an "authentic" Holy Land, Wallace creates a series of tableaus to be received in the most objective fashion possible (or so the logic goes). Posturing as supremely objective, Wallace fosters a Cult of the Image by compelling his readers to rely upon a strictly iconographic imagination.

Wallace crafts his own style by recycling the ideas of well-liked travel writers of the day, including Reverend W.M. Thomson, and tuning in to the "globe-trotting" tendencies of the Gilded Age.[6] As America's imperial gaze surveys increasingly distant lands as well distant historical periods, readers in the 1880s gravitate toward novels like *Ben-Hur*, in which an omnipotent narrator curates a visual smorgasbord of far-flung locales. This aesthetic choice supports Fredric Jameson's thesis in regards to "periodizing"; historical periods become popular styles as producers transform history into purely visual, utterly reified, consumable images. Wallace's audience gradually grows accustomed to the passive consumption of foreign vistas.

Similarly, in homiletic texts from this era, Jackson uncovers "virtual-tour narratives" designed "to simulate the intimacy and immediacy of a tour – part of the system of homiletic strategies comprising an aesthetics of immediacy" (Jackson *Word* 34, 168). But what does this emphasis upon a visuality that supposedly speaks for itself tell us about texts like *Ben-Hur* and, in related ways, *The Life of Ben Harrison*? First, we must acknowledge Wallace's investment in scientific validation. Like most of the authors considered in this book, Wallace confirms America's obsession with realism in the closing decades of the nineteenth century – although, as we shall discuss shortly, Wallace's fidelity to an ethnographic, unfiltered image departs quite radically from the realism of a figure like Howells.[7] Second, and on a related front, Wallace treats history as performative, as a spectacle that can be absorbed with almost no introspection or critical thought. The famous chariot scene in *Ben-Hur*, during which the eponymous Jewish hero defeats his Roman nemesis, demonstrates the text's dependence upon unmediated spectatorship, which is to say, the bodily thrills of a singularly visual triumph. Amy Kaplan writes, "The historical novel appeals to (…) 'spectatorial lust' by (insisting upon) the theatricalization of the chivalric warrior" (677–679). In other words, thanks to his one-dimensional ethnographic lens as well as his exploitation of "spectatorial lust," Wallace fuels a Cult of the Image in which the past serves as a series of still images to be appreciated at face value.

The religious underpinnings of this Cult of the Image reveal a great deal about how, in the late nineteenth century, historical Romances and historical accounts of Christian themes become highly popular for similar reasons. Jefferson Gatrall argues that this period's literary portrayals of Jesus, like the ones produced by Wallace, "(supplement) the gospel accounts of Jesus's life with extra-biblical narrative as well as with the detail-intensive descriptive sequences central to modern literary realism." Wallace's ethnographic sensibility proves "well suited to a realist cult of image" (110, 117). Creating a perspective that closely resembles a detached camera as it impartially hovers above historical moments to record them for a reader's mindless consumption, Wallace upholds the basic premise behind many popular works of realism from the close of the century.[8] As a result, by relentlessly documenting the appearance of the Holy Land and its occupants, Wallace arguably diminishes the theological resonance of his work in favor of a slavish devotion to colorful iconography: "The question of whether the historical Jesus was actually God was of less importance to literary portraitists," Gatrall asserts, "than the mystique of realism, which place its equivocal powers of consecration at the service of his human image" (127). Put differently, Wallace capitalizes upon the "mystique of realism" to short-cut theological or philosophical complexity and produce instead a powerful Image, thus reiterating the mantra that a picture is worth a thousand words. Vachel Lindsay appropriately describes America at the end of the nineteenth century as a "hieroglyphic civilization" in which audiences become leery of oratory but still "relatively innocent of pictorial deceit" (Troy 136). Ironically, according to Wallace, who makes his living as a writer, visual icons of a beautiful city like Jerusalem or a beautiful man like Jesus remain more "authentic" than even the most well-crafted piece of prose.[9]

Paul Gripp argues that the presentation of the Real as a flattened image by the likes of Wallace transforms history into a kind of fetish: "The historical novel form is fetishistic ... the reader fetishistically returns again and again, lured by the promise the formula advertises and never fulfills" (304). Wallace too depicts "signs of reality" that evoke fidelity without the barriers that exist within any written language (310). A word can mean many things; an image, on the other hand, unequivocally communicates its meaning without conceptual baggage. Wallace's fetishized Image – be it religious, historical, or, as we shall soon see, political – is meant to exist somehow above and beyond the gap that lingers between a text and the thing-in-itself. But critics will recognize in the attempt to bypass this inherent gap a crisis for proponents of the historical Romance: ultimately, the Real cannot be captured. Wallace's historical Romances mistake "spectatorial lust" for meaningful revelation.

Ben-Hur exemplifies Wallace's historical and religious fetishism. We might consider the scene in which Wallace pauses to survey the crowded market near the Joppa Gate in Jerusalem: "Let us take our stand by the gate, just out of the edge of the currents ... and use our eyes and ears for awhile" (24). The ethnographic mode is on full display as Wallace's gaze sweeps across the market with the indifference of a movie camera. The image of the market remains undoubtedly a moving one in its splendor – "everybody and everything seemed to be in motion" – yet the impression is meant to be consumed as a singular icon, and therefore endowed with a sense of wholeness that ignores the reality that Wallace constructs the scene from a series of disconnected shots: "All these are there; not singly, as described, but many times repeated; not in one place, but everywhere in the market" (31, 23). Wallace stringently declares "the singularity of the vision" (*Fair God* 159). The titular protagonist of *Ben-Hur* watches a Roman processional with "machine-like unity." Wallace's use of the modifier "machine-like" may be anachronistic, but it is still somehow appropriate in that it conveys the cinematic plenitude of the moment by encapsulating the apparently timeless images of a processional. The ancient processional bears an eagle as its sign, thereby creating a visual palimpsest: the proto-celluloid tapestry of a Roman empire not yet matured, overlaid with an American spirit still to come – eagles, of course, eventually serving as the nation's most familiar icon (*Ben-Hur* 78). At both the Joppa Gate and the site of the Roman parade, then, Wallace fetishizes the moving image as a historical and religious Real. Instead of playing with the gap between the images – a choice that would forecast the caesura exploited in Soviet Montage, among other filmic examples – Wallace embraces the poetic totality of his proto-cinematic tapestry.

Ben-Hur understands itself to be an ethnographic visual aid. It goes so far as to instruct readers to "take a map" and follow it down hidden roadways (100).

Wallace's visual impetus is hardly subtle: "Look up," the text commands. "Look down upon the arena." Eventually, the novel simply interjects: "Look!" (227, 235, 365). The imperial vision on display in *Ben-Hur* erases the border between interior and exterior, a border that would maintain at least a partial demarcation of the Real from the Cult of the Image. Wallace's novel flattens time and space and, in so doing, encourages its spectators to visualize everything within one bountiful frame: "Let us see what her purpose is," reads a particularly ambitious aside (280). Even interior motivations can apparently be penetrated by the gaze as when, upon staring at Ben-Hur's face, the narrator notes: "Even the reader will say (Ben-Hur) was having a vision of the woman" (154). In effect, what Ben-Hur sees with his "inner eye" becomes coopted into Wallace's (im)possible visual composite. Do any tangible differences exist between a glossy tourist brochure and the prose of *Ben-Hur*?

Very much connected to these scopophilic concerns, let us now turn to another Cult of the Image in the Wallace canon: the image of the democratic candidate. Wallace's *The Life of Ben Harrison* duplicates the ethnographic as well as proto-cinematic tendencies in *Ben-Hur*, and this overlap tells us a great deal about the shifting ground of the campaign biography. Not unlike the scopophilia of *Ben-Hur*, Wallace's *Life* portrays candidate Benjamin Harrison through unvarnished, one-dimensional images – snapshots that are meant to culminate in a full picture of the man who would be President. As Charles Hyde writes in his introduction to the Harrison biography, the text "seeks to show, not tell" and it is composed, theoretically at least, with "no embellishment" (n.p.). Wallace wishes to paint a portrait of his chosen candidate with complete verisimilitude; in the process, however, he reduces a complex human being into a fetish. When the reader completes the campaign biography, Wallace claims, "it will be possible to say and believe we know him" (*Life* 1). Compare this confident assertion with the periodic emphasis upon the unknowable in the campaign biographies considered in each of the preceding chapters by Hawthorne, Howells, and Balestier. Treating the candidate's glorified image as a shorthand for "the people's will," Wallace invites his spectator to behold Harrison and to trust unfailingly the potency of the spectacle. To see him is quite literally to believe in him.

There are countless examples in *Life* that demonstrate this iconographic impulse. In the requisite ancestry section of the biography, Wallace describes a painting that depicts the trial of England's Charles I: "There is an historical picture of the assemblage in ruffs and broad-brimmed, steeple-crowned hats, sitting solemn as ghosts, with the kind over against them face-to-face" (3). Here Wallace elects to present Benjamin's relative Thomas Harrison in a literal tableau – a supposedly unvarnished expression of the period in which the elder Harrison lived. In addition, readers are led to "authenticate" the portrait with Harrison's signature as well as his wax seal. The seal design again involves an eagle, an emblem that Wallace compares to the one later used on the half-dollar in

American currency. As he does in *Ben-Hur*, Wallace creates a palimpsest by overlaying pregnant symbols in order to channel the timeless spirit of the thing-in-itself: in this case, Benjamin Harrison's "American-ness," or even more pointedly, his innate rebelliousness in the face of tyranny. This heightened portrait of the Harrison clan, which appears to offer a window into the nation's inherent resistance to authority, presumably serves as an image of something Real to connect its spectators to an unmediated history.

Wallace represents Harrison in a manner that echoes his description of the protagonist in *Ben-Hur*. In that novel, the eponymous character appears "gentle even to womanliness" (78). Harrison, meanwhile, remains "of slight physique ... even girlish in appearance" (*Life* 28). At a practical level, Wallace compensates for Harrison's diminutive stature – standing at 5 foot, six inches tall, fellow soldiers in the Civil War nicknamed the candidate "Little Ben" – by equating physical smallness with spiritual enormity. Furthermore, Wallace makes Cultish the Image of his ideal candidate by evoking a connection with Ben-Hur and, more significant still, with Jesus Christ. Endowed with the "feminine" look of Christ, Wallace's portrait of the candidate strikes the spectator as beautiful, pure, and unpolluted. To gaze upon Harrison is apparently not dissimilar from gazing upon the face of the Lord. Capitalizing upon the fact that Harrison was a decorated soldier in the Civil War, Wallace conjures once more the sort of "spectatorial lust" triggered by the chariot scene in *Ben-Hur*, which is to say, he recreates a jingoist spectacle. A good deal of *Life* involves a careful mapping of the many battles in which Harrison has taken part. These intensely matter-of-fact scenes do not aim to romanticize the candidate – indeed, there is very little of the bravado that we see in other campaign biographies, such as Hawthorne's infamous treatment of Franklin Pierce in the Mexican War (see Chapter 3). Instead, Wallace tracks Harrison through his actual movements during the conflict and so transports his readers to another era, encouraging them to consume Civil War imagery as "objectively" as possible. The proto-cinematic qualities of these passages cannot be overstated: Wallace claims to document the Real by allowing a series of snapshots to capture Harrison's martial essence. "Throughout the foregoing narrative of General Harrison's military service the writer has purposely refrained from expressions of opinion respecting them; it was greatly preferable, he thought, to present the circumstances, and leave the reader to draw his own conclusions" (170–171). Summoning the logic employed in Wallace's historical Romances, the plenitude of the candidate's image requires nothing more than to be gazed upon and absorbed in its fullness: "(Harrison's) clothes were of good material, but plainly cut and made. He wore no jewelry on finger or shirt front ... a genuine, hearty, unaffected gentleman" (193–194). Greeted by powerful visuals at every turn, Wallace's readers glimpse an ostensibly transparent figure, stripped of all pretense by a penetrating gaze.

Through its extremely ocular prose, Wallace again borrows a good deal from popular Christian discourse from the period, since "words themselves have, in particular Protestant traditions, been perceived as something vividly incarnated and materially transformative: a literalization of the 'word made flesh'" (Jackson *Word*, 26). In Wallace's estimation, Harrison's words remain interchangeable with pictures, because their "plain style (advocates) simplicity, clarity, and lack of such ornamentation as rhetorical flourishes and figures, allegory, metaphor, metonymy, and the like" (29). In a particularly pregnant moment, Wallace declares that Harrison "never fails to make himself perfectly understood" (55). Wallace's tendency to "make the word flesh" influences the contours of his campaign biography – and, concurrently, it suggests that his campaign biography also influences the tenor of his historical Romances.

Yet every fetish, every Cult of the Image, can only sustain its illusion for so long, and the spectator must eventually confront the void between an icon and what it appears to represent. Unlike Howells, a writer who consistently acknowledges a Real that could never be manifested through the symbolic order, Wallace rarely de-fetishizes his subject.[10] "Rarely," however, does not mean never. On occasion, and perhaps unconsciously, Wallace admits that his visualizations do not completely capture the thing-in-itself. He describes the horrors of combat as "indescribable"; Harrison as a character retains "an element of (R)omance more or less defiant of control" (151, 31). In other words, *Life* cannot maintain the central premise of scientific, religious, historical, or political "authenticity" without an occasional interruption. Even though "the spectacle (is) simple enough of itself," its simplicity – its presumed purity – proves to be strained by internal inconsistencies. In *Ben-Hur*, Wallace offers "a spectacle which the modern tourist cannot see" – but, of course, now they *can* see it, thanks to the stunning panoramas of the novel. Consequently, the reader's second sight reveals itself to be neither natural nor unproblematic. We therefore rediscover an enduring gap between the unseen and the image (83).[11] In another example, Wallace's presentation of the Virgin Mary possesses "indefinable" traits that call to mind "things impalpable" (29). Perhaps seeing is not quite the same thing as believing after all.

In sum, the unthinking scopophilia of *Life* suggests that "faith (is) always more important than fact" (Gutjahr 63). In political terms, the visual image of the candidate is never merely a matter of public record; instead, representative government involves faith in a recognizable icon that could never truly manifest the so-called "will of the people." That is, a feeling of faith in Harrison's image connects the reader to what could never adopt a final form – the imagined essence that (im)possibly binds a community of individuals with highly variegated desires. And due to its inconsistencies and omissions, Wallace's portrait of Harrison unwittingly invites us to challenge the ocularcentric tenets of the author's works as well as in a broader sense the "ocular orientation of realist writing" (Moody 178). Wallace's historical Romances as well as his campaign biography unconsciously tarry around a schism between what can be articulated – the Cult of the Candidate's Image – and that which remains eternally unsaid – the surplus of the yet-to-be-articulated; seeds of iconoclasm that render the political possible by leaving open the possibility of different icons yet to come.

Self-Uttered Men and Permanent Picture-Writing

The second aspect of the historical Romance, especially in places where the genre converges with the homiletic novel, involves self-formation. These works comment upon how subjects are led to form their own subjectivity in specifically Protestant terms. The late nineteenth century produces a range of texts that blur the line between the objective and the subjective, realism and idealism. In the final section, we investigate how this complex moment informs Wallace's campaign biography by framing Harrison as iconic and iconoclastic all at once.

Wallace's historical Romance *The Fair God* creates an internal unrest by paradoxically conveying an unmediated Real through a heavily mediated series of tableaus. On the surface, the novel dwells upon the exotic visuals of Mexico, repeatedly commanding its reader to "look" and to "see" the splendor that surrounds her: "No traveler … could look unmoved on the picture" (16).[12] Yet even as the story doubles as a visual tour of an ancient place, it actively condemns the "picture-writing" of its superstitious antagonist (52). That is, the text strains to reconcile its own formal structure, a structure not unlike the picture-writing practiced by Wallace's exoticized Mexicans, with its distinctive ideological message – namely, the presumed iconoclasm that accompanies an imagined shift from Mexican monarchy to America's liberal democracy. Plagued by cognitive dissonance, Wallace's readers are left to make sense of the author's pivot from naïve belief in hieroglyphs to the supposedly sturdier belief in a faith-based freedom of self-expression: "The images were not of themselves more estimable than other stones," the hero realizes. "Their sanctity was from faith alone … I will make gods of things least godly" (429). *The Fair God* therefore celebrates a man that must learn to deconstruct tyrannous iconographies and invest in a form of self-governance, which is to say, in his ability to write his own story.

Following the precedent set by Henry Ward Beecher in 1871 with *Life of Jesus, The Christ*, and anticipating Charles Sheldon's 1896 work *In His Steps*, made famous by its rhetorical question "What would Jesus do?," Wallace follows a trend among popular novelists at the *fin-de-siècle* "to construct a highly personalized theology" (Moody 157). It would be difficult to overstate the significance of this cultural shift. More and more American Protestants begin to call into question *sola scriptura* – the belief that Scripture stands out as the only way to understand God – and erect in its place a sense of the Holy Spirit that comes from "within" rather than from "above" (159). One perhaps unexpected reason for this increasingly personalized faith is a growing dependence upon scientific discourse; as readers turn to secular texts for answers to life's questions, pastors and theologians alike respond by seeking ways to modify Christianity and render it more immediately applicable to everyday life. Another possible reason for this personalized experience of faith would be the rise of the Gospel of Wealth, in which people of faith look to apply Christian ethics to their private habits – particularly in regards to consumerism or financial speculation. In its crudest terms, the

Gospel of Wealth invokes the convention of the self-made man. Caught up in these cultural eddies, Wallace is well aware of the dominant sensibility shared by many literary realists as well as mouthpieces for a modernized Christianity: the drive to morph individuals into "agents of interpretation" by asking them to make "participatory investments" through their reading experiences (176).[13] As a result of this renewed attention to epistemological assumptions, Wallace challenges the roots of Christian consciousness at the twilight of the nineteenth century – or, more importantly for the author, a man with few religious convictions of his own, a stronger emphasis upon the evolving political consciousness of his era. Wallace's advocacy of America's liberal democracy blends with the tenets of Christian evangelism.

Before detailing how Wallace's campaign biography dovetails with the Pauline undercurrents described above, let us dig a bit deeper into the literary, religious, and political contexts of late nineteenth century America. Jackson writes, "The aesthetic innovations of literary realism emerged not only from a cosmopolitan embrace of scientific empiricism but also from this homegrown, indeed parochial, heuristic tradition of Protestant homiletics" (*Word* 14). Jackson meticulously examines how the long arc of American realism – which remains, as we have already established, the dominant aesthetic of both the Gilded and Progressive periods – is informed by a shifting set of Christian attitudes. One cannot readily separate literary realism, with its belief in science as well as its cynicism toward idealism or metaphysics in general, from the concomitant development of the homiletic novel. The shared vector that links realism to homiletics involves stress upon self-formation, a sense that idealism must be "put into action" if it is to mean anything, and a focus upon experience rather than second-hand instruction.[14] "The homiletic novel," Jackson argues, aims "to facilitate *private* devotion, strengthen moral *autonomy*, and foster social engagement through particular acts of reading" (158, emphasis mine). Wallace's texts reflect an underlying ethos of self-reliance cultivated by many of the pastors and theologians of his day.

Once again, in contrast to his ocular-centrism and ethnographic tendencies, Wallace periodically, and however unconsciously, reveals the gap between the Word and what it represents. His texts do not infrequently suggest a departure from the ontological and epistemological traditions of yesterday.[15] In their place, he urges his reader to discover the truth *within herself*. Like many sermonizers, Wallace prods his audience into "living out" the truth instead of simply observing it. But an internal conflict becomes quickly apparent: this pivot into self-governance stands at odds with his devotion to one-dimensional icons – the extreme visual fetishism described in the first part of this chapter. Undeterred by inconsistency on the question of autonomy versus blind obedience, Wallace denies his "readers a passive role, presenting instead real-life scenarios that (demand) narrative participation" (*Word* 163). His strategies involve teaching readers "to interpret their own lived experiences according to spiritual templates," compelling them into "direct action," and inspiring them "to shape themselves." In a word, Wallace attempts "to engage (readers) in a radical *imitation Christi*" via a series of Pauline exercises (189, 203–204, 189).

In other words, by departing from the immediacy of his visuals, Wallace highlights an internal process of articulating and then affirming one's own truth, of expressing faith in a habitus unique to America's liberal democracy, especially in the midst of a Gilded Age in which citizens are habitually told to cultivate proper behaviors for accruing greater wealth. Like contemporaneous homiletic writers, Wallace compels his readers to follow the disciple Paul, "not to 'conform' their lives but to 'transform' them ... to imagine themselves as participants in sacred events ... to perceive and reshape" (*Word* 33–35). On multiple fronts, Wallace readers experience a crucial disjuncture at the heart of the historical Romance: in terms of "history," they are asked to submit to a Real that has been defined for them by scientists, historians, and the mass media (a Cult of the Image); in terms of "Romance," they are asked to define themselves instead of waiting to be defined by others. What does this ongoing tension between self-actualization and uncritical spectatorship reveal about Wallace's depiction of a public candidate for office? Is Wallace's vision of a democratic candidacy imbued with the same conceptual baggage as his historical Romances?

Before investigating the emphasis upon self-utterance in *The Life of Benjamin Harrison*, however, we must step back and consider what is at stake. As we shall soon see, Wallace adopts a Pauline approach in his work, but not the Paul that has been historically "tied to Christianity's least open, most institutional aspects" (Badiou 4). Rather, Wallace seizes upon Paul's process of forming a new subjectivity in the crucible of faith, a process that originates in the transformation of Saul, in name as well as character. Paul preserves unexpected ruptures that challenge the status quo. However, Wallace cares little for institutionalized Christianity when he sits down to write *Ben-Hur*, later admitting "I have no convictions about God or Christ" (qtd. in Gutjahr, 55). It can be surmised that Wallace adopts a Pauline ethos for the same reason that contemporary philosophers like Alain Badiou turn to Paul: to talk about politics – or, perhaps more to the point, to remind his readers of what it means to speak politically.[16] *Ben-Hur* plainly states this focus: "The unhappy condition was not from religion, but from misgovernment and usurpations and countless tyrannies" (*Ben-Hur* 179). According to Badiou, the subject utters itself into being by experiencing an unplanned truth, declaring it, and then "being faithful to this declaration" (14). The subject must remain open to conversion at any moment. Paul, "although himself a Roman citizen, and proud of it ... will never allow any legal categories to identify the Christian subject" (13). If we subscribe to this kind of Pauline approach, we discover the genuine radicality of a Christian subjectivity, one that leads subjects to reinvent themselves without the comfort of custom. According to Badiou, Paul insists upon "the declaring subject" and, by so doing, undermines the supposed continuity between Judaism and what follows "the Christ-event" (77, 35). Indeed, similar ruptures punctuate the entire body of Wallace's work, including his campaign biography of Harrison. Wallace presents "declaring subjects" to encourage a broader investment in America's brand of liberal democracy.

Wallace almost always wants to write about freedom from legal restraint, and he almost always employs a specific Christian framework to make his case. He opens *Ben-Hur* by pointing out the innate problem with the Brahman: they rely upon too many rules, too much top-down discipline. Michael Dobkowski elucidates the novel's central focus upon excessive legalism: "Jews are depicted in (*Ben-Hur*) as reverent servants of the law" (169). Elswhere, the text contrasts a Jewish code of conduct, one that demands revenge, with a Christian code of conduct that maintains the freedom to forgive. At the same time, *Ben-Hur* gestures at the unacceptable condition of slavery: when I am a slave, "I am not my own" (198). Wallace charts a pivot from the consciousness of the enslaved to an emancipated consciousness with which free actors declare themselves to be free and then define themselves against the rigid expectations of the state or leaders in the temple. Ben-Hur's Roman nemesis articulates this dilemma by revealing to his enemy the shortcomings of Jewish law: "Why not step out of the narrow circle which ... is all of noble life your laws and customs allow?" (58). At the same time, he reveals the shortcomings of Roman law when he declares himself to be like a god that controls the consciousness of his loyal subjects: "I cannot name a god to commend thee to; so, by all the gods, I will commend thee to – myself!" (144). Echoing Paul, Wallace neither fully critiques the state – the novel often lauds the way that Romans conduct their business – nor does he fully reject religion (*Ben-Hur* repeatedly celebrates Judaism, particularly in its emphasis upon familial continuity).[17] Instead, Wallace cherry-picks popular theological and, even more assertively, political concepts to identify his ideal American citizen, one that can declare herself into being without waiting for sanction from authorities. *The Life of Benjamin Harrison* likewise challenges legal restraint in order to declare a free subject. In one particularly memorable scene, Wallace describes a courthouse in less than flattering terms. His would-be President encounters the realm of the law and finds it to be "dingy, gloomy and forbidding ... funereal" (43). Not unlike Ben-Hur, Harrison must somehow evade his country's oppressive legal apparatus, with all of its imposing dreariness. Wallace's heroic candidate eventually defies the law, with its funereal façade, by improvising a legal defense and thereby unshackling himself from the death-like grip of legalism through improvised self-governance.

For Wallace, the law signals death both literal and poetic. Badiou shares in this Pauline mode of resistance by stressing that Christ was "born and concurrently establishes his own date of birth by instituting year 1" (16). The story of the resurrection invokes the power to declare one's own life against the greatest restriction that could possibly be imposed by earthly forces: specifically, the power reserved by governing bodies to decide between life or death for citizens. *Ben-Hur* illustrates this resistance through the treatment of Ben-Hur's family as lepers. To be classified as a leper means that one should be "treated as dead" (265). In response, Jesus speaks an unsanctioned word "and the sick are made well" (330). Language uttered by the "declaring subject" can undo the paralysis of death experienced by subjects cataloged, and so controlled, by the state. That is, when Wallace writes of the lepers that they are "only dead in law," his readers are meant to underline the word "only" and so understand that man's law is never the final word (286).

While novels like *Ben-Hur* ostensibly utilize these utterances as a sign of personal freedom in a religious context – Jesus declares "I Am" and that is enough to undermine attempts by the Jews and Romans to name him, in a mocking fashion, "King of the Jews" – *The Life of Benjamin Harrison* underscores the acutely political valence of this radical form of subjectivity (*Ben-Hur* 369). For example, Wallace spins otherwise negative aspects of the biography, like Harrison's failure to give attention to the subject of composition while he is enrolled in school, into a positive. By repeatedly referencing Harrison's shortcoming as a writer, Wallace elevates the candidate's oral communication as a declarative as well as unmediated mode of communication to rival the mode used by the Pauline self-declaring subject. "Tricks, traps, surprises and small advantages are foreign to General Harrison's ideas of professional honor. He may not always be eloquent, but he is always logical ... he despises attempts at dramatic effect" (*Life* 54). Unlike the logocentric Harrison, Wallace's fictional Roman remains "habitually" satirical. Wallace classifies Roman-style communication as secretive, manipulative, and untrue – letters must be "burned after reading"; Roman sentries routinely intercept letters and throw into doubt their authenticity (193). A Roman map of a prison reveals itself to be "a lie" that allows Ben-Hur's family to be kept in total isolation, a revelation that illuminates the inherent subterfuge of all Roman texts (260). Wallace's fictional heroes – including, in a sense, Benjamin Harrison – invariably speak truth to power, which is to say, they insist that one's *spoken* word is one's bond. When a character asks if a contract should be recorded in writing, Ben-Hur responds: "I rest upon your word" (211). Because truth-telling separates the free man from the slave, as Wallace overtly proclaims in *Ben-Hur*, Wallace's works compel us to attend to the underlying relationship between language and power. Who exactly gets to utter himself into being, and what are we to do, then, with the iconographic quality of the written word – a quality that seems to run counter to the iconoclastic impulse behind Wallace's protagonists, including Harrison?

Perhaps nothing more accurately encapsulates the value placed upon self-utterance in Wallace's works than Badiou's statement: "It is not the signs of power that count, nor exemplary lives, but what a conviction is capable of, here, now, and forever" (30). Paul's radical form of subjectivity, Badiou continues, reminds us of the power of an unanticipated "intervention" – one that appears out of nowhere, reorients the subject, and then fosters fidelity to a new truth. Hence the ongoing issue with naming in *Ben-Hur*: Wallace's subject constantly adopts different names in order to reinvent his place in the ancient world. This many-named hero exists as "both Jew and Roman ... (he) hath tricks of language ... today a Jew, tomorrow a Roman" (165). He refuses to be named by another, and his insistence upon renaming himself serves a strategic purpose. The gap between being named and naming oneself cannot be predicted, or it would already be part and parcel of the cultural discourse that enslaves the oppressed. In *The Life of Benjamin Harrison*, Wallace describes the career of one of Harrison's relatives in a similar fashion. Harrison's relative declares himself to be a politician and, lo and behold, he becomes a politician. It is not prescribed to the Harrisons that they will be elected officials; they fall into it quite by accident. The unexpected moment arrives and so they declare themselves to be a key part of American politics. In a formulaic sense, of course, this rhetorical tactic rehashes the age-old Cincinnatus trope in which American politicians pose as reluctant to assume office rather than appear too eager to claim power for themselves. Wallace relies upon this ploy throughout his corpus, and this reliance invokes a common theological/political motive. the opportunity to rebrand oneself cannot be anticipated; it arrives in a state of grace, like a thunderbolt, and sets the stage for something completely different. As Wallace writes, "Not seldom it is the unexpected that happens in politics" (*Life* 48). After all, if the change was expected, it would be readily folded into the existing order of things, since there would exist no genuine rupture between the previous dictates of the law and the nascent formation of a "free subject." It is this Pauline possibility of perpetual rupture that sustains the political potential in Wallace's fiction, and we also find this message manifested in his campaign biography for Harrison.

Consequently, Wallace's improvisers remain undeterred in the dark halls of the legal system by coming to terms with the issue of textuality. Although Wallace's logocentric protagonists instinctually prefer the spoken word to the written document, a crucial tool of both Judaism and Roman tyranny, it is the symbolic order that best ensures power, control, and domination in the long run. "The law," Badiou reminds us, "consists above all in the letter's force of commandment" (83). Through Rome's ability to kill a citizen, literally and figuratively, through terms like "leper" (or "Jew," for that matter), Wallace presents the written text as an assertion of dominance as well as an erasure of personal agency. When Rome commandeers Ben-Hur's family home, a placard reads: "THIS IS THE PROPERTY OF THE EMPEROR" (274). When Ben-Hur forges an alliance with a Northman by giving him funds to start his own wine shop, Wallace closes the chapter with another inscription that signifies freedom over a formerly prescribed status: over the door, a sign reads "THOR THE NORTHMAN" (254). And, in yet another example, Chapter XXIV ends with the inscription of a name – this time, the name of Ben-Hur's Roman benefactor upon his triumph over the Northmen at sea (114). Wallace clearly invests a good deal in the concept of the declaring subject that writes himself into existence.[18] In the section of his campaign biography entitled "Ancestry," Wallace similarly focuses upon the relatives of Harrison that write themselves into being. One looming ancestor signs the Declaration of Independence; another extremely prominent ancestor – the former President, William Henry Harrison – controls land grants in the Northwest: "In this regard his authority was absolute ... his signature was the perfect evidence of title" (*Life* 8). To be a Harrison, it seems, means possessing the ability to legitimize a thing by merely signing one's name to it. Writing one's own name instigates a power that appears to be "perfect."

An pressing question remains: "What I declare, that I put in writing. *Is it enough?*" (*Ben-Hur* 207, emphasis mine). The friction between logocentrism and an insistence upon the power of textuality forces Wallace's readers to interrogate the gap between self-utterance and its (im)possibility, and to return once more to the uneven ground between icon and iconoclasm. Proven by the derogatory sign that designates Christ as "King of the Jews," a written text never quite captures the thing-in-itself. Ben-Hur's family property certainly does not belong to the Emperor, at least not in any meaningful way. But the land grants signed by the elder Harrison in *Life* are supposedly "absolute" on the basic grounds of his signature. What are readers to make of this inconsistency? In *Life*, Wallace draws attention to the seal of Harrison's ancestor; decorated with an eagle, prescient of "the bird on our silver dollar," this signature serves as an idol of sorts – a hieroglyph; a word made image, stripped of its rhetorical slipperiness and purified (4). Yet we have already seen how textual signatures in Wallace's works are routinely subjected to deconstruction in the name of the Real. So which will it be: iconography or iconoclasm? Rigid visual history or the unspeakable absences of the dark Romance?

Wallace never fully commits to the promise of self-utterance in America's liberal democracy. This moment of authorial indecision speaks volumes to the conflicted vision that we have been tracking throughout the development of the campaign biography. Even as certain campaign biographies sustain a radical openness, that is, a refusal to fetishize, or fix in place, an avatar for "the will of the people," many of Wallace's works reconcile readers to a comforting sense of closure. On the one hand, as this section has illustrated, *The Life of William Harrison* remains a relatively rich text thanks to its place within a larger constellation of generic uncertainty (the historical Romance; the homiletic novel); it is the story of a candidate that declares himself into being while simultaneously understanding the (im)perfection of language as a tool of legalism. On the other hand, this tension appears to be "not enough" in Wallace's campaign biography, and so the text ultimately denies what Badiou would describe as a revolutionary "doctrine of the Real" in its attempt to resolve potential loose ends (69). The Harrison text fails as a true intervention, one that would highlight the gap between the Real and the thing-in-itself, because it succumbs to an inertia of certitude that is becoming all-pervasive at the twilight of the nineteenth century.

A Perfect Circle

Whereas one might argue that the friction between iconography and iconoclasm throughout Wallace's works evokes a useful dynamism – in so far as the dynamic encourages a better understanding of how readers must grapple with the inherent slipperiness of American democracy – his work ultimately refuses the radical openness that it occasionally invokes. Although we can track Wallace's reliance upon the counter-cultural aspects of Christian aesthetics as well as literary realism from the period in question, we cannot forget Wallace's stubborn insistence upon a fetishized Real. That is, despite their momentary openness, Wallace's works nevertheless push readers to revere what the texts present to be "authentic" and "immediate," thereby encouraging them to venerate ethnographic, religious, and political icons. In turn, even as Wallace's campaign biography of Harrison illustrates how candidates serve as one-dimensional avatars as well as elusive signifiers that leave unfinished a potent democratic order in their resistance to imposed meaning as well as their celebration of self-utterance, Wallace's *Life* finally undermines its own ambivalence in favor of a fixed Real to be consumed with precious little introspection. Wallace's campaign biography accomplishes this feat in a number of ways, including through its deference to social evolution as well as its enclosure of "radical" events within larger predictable patterns. Although Wallace's *Life* flirts with a radical, iconoclastic understanding of democracy, it ultimately restores the hagiographic sensibilities that have led most critics to foreclose analysis of the campaign biography as literature.

Foley describes Wallace's type of foreclosure as follows: "There is little attempt to present character and event as issuing from the contradictions of the historical dialectic" (162). Unlike the well-known celebration of realism issued by Georg Lukács, in which literary realism exposes the internal dynamics of lived history, Foley demonstrates how many so-called realists, including Wallace, never achieve anything close to this level of dynamism. In the fictional worlds created by Wallace, history is not a dialectical machine run by internal contradictions, but "a remote and exotic ground for the incarnation of religious truths and timeless human passions" (Foley 162). Said another way, Wallace removes the possibility of a complex understanding of history – or politics, for that matter – in order to establish easy-to-digest Truth: a vision that remains ostensibly remote, eternal, and driven by feverish passion instead of philosophical reflection. As a tour guide for the self-made men of the Gilded Age, Wallace excels; as a commentator on the messy human condition, he falls well short of his target. Wallace's "aesthetics of immediacy" dulls the teeth of his iconoclastic perspective because he dwells upon the arguably less compelling elements of the historical Romance – namely, its ethnographic certitude in a scientific Real alongside its quiet submission to a Real of the pseudo-metaphysical variety. The interesting attributes of the historical Romance – history as a dialectical dance; Romance as a chasm between what can be pictured and what is eternally formless – are all but abandoned by the time the reader arrives at Wallace's highly reductive resolutions.

To illustrate this widespread abandonment of the tensions that we outlined in the previous sections, let us turn to Wallace's reliance upon social evolutionism. On this count, Wallace expresses a hunger, shared among many of his fellow American realists, for "evolutionary determinism" (Jackson *Word*, 13). Despite his numerous borrowings from the homiletic tradition, Wallace does not hesitate to make extensive references to evolution, a concept that is still quite novel in the late nineteenth century. Wallace coopts the language of genealogy to render his Biblical claims, as well as his claims about the Harrisons, more "scientifically accurate" (Gutjahr 61). To do so, Wallace synthesizes the Darwinian premise of natural selection with the growing readerly interest in religious symbolism. The resultant amalgamation proves to be, in the final tally, propelled not by the ruptures that remain so vital in Paul's radical subjectivity; rather, Wallace preserves a neat-and-tidy teleology in which everything that does unfold was always-already meant to unfold. This determinism appears most palpably when Wallace diverges into overtly political matters. In the early sections of *Ben-Hur*, for example, the narrator/tour guide pauses to survey the marketplace of Jerusalem and sees "all the sects among whom the ancient faith has been parceled and refined" (26). The text's assumption here is that sectarian divisions are somehow the result of a natural – and benevolent – process of "refinement." Wallace then applies this logic of natural selection to the geopolitics of the region:

> There is no law by which to determine the superiority of nations. A people rise, run their race, and die either of themselves or at the hands of another, who, succeeding to their power, takes possession of their place, and upon their monuments write new names, such is history. (67)

Wallace aims to legitimize a hierarchy of nations by declaring Western supremacy – especially for the burgeoning United States – to be inevitable, which is to say, the way things "must be."

Wallace reiterates this evolutionary premise in his campaign biography of Harrison when he indulges in a long diatribe concerning the so-called natural selection of political parties. "The best evidence of genuine political liberty," he concludes, "is the existence of political parties. They are in fact the organized expression of opinion permissible only in a state of freedom" (*Life* 183). Like the sects of Jerusalem that have been gradually polished over time, political parties prove the existence of an organic refinery beneath a protean social order: "A political part cannot be manufactured ... (and) cannot succeed upon a question of morals purely and singly" (183). Posturing as an impartial ethnographer, Wallace argues that the Republican party came into being, and other parties subsequently fell out of favor, because there was simply no other way that things could have unfolded. The political party serves as "the natural output of political conditions," as lesser parties "died, and died early, in instances because there was but the beveled edge of a plank for them to live upon; more plainly, because there was no necessity for them ... (no) necessity calling them to organize" (184–185). In this way, Wallace incessantly repeats the terms "natural" and "necessary" in his summation of America's party system. He does so not to emphasize unexpected ruptures, as when the Whigs dissolve and the Republicans materialize in their place, but to contain everything within a comprehensive, prearranged narrative. Just as the Old Testament anticipates the New, Benjamin Harrison and the Republicans are presented as the natural and necessary inheritors of the Presidency. Wallace conveys the story of the whole not to stress dialectical energies, but to facilitate in his readers a belief in omnipotence, a belief in the promise of totality. Seeing is almost always believing for Wallace, and a purified essence remains immediately accessible to even the most untrained spectator.

Wallace's illusion of totality becomes quite literally circular as it reduces the Real to a painless and vague sensation that can be achieved if one sacrifices precision for generalized "good tidings" (Foley 151). Wallace's account of world history strikes the reader as flat and one-dimensional as it promotes a palimpsest of universal values. A line from *Ben-Hur* that might otherwise serve as a critique of such fetishism actually affirms the shortcoming of Wallace's historical Romance: "(Ben-Hur) is what his ancestor was in the beginning. In this sand I draw you a circle – there! Now tell me what more a Jew's life is! Round and round" (55). In this moment, Wallace maintains the circularity of *Ben-Hur* by positioning the "unexpected" event – the rupture of the crucifixion, with its radical revision of Jewish and Roman laws – not at the beginning of the text, but at the very end. Because Ben-Hur comprehends the importance of self-utterance prior to his witness of Christ's final moments, we must read Wallace's text as self-enclosed – that is, as a work that folds in upon itself and anticipates its own climactic revelation from the very first page. According to Badiou, the Christian event occurs, it is declared, and then one must be faithful to that declaration. Less interested in what follows the event – the hard work of building a faith – Wallace surveys a character before the colossal event that Wallace's readers will inevitably anticipate. The end has been there since the start. With neither genuine surprise nor genuine tension, then, Wallace's historical Romances depend upon a superficial impression of wholeness. The unpredictability of Paul's self-utterance is undermined by a transcendent orb designed to leave the reader dumbstruck. This utter circularity leaves no room for substantive engagement beyond the realm of hazy impressionism. Everything is "as it should be" and so it simply exists to be gazed upon.

The Life of Benjamin Harrison reiterates this circular structure. After bestowing the highest level of praise upon the candidate by effectively arguing for Harrison's "absolutely stainless" essence, Wallace amplifies the self-enclosure of his hero by ending the text as follows:

Whether he is chosen or set aside by the people, (Harrison's) future will always be in perfect harmony with his past. In other words, the writer who finishes this biography, beginning where we leave off, will find his subject exactly what it has been. (267–268)

Once more, Wallace affords us no room for surprise, and certainly no room for ambivalence; such surprises might be found in other campaign biographies, like the Lincoln biography by Howells, but this uncertainty quickly fades in Wallace's iteration. Gone is a "complex, non-positivist Real"; almost entirely erased by the book's conclusion is "the negativity which marks the radical limit of symbolization" (Barrish 136, 149). Through their encounter with a single, reified portrait, Wallace's readers witness what the ideal candidate was, is, and will be again: a sense of circularity enhanced by the enduring legacy of the Harrisons in American politics. There is little left for the reader to do but express amazement and admiration for the glossy picture on display.

By placing *Life* into dialogue with Wallace's fictional output, we can understand better how the campaign biography informs, and is informed by, its complex cultural moment – in particular, by popular trends in ethnographic realism, homiletic literature, and the historical Romance. In turn, we can revisit *Life* as a more internally conflicted text than critics have heretofore acknowledged. Through the text's oscillation between icon and iconoclasm, Wallace's biography of Harrison unconsciously speaks to an ongoing vision of America's democratic candidates that cannot fully suppress its open-endedness. Nonetheless, it would be a step too far to claim that *Life* functions in the precisely same way as the campaign biographies of Hawthorne, Howells, or Balestier, since Wallace condones a fashionable rush in American letters to achieve "unmediated access to (an) inexpungible" Real (Jackson *Word*, 32). We might return to a eulogy for literary realism given by Raymond Williams:

The old naïve realism is in any case dead, for it depended on a theory of natural seeing … When we thought we had only our eyes to see a common world, we could suppose that realism was a simple recording process … (but) the old static realism of the passive observer is merely a hardened convention. (314)

Through his hardened depictions of the Real, Wallace strips away intricacies and contributes to a more rigid sense of electoral politics. His campaign biography for Harrison claims to be "historical" without the actual dynamism of history, just as it lacks a sustained appreciation for the dialectical roots of Romanticism. As such, *Life* speaks to the easy-to-digest political imagery that we continue to consume in an effortless fashion today. Wallace's campaign biography thus leaves us with a set of fair but flimsy fetishes.

Notes

1 Another writer known for his historical novels, Kenneth L. Roberts, author of *Oliver Wiswell* and *Northwest Passage*, is recruited to pen a campaign biography for Calvin Coolidge in 1924.
2 Howard Miller writes, "Americans in the late Victorian era ... embraced many aspects of modernity without rejecting religion" (154).
3 As Phillip Barrish notes, "The position of 'the Real' in realist texts is more variable, more flexible, than has been assumed" (8).
4 Filmmaker Sergei Eisenstein regards realist literature as proto-cinematic: "An emphasis on visuality, whether literary or cinematic, promotes spectatorship as a dominant cultural activity" (Jaffe 254). Philosopher John Dewey calls this "the kodak fixation" (qtd. in Westbrook 129).
5 Foley summarizes this critique of the historical novel: "The bourgeois protagonist 'stands for' the dynamic totality of society in a way that sloughs over very real historical contradictions among very real social groups" (154).
6 For a detailed study of this imperial gaze, see Mary Louise Pratt's *Imperial Eyes: Travel Writing and Transculturation* (New York: Routledge, 2007).
7 Gregory S. Jackson describes a growing appetite in this period for "religious realism": "Increasingly supplemented by archaeology, ethnography, and historiography, such works depicted the Mediterranean world in evocative detail" ("What Would Jesus" 646).
8 Jefferson Gatrall adds, "In literary portraits of the historical Jesus, there is no incidental or insignificant detail. On the contrary, every detail is potentially a sight of the sacred" (115).
9 According to Howard Miller, Wallace's ethnographic approach was thought to make the story of Jesus Christ "even more believable" thanks, in large part, to the "fidelity" of the author's descriptions (160).
10 This argument contradicts the case made by Michael Davitt Bell that Henry James subverts Howellsian realism by producing a realism "designed to fail." To make such a claim implies that Howellsian realism does not in itself, at least on occasion, undercut the faulty premise of a knowable Real. But as we discuss in Chapter 3, Howells frequently engages in meta-realism, underlining the impossibility of capturing reality. His works, too, appear to be at times, though certainly not always, "designed to fail." For an extended discussion, see Michael Davitt Bell's *The Problem of American Realism* (Chicago, IL: University of Chicago Press, 1993).
11 Gregory S. Jackson comments, "Homiletic novels simulate the evidentiary crisis of the reader's sudden shift from material knowledge to initial blindness (often figured by Paul's conversion) in the spiritual world, where the senses have little traction" (*Word* 209).
12 Of note, the novel's protagonist articulates the power of pictures: "I have an argument stronger than the vagaries of pabas or the fancies of warriors, - *a visible argument*" (Wallace *Fair* 176, emphasis mine).
13 Nathaniel Hatch calls this phenomenon "the democratization of American Christianity" via a "highly individualized personal theology" (qtd. in Moody, 177).
14 Gregory S. Jackson comments, "Religious adherents of homiletics assumed personal experience, illuminated by spiritual insight, to be the measure of reality" (*Word* 11).
15 In Wallace's *The Fair God*, this impulse to negate takes center stage: "My picture of the entertainment will be feeble, I know, and I give it rather as a suggestion of the reality." Late, the narrator admits: "The imagination of the reader will give the floating garden richer colors than lie within compass of my pen." And in yet another instance, he continues: "If my reader has been in battle, he knows the effect of that fire too well to require description of me ... I leave the scene to his fancy" (120, 364, 404).
16 In the context of the early twenty-first century, Badiou notes that "the word 'management' obliterates the word 'politics'" (12).

17 Importantly, *Ben-Hur* admires Jewish patriarchs and its protagonist trains his fellow Jews "after the Roman pattern," a sign that the novel does not wish to disavow Roman-style governance entirely (293).
18 From *Ben-Hur*: "In the haughty Roman idea, the sententious announcement was thought sufficient for the purpose – and it was" (80).

Works Cited

Badiou, Alain. *Saint Paul: The Foundation of Universalism*. Trans. Ray Brassier (Stanford, CA: Stanford University Press, 2003).

Barrish, Phillip. *American Literary Realism, Critical Theory, and Intellectual Prestige, 1880–1995* (Cambridge: Cambridge University Press, 2001).

Dobkowski, Michael N. "American Anti-Semitism: A Reinterpretation." *American Quarterly*, vol. 29, no. 2, 1977, pp. 166–181. *JSTOR*, www.jstor.org/stable/2712357. Accessed February 26, 2021.

Foley, Barbara. "The Historical Novel," in *Telling the Truth: The Theory and Practice of Documentary Fiction* (Ithaca, NY: Cornell University Press, 1986), pp. 143–184. *JSTOR*, www.jstor.org/stable/10.7591/j.ctt207g5pj.9. Accessed February 25, 2021.

Gatrall, Jefferson J. A. "The Color of His Hair: Nineteenth-Century Literary Portraits of the Historical Jesus." *NOVEL: A Forum on Fiction*, vol. 42, no. 1, 2009, pp. 109–130. *JSTOR*, www.jstor.org/stable/40267756. Accessed February 25, 2021.

Gripp, Paul. "When Knighthood Was Progressive: Progressive Historicism and the Historical Novel." *The Journal of Narrative Technique*, vol. 27, no. 3, 1997, pp. 297–328. *JSTOR*, www.jstor.org/stable/30225473. Accessed February 25, 2021.

Gutjahr, Paul. "'To the Heart of Solid Puritans': Historicizing the Popularity of 'Ben-Hur.'" *Mosaic: A Journal for the Interdisciplinary Study of Literature*, vol. 26, no. 3, 1993, pp. 53–67. *JSTOR*, www.jstor.org/stable/24780566. Accessed February 25, 2021.

Hyde, Charles. "Reconciling Benjamin Harrison," in *Life of Benjamin Harrison: Commemorative Edition* (Crawfordsville, IN: General Lew Wallace Study and Museum, 2017), n.p.

Jackson, Gregory S. *The Word and Its Witness: The Spiritualization of American Realism* (Chicago, IL: University of Chicago Press, 2009).

Jaffe, Audrey. "Spectacular Sympathy: Visuality and Ideology in Dickens's *A Christmas Carol*." *PMLA*, vol. 109, no. 2, 1994, pp. 254–265. *JSTOR*, www.jstor.org/stable/463120. Accessed February 26, 2021.

Kaplan, Amy. *The Social Construction of American Realism* (Chicago, IL: University of Chicago Press, 1992).

McKee, Irving. "The Early Life of Lew Wallace." *Indiana Magazine of History*, vol. 37, no. 3, 1941, pp. 205–216. *JSTOR*, www.jstor.org/stable/27787249. Accessed February 25, 2021.

Miller, Howard. "The Charioteer and the Christ: Ben-Hur in America from the Gilded Age to the Culture Wars." *Indiana Magazine of History*, vol. 104, no. 2, 2008, pp. 153–175. *JSTOR*, www.jstor.org/stable/27792886. Accessed February 26, 2021.

Moody, Lisa. "The American 'Lives' of Jesus: The Malleable Figure of Christ as a Man of the People." *Christianity and Literature*, vol. 58, no. 2, 2009, pp. 157–184. *JSTOR*, www.jstor.org/stable/44314016. Accessed February 25, 2021.

Reynolds, David. *Faith in Fiction: The Emergence of Religious Literature in America* (Cambridge, MA: Harvard University Press, 1981).

Troy, Gil. *See How They Ran: The Changing Role of the Presidential Candidate, Revised and Expanded Edition* (Cambridge, MA: Harvard University Press, 1996).

Wallace, Lew. *Ben-Hur: A Tale of the Christ* (London: Wordsworth Classics, 1995).
Wallace, Lew. *The Fair God: Or, the Last of the 'Tzins- A Tale of the Conquest of Mexico* (New York: Popular Library, 1962).
Wallace, Lew. *Life of Benjamin Harrison* (Philadelphia, PA: Hubbard Brothers, 1888).
Westbrook, Robert. *John Dewey and American Democracy* (Ithaca, NY: Cornell University Press, 1991).
Williams, Raymond. *The Long Revolution* (New York: Penguin, 1965).

6
JACOB RIIS, THEODORE ROOSEVELT, AND THE ART OF ADORATION

Jacob A. Riis adores Teddy Roosevelt. After reading Riis's most popular work, *How the Other Half Lives* (1890), Roosevelt seeks the immigrant from Denmark to pick his brain about the grim situation in New York City's tenements. As the city's Police Commissioner (1895–1897), Roosevelt prides himself upon reforming the plight of the urban poor, and he does so with the frequent aid of his new friend. Riis therefore does not hesitate when in 1904 Roosevelt asks him to pen his campaign biography. The subsequent text reflects a complicated period in American history, informed by popular works of literature such as Christmas stories concerning urban poverty and tales about the fraternal bonds between male friends.[1] Far from a formulaic or disposable treatise, Riis's *Theodore Roosevelt, The Citizen* reveals a convergence of political and literary concerns. Riis employs a democratic candidate to embody the fullness of Americanism, with its "melting pot" ideal, while simultaneously signaling an emptiness, an absence, a crucial gap that preserves democracy as an eternal work-in-progress.

While many critics regularly refer to Riis as a representative of the reformism on display at the *fin-de-siècle*, few have placed his output into conversation with the literary preoccupations of the Progressive Era. Richard Tuerk observes, "Authors do not even try to place Riis in the context of literary history" (259). But when they do take place, these conversations greatly enhance our understanding of Riis's literary contributions as well as his voice in the larger political discourse – indeed, as we shall soon see, these roles cannot be readily disentangled from one another.[2] Upon first blush, Riis closely resembles the subject of the previous chapter, Lew Wallace, due to his scopophilia and ethnographic mindset. Both men navigate a thin line between the veneration of unvarnished scientific fact as well as the allure of bald sentimentalism. A significant amount of scholarship on Riis dwells upon his amateur photography and the misguided

DOI: 10.4324/9781003132448-7

methodology that he employs when examining urban poverty. This chapter similarly scrutinizes Riis's race to fetishize the Real – that is, his efforts to expose something "more Real," hidden beneath the surface of things, and then ultimately champion its static portrait: "the Christmas Spirit"; a transcendent love; the populist candidate as a fixed avatar of "the people." Riis's reified ideals, which supposedly capture a sense of metaphysical fullness, prove to be problematic because they almost always lead readers into the trap of blind nationalism or racial taxonomy.[3] Nonetheless, it would be an error to misread Riis's work as just another reheated version of Wallace's mostly one-dimensional output, primarily because Riis seems never quite so confident as Wallace in his singular vision. Instead, as a former immigrant himself, and as someone who vocally disagrees with Roosevelt on myriad political points, Riis's prose periodically slips from iconography to iconoclasm, oscillating between a rigid notion of the Real – the candidate as a permanent manifestation of something vast – and a fluid, deconstructive notion of the Real – the candidate as a temporary placeholder for something that could never be articulated with any finality. By placing Riis "loosely in the camp of William Dean Howells" – a categorization that already speaks volumes about Riis's campaign biography – we can recognize unresolved tensions within the writer's corpus (Tuerk 261).[4] Simply put, *TR The Citizen* reflects Riis's ongoing struggle to present the nation as an expansive whole and, at the same time, to preserve its democratic roots: the promise of pluralism and genuine egalitarian thought.[5]

By attending to the unevenness of Riis's body of work, including his campaign biography, we can also reconsider the intellectual and imaginative foundations of Roosevelt's ascent to the highest office in the land. Multiple historians observe that Roosevelt's candidacy breaks new ground in a variety of ways, including his willingness "to avail himself of the new machinery of image-craft" (Greenberg 1082).[6] In particular, Riis illuminates how Roosevelt's unique brand of populism wavers between a "communitarian approach," in which Roosevelt represents a broad entity called "the people," and radical democracy, in which Roosevelt's presence opens avenues for ever greater participation in the electoral process by reminding the so-called establishment of what they can never totally repress: "The particular, the multiple, the heterogeneous" (Mouffe *Return*, 13). Riis's account of Roosevelt emphasizes consensus, typically as a secular universalism (as in the Christmas story), or as an expression of fraternal devotion, a response conditioned by "romantic friend fiction," in which a wiser male companion fosters an unconditional sense of what is "just" or "right" in his impressionable devotee. In many of his texts, Riis marks this imaginary consensus with the vague term "key-note" (*How* 153). Slavoj Žižek calls this approach "arche-politics": belief in a homogeneous social space in which the variegated desires of a diverse populace magically align.[7] Yet despite these vague claims of consensus, Riis's campaign biography recognizes that political identity is "something to be constructed, not empirically given" (Mouffe *Return*, 66). Chantal Mouffe contends that "antagonistic forces will never disappear," and so "we should reject today the idea of a political community unified by an objective moral order" (69, 55). That is, even as *TR The Citizen* fetishizes a community made whole in Roosevelt's image, it still remains fueled by excesses and violations of the status quo, which is to say, it stubbornly resists symbolization. Unable to contain the surplus of populist sentiment that Roosevelt makes visible, Riis's campaign biography retains traces of a democratic truth that this surplus underscores: "Things could always be otherwise and therefore every order is predicated on the exclusion of other possibilities" (*On the Political* 18). Roosevelt's embodiment of "the people" is in effect only ever a solitary figuration. Populism plays a pivotal role in reminding a citizenry that established orders are fragile things and liable to be overturned, sometimes at a moment's notice. It is not as though Riis's portrayal of Roosevelt as transcendental "fullness," then, should be discarded as mere empty-headed propaganda. When Riis depicts urban life, he promotes empathy with otherwise invisible populations, thereby building emotional connections and invaluable political alliances among a diverse population. In turn, this chapter does not exclusively critique the populist undertow that accompanies Roosevelt's campaign or its chronicle; rather, Riis's campaign biography reveals American populism to be dialectical at its heart, since it enables readers "to have a real purchase on people's desires and fantasies (via) forms of identification" and, concurrently, it never allows them to lose sight of any candidate's inevitable constructed-ness (28).[8] In sum, Riis conveys the latent dynamism of the campaign biography as we have seen it germinated by Nathaniel Hawthorne and polished by Howells. The genre advances a candidate as a fixed emblem, a nascent constellation of political interests, as well as a floating signifier – that is, the specter of democracy's inevitable restlessness. The Real as permanent essence versus the Real as perpetual lack.

This chapter starts by examining the literary surpluses of *TR The Citizen* in dialogue with the rest of Riis's output, before turning to the issue of how these excesses serve as fossilized fixtures as well as radical remainders. By tracking Riis's excesses, a byproduct of his genuine affection for the candidate, we can understand better the promise and peril of Roosevelt's populism as well as the campaign biography as a distinctly literary enterprise. Through its complicated engagement with the Real, Riis's *TR The Citizen* sheds light upon major cultural concerns from the Progressive Era – not as distinctive points, but as mutually-informed, contiguous provinces.

Populist Candidates and the Spirit of Christmas

Not unlike other American realists from the *fin-de-siècle*, Riis habitually employs the imagery of Christmas in his writings, fictional and nonfictional alike, to petition for social reforms.[9] An immigrant from Denmark, Riis maintains strong cultural ties to the holiday that initially arrives in New York via Dutch immigrants. In the early days of the twentieth century, Christmas stories prove incredibly popular with reading audiences. Katherine Allyn See contends that in the United States the Christmas story serves as "a minor literary genre" in its own right (v). Correspondingly, Riis capitalizes upon the trappings of this "minor genre" in his campaign biography in order to cultivate the image of his chosen candidate. In particular, Riis draws from Christmas stories for three primary reasons, all of which play a vital role in the political treatise that he writes on behalf of Roosevelt: to instill an important interplay between the so-called material Real – the abject poverty that Riis "scientifically" exposes – and the so-called spiritual Real, which is to say, the Christmas Spirit that transcends everyday concerns; to blend the myth of the President and the metaphysical circle that purportedly binds Roosevelt to "the people" via the story of Santa Claus; and, relatedly, to express the need for a universal Truth to orient the increasingly diverse demographics of the United States in general (and New York, more specifically). In a word, Christmas stories provide Riis with precisely the kind of sentimental surpluses that he requires to deify his populist candidate.

Penne Restad argues that late nineteenth-century American Christmas narratives aim to generate a stronger sense of community in the face of industrial atomization. Early writers like Washington Irving – another figure famous for defining Christmas as well as Presidential biographies (see Chapter 1) – view the holiday as an opportunity to promote interpersonal bonds, especially in the face of the nation's growing pluralism. For Riis, Christmas narratives approximate a sense of wholeness across diverse races and religions, because to foster the heightened emotions of the holiday involves concomitantly consolidating a coherent national story. Christmas provides "a crucial key to the unity of the nation" (Restad 92). And so the goals of Riis's Christmas tales dovetail rather seamlessly with the outlook of his campaign biography. Consider Riis's most famous Christmas story, "Nibsy's Christmas" (1893), in which Riis tracks a young newspaper boy named Nibsy, who models the values of Christmas, as he secures treats for two younger street urchins before reminding them to believe in Santa Claus. This narrative establishes a clear binary between the harsh material world as it truly is – impoverished – and the even deeper, metaphysical reality that Riis describes as the Christmas Spirit. On the one hand, "Nibsy's Christmas" offers a realist's account of life on the streets of New York that foreshadows the tenets of literary naturalism soon to come: darkness "closes in," light "struggles" to get through the grime, and the wind "forces" its way into unsanitary spaces (138). Riis cuts through the gilded frame of a bourgeois Christmas to expose his readers to an ugly urban reality. Against the superficial "clink of glasses" and the "tinkling bell" of wealthy parties, against the windows stuffed with goods that remain just out of the children's grasp, "as if in a dream," readers encounter the brutal undercurrent of "the great treadmill." At the open of the story, "Christmas welcome had turned to dread" (138, 141–142). For Riis's mostly bourgeois audience, the author's juxtaposition of abject poverty and the luxuries of Christmas is meant to spur readers, in Dickensian fashion, into greater awareness of urban suffering. At the close, Nibsy falls asleep on a steam grate near a printing office just as the office explodes with "a cry of mortal terror and pain ... echoed by a hundred throats" (147). But this story cannot be classified as straightforward realism if by the term we refer exclusively to the exposure of readers to harsh industrial conditions. The tale ends with one of the urchins that Nibsy helped attending Nibsy's funeral and bringing him a hemlock branch: "It's from Santa ... Nibsy knows" (149). Beyond the material reality of the grotesque tenements, then, Riis uncovers yet another Real – this one in a vague, ethereal realm.[10] Riis ties what Nibsy "knows" – the secret that he manages to hold upon his death – to a Christmas season defined by blind faith and sacrificial gift-giving. A twofold excavation thus unfolds: first, Riis's bourgeois reader uncovers the gritty Real beneath her frivolous and privileged existence; then, a saintly character uncovers a still more significant Real, linked to the idealism of the holiday season. As the supposed Real of Christmas surpasses the supposed Real of investigative journalism, Riis forfeits the illumination of class difference in favor of something far more metaphysical. As a result, the so-called Spirit of Christmas and its impression of consensus nearly erases the unsettling qualities of Riis's journalistic exercise.

Riis's self-described Christian attitudes guide him from the material Real into the realm of bald idealism. According to Gregory S. Jackson, Riis claims "the ability to see what lies beyond the sensual trappings of the merely 'realistic', to the spiritual Real" (*Word* 228). When Riis pursues "a reality beyond the senses ... glimpses behind the veil," he encourages his readers to engage in a realist enterprise infused with his own religious sensibility. Although Riis's spiritual Real may strike contemporary readers as a byproduct of his "sentimentality" – and many critics do indeed attack him on these grounds – Jackson insists that Riis must be recognized as part of a much broader moral reform movement (230).[11] Still, neither Jackson nor other critics address Riis's extensive reliance upon the tropes of Christmas – a version of Christmas, as we shall see, stripped bare of its uniquely Christian message to be made palatable to a secularized audience. For Riis, Christmas heralds pure excess: the sentimentalism of "slumming literature" as well as a sentimentalism tied to this particular holiday, characterized by a set of ill-defined concepts such as love, good cheer, and childhood devotion.[12] Appealing to the invisible spirit of Christmas, Riis clings to a sense of moral uplift that his critics repeatedly denounce in the years to follow. To call it "realism" at all, they claim, is a blatant mischaracterization.[13] Nonetheless, whether his readers describe his work as realism or rely upon some other designation, difficulties persist as Riis attempts "to mediate the heady distractions of materialism and the steady tug of Christian piety" (Fried 8). The "minor genre" of the Christmas story allows Riis to posit material as well as spiritual Reals that can somehow coexist with one another. In 1904, Riis returns to these two abstract Reals in his campaign biography for Theodore Roosevelt.

In Riis's *TR The Citizen*, the Christmas Spirit undermines a political establishment rife with corruption. Whereas "the soul has gone out" of the political machine, Christmas supposedly sustains an innate sense of wholesomeness within American communities (99). Riis's narrator discovers that political gamesmanship threatens the ability of a clerk to be able to afford a tree for his family and so he rejects politics entirely: "It was the Christmas tree that settled it with me ... not with my Danish pedigree of blessed Christmas-trees ... never!" (105–106). More importantly, Riis evokes Christmas to trigger revelries concerning Roosevelt – a spirit that moves the once and future President; a muse to invoke cherished memories. "The Christmas bells are ringing as I write this," Riis's narrator states. "And they take me back to that holiday season, half a dozen years ago" (358). Throughout Riis's campaign biography, Christmas serves as a spiritual adhesive, one potent enough to underwrite the entire text and to endow a rapidly pluralizing American with an illusion of unity. Riis uses the Real associated with Christmas to expose readers to the hollowness of soul-sucking industrialism. The Real of Christmas endures even as joyless capitalist cabals threaten to sacrifice it at the altars of profit. And the Real of Christmas infuses life with greater meaning: a veritable fount of happiness and nostalgia to disrupt the reader's laborious hours. Even as Riis rushes to capture the candidate in an "authentic" manner – for example, he entitles chapter XI "What He Is Like Himself," a header that raises questions concerning what Riis's readers have been up to for the previous 250 pages – this level of journalistic realism pales in comparison to the recurrent spiritual Real that Riis connects to Christmas. Dependent upon Christmas stories as a significant source of inspiration, Roosevelt's campaign biographer endows its subject with grand metaphysical weightiness.

The mythical figure of Santa Claus further accentuates Riis's conjuring of the Christmas Spirit on behalf of a democratic candidate. Indeed, in *TR The Citizen*, Riis's two favorite larger-than-life heroes, Roosevelt and Santa Claus, methodically merge into a singular composite.[14] In *Is There A Santa Claus?* (also from 1904), Riis recycles one of his favorite Roosevelt anecdotes from his campaign biography, in which the candidate gives him "the very greatest Christmas gift any man ever received" by calling Riis's mother and making her feel "ten years younger." As a result, "I had to pinch myself to make sure the President was not Santa Claus himself" (13–14). Both mythical beings inspire progressive reform in the face of an urban commerce that encroaches upon "traditional" models of community. In his short story "Merry Christmas in the Tenements," Riis again generates an amalgamation of Father Christmas and the American Presidency. A teacher asks, "Who is the King?" A student blurts out, "McKinley!" And then, without further discussion or clarification, they all enjoy some ice cream: "The poorest, the shabbiest, the hungriest – the children Santa Claus loves best to find" (63). A bit further on in the tale, Santa and his wife are imagined to "stand in state" (66). By directly juxtaposing the President and Santa Claus, Riis crafts a public persona that greatly benefits Roosevelt during his campaign. "Faith in

Santa Claus is established" by Riis, and – we might hasten to add – so is "the people's" faith in Teddy (64). In *TR The Citizen*, Riis recycles a portion of his story "Merry Christmas in the Tenements," in which a group of poor children steal some pies, mistake Riis for Roosevelt, and then return the stolen goods, thoroughly chastened. Here we discover that Santa Claus and Roosevelt share vital characteristics – and, in turn, we start to understand why Christmas plays such a prominent role in Riis's campaign tract. "The people" believe in both mythical figures, and both mythical figures believe in "the people" – a reciprocity to which we will return shortly. Each figure graciously delivers charitable gifts while concurrently issuing stern judgments about what the "deserving poor" should, or should not, receive. Finally, Santa Claus and Roosevelt each remain suspended above the masses, without any accountability to the starry-eyed "children" that they serve. Both men are at heart policemen, not politicians. Far from being merely suggested in his campaign biography, Riis proclaims this parallel quite plainly: "Mr. Roosevelt made a good Santa Claus" (326).

Riis presents Santa and Roosevelt as equally self-enclosed figures. Their chronicler imagines them to be avatars for "the will of the people," and so the degree of separation between Roosevelt and Father Christmas remains quite small. In fact, because Santa is often said to be "inside" all of us, we cannot readily isolate the believer from her deified leader. Historians consider New York, formerly New Amsterdam, to be the birthplace of the American Santa Claus. This setting serves as a bridge between Santa's Dutch roots and his role in the United States as "protector, disciplinarian, and gift giver" (Forbes 94). Like his earlier incarnation, St. Nicholas, the American Santa watches over "the people," protects citizens from danger, shepherds them along a moral pathway, and rewards them when they fulfill their civic responsibilities. In *TR The Citizen*, Riis appears to be aware of the mythological overtones that he applies to Santa as well as Roosevelt. Yet his acknowledgment of this mythologizing function does little to dissuade Riis; instead, his narrator persists in recalling his boyhood love of John Halifax, a prototype for Horatio Alger's Ragged Dick, and, as a result of this adoration, he suffers "many taunts" from his mates. Nonetheless, he notes, "I have been happier than they, it seems" (*TR* 445). Riis thus heartily encourages hero worship. Neither Santa nor Roosevelt requires rigorous scrutiny to establish the veracity of their greatness, because the twin figures necessitate faith in themselves, which is to say, their stories encourage belief in fictional heroes against the pull of cynicism. On this count, at least, it would be difficult to peg Riis as a straightforward realist. When it comes to these mythic giants and their followers, what matters most is blind obedience to an ideal.[15] This process becomes increasingly insular as the belief in Santa or Teddy reveals itself to be the belief in oneself (and vice versa). Roosevelt expresses "his trust in the people" and, in response, he is greeted by "a genuine shout for the leader who spoke with their tongue, to their hearts" (234–236).[16] Riis reinforces his correlation of the would-be President with Father Christmas by pointing out that the elder Roosevelt, much like his son Teddy, shares an intimate connection with children: "He knew them by name ... and they loved him" (442). As Riis imagines the Oneness of the desires of an electorate, he simultaneously underscores a populist fantasy that remains ostensibly synonymous with the Christmas season.

From one point of view, Riis's synchronization of the future President and "the people" reduces the chosen candidate to a mere symbol, a vessel to be filled by the will of the electorate, while exposing "the people" to be child-like, naïve, and dependent upon what eventually proves to be a rather flimsy fetish. Belief in populist candidates, like belief in Santa, can be viewed as proof of one's gullibility. Riis strongly links the idol of Roosevelt to his worshippers in an all-consuming fashion – hence the youthful veneer of Roosevelt's followers, whose innocent embrace of the leader is made "beautiful" because it is likened to the unconditional love expressed by children in the presence of Father Christmas. Like Kris Kringle, Teddy can "read" children and children can "read" him back: "(Roosevelt's) character is all over (his handwriting): a child could read it" (*TR* 114). Riis's campaign biography frequently comments upon Roosevelt's psychic link to children. Riis's narrator observes: "I must not be tempted to write about (Roosevelt's) children ... I might even be led to betray the secret of the morning battles with pillows" (331). Santa's excessive mirth makes him privy to the secrets of childhood, and this invisible bond irrevocably joins Santa's desire to please the children with the longing of children to please him in return by behaving in an appropriate fashion throughout the months that precede Christmas. The jolly elf and the children take to one another in "perfect good faith" (346).

Like Santa, Roosevelt cultivates the persona of a militant figure when it seems necessary, and so he must not be mistaken for a feather-weight fighter. Like Santa, the would-be President represents "the greatest of moral forces" – not a man, but an a priori constant, a measuring stick against which righteousness must be measured (we might recall Howells's Lincoln from Chapter 3): "It commended itself to him as right, and that was enough" (36). A discerning fatherfigure that can always distinguish the naughty from the nice, Riis's ideal candidate stands intimately connected to "the people" even as he operates from a relatively detached position. After all, neither Father Christmas nor Teddy solicits feedback or invites dialogue with their wards; these populist mouthpieces instead offer the final word on any subject and act as judge, jury, as well as executioner.

Even so, the imagined Santa acts as a transcendental wash, removing all signs of difference and instilling a kind of universal "goodness." Bruce David Forbes argues that the Americanized Santa Claus provides "a generalized spirit of Christmas" and serves as a spiritual pillar "around whom everyone could rally." Both the religious and nonreligious public "could embrace" this benevolent fetish for "all people" (95–96). The universalism of Father Christmas speaks to a broader demand for consensus, captured at the *fin-de-siècle* by the poetic image of the American "melting pot." For Riis, the Teddy–Santa composite conveys "a broad Americanism that cares nothing for color, creed, or the wherefrom of the citizen, so that, now he is here, he be an American in heart and soul; an Americanism that reaches down to hard-pan" (*TR* 256). Riis's fabled spirit of Christmas envelops the segmented society of urban New York and, by extension, the entire country in order to concoct feelings of national solidarity – a fiction that is also aggressively cultivated by the Roosevelt campaign. Blending tropes from the Christmas story with his fictionalized depiction of his ideal candidate, Riis intervenes in the campaign biography with a set of stock Christmas characters and plot devices to imbue his prose with a powerful, if obscure, idealism: "The human feeling that levels all differences" (275).

Riis perpetually petitions for an America "made whole" by the invisible ties that bind. "The Little Dollar's Christmas Journey," for instance, marries faith in Christmas cheer to faith in a government under Roosevelt. It is a story about a coupon, which serves as legal U.S tender, as characters pay it forward through charitable acts during the yuletide season. The narrative advocates belief in a sort of boundless Americanism: "Don't be afraid to trust Uncle Sam where you see his promise to pay," it insists. The story therefore remarks upon the nondenominational pleasures of the holiday season: "There was Christmas in the air" (29–32). Riis deliberately synthesizes the imagined essence of the nation with the imagined essence of Christmas. By story's end, the coupon finds its way back to the original owner, thereby underlining the premise that charity brings its own reward. "The Little Dollar's Christmas Journey" promotes a united front by tracing unseen connections between all Americans, and it does so by highlighting the very feverish activism that would have resonated with Progressive Era readers: "It was just impossible for the little dollar to lie still in the pocket while there was want to relieved ... For all I know, it may be going yet. Certainly it is a sin to stop it" (31–32). Analyzing several of Riis's contemporaries, Jana Tigchelaar gestures at the subgenre of "neighborly Christmas" tales concerning gift exchange that celebrates the moral economy in which Riis also invests: "Reciprocity is essential in order to preserve social ties ... encouraging readers to be empathetic and community-minded" (253). Riis's narrative about a government coupon on its Christmas journey conveys an impression of wholeness that ignores political antagonism in pursuit of "permanent peace" (Riis *TR*, 221).

In "Merry Christmas in the Tenements," Riis appeals to a vague sense of Oneness to remove sectarian barriers as well as partisan passions and stress an "undenominational zeal" for the holiday, or a "Christmas gospel of peace ... the spirit of mutual help, of charity, and of the common cause against the common enemy" (60–62).[17] *TR The Citizen* likewise produces transcendental fogginess – a populist ploy, as we shall soon see, designed to cut down the so-called establishment and tap into a supposedly unspoiled Real. In both the Christmas story and the campaign biography, Riis claims to uncover "authentic" ground, only to bury it once more beneath his whitewashed vision of the holiday season. Not unlike his campaign biography, his Christmas stories soften "all the hard and ugly lines, and throws the spotless mantle of charity over the blemishes, the shortcoming"

(70). For Riis, literary treatments of Christmas circumnavigate politics and, in turn, by borrowing from this tradition, he effectively romanticizes his "unblemished" candidate of choice.

Teddy Roosevelt, a Romance

Riis's narrator in *TR The Citizen* professes his appetite for unambiguous resolution in a memory of Christmas at the White House: "There should be a law," the narrator suggests, "to make all loves happy in the end" (336). Readers will not find Riis to be a Romantic in the negative mold of American writers like Hawthorne; Riis's unyielding reliance upon sentimental, sometimes downright saccharine prose lacks the internal resistance that Herman Melville locates in the best works of Hawthorne (the subject of Chapter 2): "He says No! in thunder." That is, Riis rarely confronts existential voids that captivate earlier American Romantics, opting instead to highlight a spiritual Real that seemingly completes the individual, making him whole again. Nor does Riis remind readers of that "Dean of American Letters," Howells, or his protégé, Wolcott Balestier (the subjects of Chapters 3 and 4, respectively), due to Riis's limited efforts at shifting back and forth – at least, in any substantive manner – between realism and Romanticism. Broadly speaking, Riis is more like Wallace (the subject of Chapter 5) because his writing appears to be what Howells derisively deems "romanticistic": "What I object to is the romantic thing which asks to be accepted with all its fantasticality on the ground of reality" (qtd. in Budd, 36). By confusing the ground of reality with the realm of the fantastic, as when he blurs the line between unearthed urban poverty and the universal Christmas Spirit, Riis reflects the "romanticistic" tendencies of late nineteenth-century popular American prose. This tendency bleeds over into Riis's campaign biography.

In his "romanticistic" portrayal of Roosevelt, Riis relies upon a number of themes derived from a loose assemblage of works classified under the term Romanticism. For one, Riis presents Nature as a counter-force as well as a compliment to Western civilization. Roosevelt famously defines himself through his engagement with a vast, unknowable Nature – namely, the American frontier, a sublime landscape that he believes to resonate with his own vast, internal vistas. In Whitmanesque fashion, Riis's candidate knows no borders. Yet even as Riis's Roosevelt longs to be One with Nature in its sheer openness, he concomitantly conquers Nature, taming it and declaring his mastery. Furthermore, Riis capitalizes upon another derivative trait of Romanticism: the idealization of, and near total submission to, a love interest – in this case, a male companion. Through his gestures at Nature and "romanticistic" entanglements, then, Riis brings a host of popular fictional tropes from the Progressive Era to bear upon the composition of his campaign biography. Once more, the common thread proves to be encounters with excess, external as well as internal. *TR The Citizen* cultivates an approach to democratic candidates that remains heroic, dreamy, and utterly decoupled from "reality."

On several occasions, Riis diverges from the task at hand to take the reader on a tour through lush green pastures and craggy forests. These recognizable sites of "romanticistic" revelry offer Riis an opportunity to penetrate into the psychic life of his candidate by juxtaposing Roosevelt's interior wildness with his managerial bravado. This tension manifests in Riis's *mise-en-scene* of choice, at least, when he does not linger in urban alleyways: Roosevelt's New York countryside estate, Sagamore Hill. Riis paints visually stimulating tableaus of the estate that rival his most colorful Christmas set pieces: "Roses were blooming still, and heliotrope and sweet alyssum, in Mrs. Roosevelt's garden, and down at the foot of the long lawn a wild vine crept caressingly over the stone" (*TR* 315). In formulaic fashion, Roosevelt's biographer utilizes the contrasts of Nature to stress the multitudes that reside within his multivocal subject. The beauty of the cultivated – the symmetrical roses, curated in the domestic sphere – appears to be at odds with the uncultivated – a wild vine, seducing us away from the disciplinary guardrails of the garden and out into the unkempt freedom of the forest. The mythical Roosevelt idles in this liminal space, holding court as both judicious policeman and rowdy cowboy. When McKinley is shot, vice President Roosevelt goes out into the woods to seek clarity; like many pseudo-Romantics before as well as after him, Riis capitalizes upon the candidate's natural surroundings to convey Roosevelt's anguish – an attempt, we might conjecture, to combat the perception that Teddy was too ambitious and accepted the office without considering the difficulties of the challenge at hand. In this highly decorative scene, Riis lingers on Roosevelt as he wrestles with the enormity of the position into which he is thrust. The candidate appears to be caught between the sunshine of the summit and the fog in which he finds himself, lost and alone: "All the world lay wrapped in a gray, impenetrable mist … the gloomy forest" (244–245). When he receives word of McKinley's dying breath, the once and future President leaps into a carriage and begins a ride that plunges Riis's reader down the twists and turns of a distinctly Gothic mountainside:

> Through narrow defiles, over bare hillsides … on perilous brinks hidden in the shrouding fog … a bog hole … once more the gloom and the forest; once more the grim traveler ahead, ahead, as if he would pierce the veil of fate … trees and rocks whirling past took on dim outlines. (248–249)

Riis evokes Roosevelt's dread not through dialogue or free indirect discourse, as critics of the campaign biography might assume, but through projection of this dread onto the world around him, a common practice among heavyweight Romantics and sentimentalists alike. The reader never fears that his carriage will crash, or that Roosevelt will be paralyzed by fear; instead, she sees the future President moving boldly forward: "Go on – go right ahead!" (247). At this moment, Riis's Roosevelt most closely resembles Howells's Lincoln, because he too remains, in aesthetic terms, picturesque. Deftly dancing on a fault line between the beautifully cultivated garden and the sublime mountainside, Riis's candidate sits undeterred upon a "fallen log" (244). Riis conjures an image that may as well have been painted by an artist from the Hudson River Valley school, such as Thomas Cole with his "The Oxbow, View from Mount Holyoke, Northampton Massachusetts, After a Thunderstorm" (1836), a painting in which the spectator stares out at the sublime expanse of the frontier, emphasized by impending storms, from a position of relative ease. Cole provides a downed tree for his viewer upon which his spectator can figuratively find her repose. Similarly, Roosevelt's "fallen log" demarcates the civilized world, with its innate orderliness, from the unbridled chaos of the wilderness. Roosevelt maintains a foothold between these worlds as he engages in his "manly" adventures. This site therefore serves as a poignant backdrop against which readers view Roosevelt at the precipice of his impending Presidency.

However, not all of Riis's "romanticistic" displays of Nature manifest at the outermost physical or psychic perimeters; indeed, in one particularly pregnant moment, Riis employs a pastoral backdrop defined by relative tranquility and contemplative candor. This scene portrays Riis's narrator and Roosevelt in a moment of reprieve from their life amongst the Rough Riders: "We were lying in the grass at his tent, under the starry August sky. The Colonel's eye wandered ... a bright meteor shot athwart the sky ... we watched it in silence. I know what my thoughts were. He knew his own." Roosevelt then muses, "All things pass away. But they were beautiful days," before Riis's narrator extinguishes his pipe and the two men head in for the night (199–200). American Romantics constantly chronicle characters that wander through gloomy settings with a "melancholic soul" (Ferber 20). Riis's depiction of Nature outside of their shared camp is certainly melancholic: caught in a bout of extreme nostalgia, the biographer and the would-be President leisurely watch a streaking meteor and contemplate the finitude of their existence. At the threshold of autumn, they sigh deep sighs and allow their eyes to wander across Nature's expansiveness. No words are spoken. The panorama says it all. In this instance, Riis turns to Nature as a striking reminder that all things must pass. Yet the grandeur of the night sky also renders more acute the connection between these two men. Even though Riis depicts these characters as hyper-individualists, in a different, gloomier register, their separate thoughts begin to blur together. When Nature's deathless dance unfurls before them, they become fused together by their awe-inspiring surroundings and come to share an appreciation of "beautiful days." In a word, Riis's star-crossed "lovers" grow ever more intimate as they confront Nature in one another's safekeeping.

I hasten to add that when I use the term "lovers" in this context I do not wish to imply a homosexual relationship between Riis and Roosevelt. The sexuality of these historical characters is of no consequence to my larger argument. Nevertheless, when one reads *TR The Citizen*, one cannot help but recognize an undercurrent missing from the other campaign biographies addressed in this book. We might interpret this particular undercurrent as a prevalent surge of "romantic, irrational longings for new sources of virility" during the Progressive Era – a surge meant to aid men in particular in their imaginary escape from industrial ennui (Watts 3). Riis draws his male readers to Roosevelt's intensity and, in turn, the raw emotionalism of the candidate's rhetoric converts libidinal energies into American politics via the reader's awakened sensorium. Whether we designate Riis's style as florid, overly wrought, or as predictable window dressing borrowed from other "romantic friendship" narratives of the day, Riis draws liberally from a robust body of fiction in *fin-de-siècle* America that involves re-defining masculinity through the surpluses of male companionship.[18]

TR The Citizen primarily provides the story of an evolving friendship. Laura Fisher frames the *fin-de-siècle* focus upon fraternity as a "politics of proximity."[19] Throughout the Progressive Era, cultural voices amplify the invisible ties that bind male relationships: "Friendship remain(s) central to the reformist zeitgeist into the twentieth century ... (a) passionate homosocial amity" (Watts 11, 19). With nods to the subgenres of domestic and sentimental novels, Riis's campaign biography places a heavy emphasis upon the tight knit bonds of male friendship – a literary focus that Axel Nissen describes as "friendship fiction" and which remains, alongside the Christmas story, one of the most recognizable "minor genres" from America during this period (13). "Friendship," Nissen states, "is integral to the plot and forms one of the chief preoccupations" of the characters that populate these narratives. The power of male friendship provides "a guiding myth" for individuals in pursuit of "the emotional, intellectual, and – dare I say it – *spiritual* aspect of interpersonal relations" (8–9, author's emphasis). Riis's narrator gushes about his chum Roosevelt: "I would rather stand with (Roosevelt) and be counted than anywhere else on God's green earth ... his example and his friendship have taught me to love" (*TR* 305). Although other campaign biographers count the candidates that commission them as friends – see, for instance, Hawthorne (Chapter 2) and Wallace (Chapter 5) – none of these writers confess their affection as earnestly, or with as much intensity, as Riis does for Roosevelt.

In the national imaginary of this age, few boundaries remain between Roosevelt's natural body and the body politic, a fusion that confirms a level of excess intimacy never before seen in campaigns or their relevant biographies. We need only glance at the characteristics of romantic friendship fiction to appreciate the degree to which *TR The Citizen* comports to its central framework. As Nissen outlines, this subgenre focuses upon:

> The uniqueness of the relationship; the sense of intimacy, the need to know each other deeply, and reveal oneself as no one else; the idealization of the partner; the promise of faithfulness until death; the sense of intellectual and spiritual companionship; and, finally, an aesthetic admiration of the lover's beauty of form and feature that may occasionally shade into the overtly homo-erotic. (24)

The narrator of *TR The Citizen* presents relevant materials as though they are compiled not for a public campaign, but for a private diary. As a result, the text reads as a deeply personal exposition (and, consequently, a somewhat unreliable one – but we shall return to this point later). For example, like many campaign biographers, Riis includes in *TR The Citizen* a hearty slate of excerpts from Roosevelt speeches. And yet, in setting up these quotations, his narrator adopts a distinctively subjective tone: "I am going to set down a few of the extracts here. Very likely they are not the ones that would appeal to many of my readers. They did to me; that was why I wrote them down" (415). At times, Riis appears to ruminate on his friend not to help him secure elected office, but to confess a simple and abiding love for the man. That is, regardless of what "appeals" to readers, Riis's narrator insists upon rhapsodizing. This self-indulgent rhapsody strikes the reader as dream-like, as though the narrator, caught in a revelry, muses to himself about a love interest. He trails off whimsically: "As I am writing now, there comes to mind …" (268). In another example, the narrator expresses his distress about his friend being out at sea as he impatiently awaits Roosevelt's return: "I'm going to tell you now, – at least, I am going to try. Here, a whole week, have I been walking about the garden, upon which winter had laid its rude hand" (254). Once more, Riis conjures the image of a nervous, pacing lover. In contrast, readers never witness Hawthorne's narrator anxiously wringing his hands about his subject's well-being, nor do they spy Wallace's narrator swooning. Although the narrator knows what he "ought to remember," he remains too enraptured by his "love interest" to stay on task (227). Fond and fuzzy recollections intrude into Riis's ostensibly objective account of the candidate.

One stylistic choice sets Riis's campaign biography apart from its peers: for a variety of reasons, his narrator, unable or unwilling to remain a passive or objective observer, serves as an active character within the text. Riis's narrator occupies the spotlight of the campaign biography in order to elevate Roosevelt by contrast, which is to say, by producing a study in "masculine contrasts," Riis idealizes his candidate as a man worthy of great admiration (Nissen 17). To emphasize this difference, Riis positions himself as a strawman for readers to trivialize through comparisons to his ideal candidate. This approach taps into the romantic friendship subgenre's formulaic imbalance between a "worthy man" and his aspiring companion.[20] In turn, Riis capitalizes upon the gender politics of the era as he elevates Teddy's masculinity while, in the same breath, degrading – or, at least, undervaluing – corresponding notions of femininity. Simply put, he "feminizes" himself as narrator in order to highlight the conduct of a "real man" and, of greater import in this context, a "real President." One method with which Riis "feminizes" his narrator is the stress that he places upon a sort of literary impotence. The first line of *TR The Citizen* reads as follows: "Perhaps one of the kindest things the years do for us as they pass is to show us what things we cannot do" (3). Whereas Roosevelt's rhetoric receives endless praise, Riis's narrator habitually undermines his own capacities as a rhetorician. Notably, Hawthorne and Howells likewise question their own aptitude as biographers - but Riis heightens his inability to "measure up" to an extraordinary degree. Later, amidst stories of Teddy's prowess as a hunter with a "stout heart,"

Riis's narrator elects to tell a follow-up tale that emasculates himself: an anecdote in which he accidentally mistakes a porcupine for a baby bear (89). Then, to add insult to self-inflicted injury, Riis's narrator follows a story of Roosevelt's ingenuity and honesty with a tale of his own ineptitude in which, as a young man, he seeks, and ultimately fails, to lure a neighbor's hen into his yard so that he can harvest its eggs. "No one," he confesses, "would ever think of making me President" (92). In yet another instance, the narrator recalls a summer trip that he took with Roosevelt to the sweatshops of lower Manhattan and, in so doing, he emphasizes his own weakness to boost the candidate's prowess: "It wore me out completely, though I was used to it. Him it only gave a better appetite for dinner" (217). Riis's narrator delegitimizes himself as a "man" to further romanticize his vivacious companion.

Riis frequently "feminizes" his narrator by triangulating the relationship between himself, Roosevelt, and their respective wives. Riis aligns his narrator's eyeline with the eyeline of his own wife as well as Roosevelt's. Given the period's literary concern with intimacy between benefactors and their wards, Riis opts to perform the role of emotional as well as financial recipient by stressing his own status as immigrant, and to place Roosevelt in the position of loving patron. This dynamic is broadly deployed in literature from the Progressive Era. These realignments typically occur when members of the "feminine" group, including children, wives, and Riis, find themselves caught off guard and the "dominant male" (in this case, Teddy) demonstrates a surprising degree of bravado. For example: "I, taking tea peacefully with Mrs. Roosevelt and the children, was suddenly catapulted ..." (226). In another scene, *TR The Citizen* cuts directly from a jingoist celebration of the Rough Riders to Riis's narrator and his wife reading that particularly "splendid story" over breakfast: "We read it together, she and I, excited, breathless" (170). Later, at a White House event, the once and future President escorts the narrator's wife – again, quite excited and breathless – into the event, while the narrator stands back and vicariously enjoys the pageant: "I do not think I ever saw a prouder woman than my wife when the President took her in to dinner" (281). Rendering himself as an unfazed cuckold, Riis's narrator expresses a desire for his intimate friend through a divergence into the perspective of his own wife – a rhetorical move that transfers the narrator's excitement, his breathlessness, onto a female and so further enhances the emotional response without forfeiting his aspiration to be "manly" like his mentor.

The tone of the prose changes significantly in these instances, and the campaign biographer reveals himself to prefer a "romanticistic" tone. Specifically, the emotional excesses of Riis's text conform to what Sarah Boyd discusses in her examination of the romantic friendship subgenre: "The aesthetic pleasures of masculine creativity and desire" dovetail with "the florid literary style often associated with nineteenth-century women's fiction" (1–2). This subgenre's "highly wrought" vocalizations, Boyd continues, reflect a longing by male narrators to be "possessed by the feminine ideal," to drink in its apparently "generative powers" (4–5).[21] Immersed in the elevated sensations purportedly tied to gender and sexuality, Riis's narrator moves back and forth between so-called masculine and feminine points of identification, intoxicated by the openness of wide-ranging affections. Of course, in addition to his passion as well as his fondness, we must not forget how Riis's narrator problematically embodies the stereotype of the "worried wife" in a manner that accentuates Roosevelt's separation from a domestic sphere that threatens to tame him. After Teddy takes a bold risk with his life, the narrator joins "Mrs. Roosevelt the next day in demanding the President's promise" to be more cautious (283).

Also problematically, Riis "feminizes" his narrator by gesturing at the assumed extremes of homoeroticism. Again, this chapter puts no stock in pseudo-psychoanalysis of the two historical figures. However, because we are examining how Riis's campaign biography tarries with romantic friendship, we simply cannot ignore how the text – like the various subgenres from which it derives its eclectic structure – ventures into the realm of homoeroticism. Nissen contends that male characters in the subgenre of romantic friendship stories almost always "comport themselves with a greater degree of physical license than" cross-sex couples (38). And so it is with *TR The Citizen*: in one episode, Riis's narrator and his ideal candidate go for a stroll together in the woods: "To him it was lovely, and so it was to me ... his boyish hand stole into mine with a new confidence. We were chums now, and all was well" (323). Elsewhere, the narrator wears a special item to an event held on Roosevelt's behalf, and he feels embarrassed to have "over-dressed," before Roosevelt "slip(s) up behind me ... and (says) in my ear" that it was a lovely gesture. Comforted that his bosom friend knows that he is wearing something special just for him, Riis's narrator expresses his relief: "He knew, and it was all right" (282). Elsewhere, in a particularly confidential vision of their friendship, Riis's narrator sits at the edge of a bed in Teddy's hotel room as the Rough Rider playfully exerts his dominance: "Between bubbles of soap he blew at me he made clear what had been dim before, until I marveled that I had not seen it" (216). The intimate wording of these passages – the boyish hand stealing into his; the slipping up behind him; the frothy bubbles on a hotel bed – leaves little room for doubt that Riis intends to walk right up to the line of blatant homoeroticism. These eroticized encounters further strengthen the case that *TR The Citizen* bears intertextual markings from a select group of texts written contemporaneously that concern the sensual bonds of male friendship. By tracking Riis's broader debts, we understand better how the author's literary preoccupations bear upon his campaign biography – and how his political tract subsequently informs the rest of his output.

A Permanent Peace/Piece

From the all-encompassing Spirit of Christmas to an all-consuming fraternal love, Riis imbues his tract for Roosevelt with impressions of transcendence. This impression manifests for Riis's reader as "romanticistic" fullness, an incontestable, metaphysical totality that overwhelms her, or, perhaps more to the point, as a circular relation between the candidate and "the people" that leaves little room for difference. To speak with One tongue to One heart: it is the utopian undercurrent beneath all populist sentiments. Riis's writings regularly conjure consensus by rendering the particular — namely, the democratic candidate as a fetish — as though it remains inclusive of *all* people, even the immigrant and the pauper. As a result, many of Riis's critics, then as well as now, deride the author as a covert custodian of the hegemonic order. However, when we place his other works into dialogue with *TR The Citizen* — that is, when we revisit his other works with this political text as a map key — we start to see how Riis's surpluses make a conformist, "romanticistic" appeal while, at the same time, offering points of departure. In the final tally, Riis's literary surpluses are not just complicit in the dominant ideology of the day; they also reflect the possibility of radical reform.

Riis composes his campaign biography in a populist style that effectively complements the Roosevelt agenda. Populist style points to "a partiality which wants to function as the totality of the community" (Laclau 81). Populists like Roosevelt and Riis wish to speak to, and ultimately on behalf of, a fictional entity known as "the people." In so doing, campaign image-makers suppress the fact that members of any group of individuals possess variegated desires. Undeterred by this undeniable obstruction, both the candidate and his chronicler maintain "a certain particularity which assumes the role of an (im)possible universality" (115). According to Ernesto Laclau, populism peddles in the illusion of fullness, as when Riis's Roosevelt stands in for abstract concepts like "justice" or "common sense." Indeed, *TR The Candidate* declares an exclusive access to a Real America that has been all too frequently ignored by so-called elites (it nearly goes without saying that Roosevelt's extremely privileged upbringing never prevents Riis from portraying the candidate as a blue-collar hero). To tap into the presumed Real of "the people," populists evoke "the 'emotive' over the 'rational'," thereby "freeing instinctual impulses that social norms usually keep under control" (39, 33). In other words, the excesses of Riis's corpus signal a populist swell that assumes an underlying absolutism within the United States: what is "right" in all circumstances, for all people. "Riis generate(s) a narrative of 'national' identity whose central features universalize middle-class values" (Twigg 310). Through specific literary forms like the Christmas story and tales of romantic friendship Riis's campaign biography transposes the populist swell surrounding Roosevelt into an illusion of political as well as aesthetic consensus.

Riis emphasizes consensus as the remedy for what he claims to be a broken and corrupt political establishment. Early in *TR The Citizen*, Riis's narrator gestures at "the foundations broad and deep of that abiding Americanism ... the very heart's blood of his being" (12–13). On the theme of Americanism, Riis's preferred candidate does not hesitate to declare that every individual ought to drop her affiliation with racial or religious distinctions "if we want to be good Americans" (65). Painting images of the proverbial "melting pot," this campaign biography expands conceptualizations of "the people" for the advantage of a specific mouthpiece: Roosevelt. This "melting pot" imagery promotes a secular embrace of Christmas as well as the holiness of two men, two kindred spirits, in repose under a vast starry sky. To achieve this feeling of totality, Riis degrades politics as an abnormal exercise and replaces "political plotting" with a militant righteousness that he refers to as "just war" (134). In the Roosevelt campaign biography, to fight on behalf of the "right" cause – that is, on behalf of "the people" – involves fostering anti-political sentiment. Riis's narrator insists that he hates "stupid politics" and seeks, with his endorsement of Roosevelt, a chance at "real non-partisanship" (213). Of course, Roosevelt is a politician, and Riis is composing a blatantly political tract. But populists habitually insist that they desire to circumvent politics in order to connect directly to a fictional entity that they describe as "the people." Since "romanticistic" consensus has always been there, they claim, just waiting to be recovered, politics becomes a rather straightforward act of recovery.

Although populism can sound democratic in its call to be all-inclusive, in truth it frequently proves to be a vehicle for authoritarian sentiments. Riis's preferred candidate elevates duty over deliberation, despite the primary role that deliberation plays in any democracy. For example, Riis celebrates Roosevelt's much ballyhooed connection to the New York police department to make his candidate's image both of "the people" and elevated above the same lot. This populist paradox comes into the light when Riis's narrator recounts his work as a surrogate on behalf of Roosevelt. In this story, Riis's narrator confronts Roosevelt's dissenters at a speaking event. He discounts any Roosevelt critic as a "pedantic spectacled loon," "invariably" drunk and obstinate. Foreshadowing rallies on behalf of the contemporary populist Donald Trump, Riis's narrator commends a loyal follower of Roosevelt for physically assaulting a vocal dissenter: "It *was* enough, and just right" (240, author's emphasis). There are no signs of irony as the narrator continues: "(Roosevelt's) critics never by any chance get any other side of a subject than their own" (241). This statement could be easily applied to Roosevelt himself, since his campaign biography incessantly reiterates that the once and future President does not need advice from anyone. In other words, if democracy demands artful negotiation, Riis's brand of populism tamps down the very mode of argumentation that democracy requires. Riis's narrator states that his candidate's policies are "the plain expression of his character," while the government only exists to blockade Roosevelt, a moral force in his own right, from "the people": "The man who single handed bade defiance to the whole executive force of the Government, when the knowledge that he was right was his only weapon" (365, 111). Like Santa Claus or a sacred lover/friend, Riis's Roosevelt exists above reproach. And to condemn him would also require condemning "the people" with whom he purportedly coalesces as well as the inevitable consensus that he embodies.

Importantly, however, unlike Lew Wallace, Riis never really resolves the inconsistencies within his campaign biography. Consider for instance his suggestion of a "*living democracy* that in its fullness shall make of (Roosevelt) a *king* in his own right"; or, his contention that Roosevelt remains "the most democratic of men," but maintains "a full measure of dignity" (272, 274; emphasis mine). Riis's ideal candidate believes in "the people," yet he also wishes "to belong to the governing class, not the governed" (48). How is it that a "living democracy" perpetually produces its antithesis – namely, a king? From one vantage point, Riis's emotive universalism, wrapped up in the dressing of romantic friendship fiction as well as evergreen Christmas stories, exposes the worst of America's populist impulses: the vision of a society that has been stripped bare of its messiness and placed under the sway of a benevolent tyrant. Nihad Farooq summarily denounces Riis's corpus as "an assimilationist rite of passage," a body of texts designed to "expand western influence" and "steer and contain" the excess of difference that he exposes in urban New York (74, 88). Other detractors lambast Riis for constructing "a wall of difference" – his "romanticistic" reliance upon Otherness and exoticism – in order to enact covert forms of social control (O'Donnell 15). Recycling a routine denunciation of American Romantics and realists, especially of the Howells variety, many of these critics dismiss Riis because he elevates bourgeois values under the cloak of a benign pursuit of "justice," or what is "right." Christopher Carter describes this tendency as a "new way to frame old conclusions" as well as a "conservatism posing as social innovation" (139). Of late, it has become increasingly difficult to track down an analysis of Riis's output that does not roundly decry him as a failed realist or, relatedly, as an "anachronistic (R)omantic" (J. Lane 45). However, by teasing out the complexities of Riis's populist style as displayed in his campaign biography, we can comprehend how these oft-volatile interactions preserve a political openness that actually refuses "romanticistic" enclosure.

To acknowledge Riis's populist style need not exclusively lead us to attack the biographer's idealism or his naïve compliance with the status quo; instead, to analyze *TR The Citizen* in these terms means highlighting once again the irrevocably political nature of American campaign biographies, which have been discarded as hagiographic. Simply put, for all of its illusions of consensus, Riis's biography of Roosevelt incessantly interrupts itself by gesturing at a Real that refuses to be fetishized – a true excess. In this way, the text shares an impetus with populism itself: it unconsciously concedes that the restless reinvention of American politics cannot be stilled, and so the concept of a democratic candidacy remains eternally incomplete. Riis's literary excesses, "romanticistic" as well as perpetually unfinished, underscore the dynamic inner workings of the campaign biography as a genre.

According to Laclau, the dialectical propulsion of populism reflects the heart of American politics – indeed, the heart of politics in general. Populists invest in "an unachievable universality," but they also remind us that political organizations can be radically overturned on a dime (111). Despite its rush to absolutism, Riis's work continually returns to the (im)possibility of such a proposition, even when Riis himself does not appear to be conscious of making such a claim. "If the names of 'the people' constitute (the populists') own object – that is, give unity to a heterogeneous ensemble – the reverse movement also operates: they can never fully control which demands they embody and represent" (108). Said another way, because Roosevelt-as-populist cannot truly speak for all peoples due to the diverse desires of the American population, Riis's campaign biography operates always at the very edge of symbolization. If every desire could be satisfied, after all, politics itself would no longer be necessary. Nonetheless, Riis and his version of Roosevelt persist in seeking this all-inclusive utopia, this "mythical fullness," in vain (119). For one, to construct Roosevelt's chosen "people" invariably means excluding certain groups. Furthermore, Riis himself admits in *TR The Citizen* that he sometimes disagrees with Roosevelt on political matters, so he prefers to focus on the man himself, or "the citizen." The campaign biography therefore echoes Laclau's assessment of populist rhetoric:

> There is the experience of a *lack*, a gap which has emerged in the harmonious continuity of the social. There is a fullness of the community which is missing. This is decisive: the construction of 'the people' will be the attempt to give a name to that absent fullness ... a demand which is not met. (85, author's emphasis)

As the case of Teddy demonstrates, even the broadest figuration of a candidate cannot repress the fissure between an impression of fullness and a campaign's fictional underpinnings: a tension that Laclau aptly describes with the paradoxical phrase "empty fullness" (106).

In effect, just as populism involves performing a sense of wholeness where none could ever exist, *TR The Candidate* depends upon imagined essences: Christmas; Nature; Love. Yet it never becomes as literal or as conclusive as Riis's readers might assume.

Scholars emphasize the innate slipperiness of Riis's prose. According to Jackson, Riis habitually shifts from the literal to the figurative and then back again, fostering a sense of "incongruity ... to alienate his audience from the comforting stasis of a prescribed sentimentalism" (238, 269). In *How the Other Half Lives*, Riis resorts to a similar kind of deconstruction: in one moment, he declares that "the one thing you shall vainly ask for ... is a distinctively American community"; in the very next moment, Riis refers to America as "this queer conglomerate mass of heterogeneous elements, ever striving and working like whiskey and water in one glass" (15–16). Like Jackson, Farooq classifies Riis as an agent of chaos because Riis's works maintain "an inherent and essential foreignness which is the foundation of all ideologies of nation formation" (89). That is to say, although Riis outwardly attempts to forge consensus among his readers, he never actually achieves "an 'historically organic' ideology likely to elicit mass 'spontaneous consent'" (Saveth 68). Perhaps no critic better demonstrates this complication in the reception of Riis's work than Bill Hug, who revels in Riis's "double-consciousness" and calls to task critics that ignore the crucial tensions within his writing. As a former immigrant, Hug argues, Riis does not whole-heartedly embrace nativism of the Roosevelt variety, the candidate's spellbinding metaphor of the "melting pot"; instead, Roosevelt's biographer utilizes what Mikhail Bakhtin describes as *heteroglossia* – a "conscious interplay" of diverse voices (Hug 132). For Hug, Riis's narrator acts as a shape-shifter, "employing the complexities of his predicament to his own rhetorical advantage" (141–142). This account of Riis's "rhetorical gamesmanship" might inspire us to revisit *TR The Candidate* and consider it less as an expression of decadent but compliant nativism and more as a text that a bit subversively refuses to fetishize the Real through any singular icon.

Hug's analysis reveals new possibilities for reading Riis's campaign biography by reminding his readers that populism is, in fact, always built upon (im)possibilities over which we cannot satisfactorily gloss. Visions of "the people" never stagnate because they must be "constantly reinvented ... This intrinsic slipperiness remains the very definition of the political itself" (Laclau 154). In any functioning democracy, officeholders must remain temporary – by their very constitution – and so vulnerable to sudden ejection. Populism periodically reminds American audiences that politics is not a business to be managed, or a utopian foreclosure of collective ambition, but an open-ended antagonism that mercifully never ends, be it with the election of Teddy – or any other public figure, for that matter. To further clarify this point, let us call to mind again Riis's Christmas stories. Although these yuletide texts do promise emotional fullness via the so-called Christmas Spirit, they concomitantly rely upon an ongoing dissatisfaction among middle-class readers. When these stories try to capture the ecstatic joy of impoverished children that become beneficiaries of the Christmas Spirit – the extreme pleasures (*jouissance*) of Christmas that overwhelm young street urchins – we must ask why Riis's privileged readers pursue this missing fullness in the first place. In Stephen Nissenbaum's estimation, Christmas stories from this period unveil "a need to experience spontaneous affectionate gratitude *in itself*; to participate in social interactions that (evoke) a powerful emotional response that (is) difficult to achieve within middle-class life" (248, author's emphasis). Because the material comforts of the Gilded Age do not provide ultimate resolution or satisfaction for the middle-class, Riis's holiday stories tarry around an emptiness that endures despite the era's growing number of "utopian fantasies" (249). Excessive emotions felt by others, like the covetous paupers that discover seasonal joy, become just one way for privileged readers to cope with what lacks in their own gilded lives. The excessive joy of a poor child redeemed by Santa infuses the reader with a stronger sense of intimacy with marginalized peoples as well as exuberant sensations to awaken her from her complacent slumber and, in the process, it reveals a good deal more about the reader than the protagonist. Tales about the perfect gift for a pauper serve as "cathartic exercises in selflessness" by extending "only symbolically" the illusion of unity to all parts of society (Restad 133). The fetishes of Christmas for an abiding existential lack. If Riis could in fact resolve the issue of a glaringly absent Christmas Spirit, he would effectively deny the impetus that fuels the need for these kinds of Christmas stories in the first place. In truth, this lack does not exist to be overcome; rather, it is only because of this lack that the fantasy structure endures. At various levels, the idea of Christmas is built upon absence, not presence. Similarly, let us once more call to mind the romantic friendships in Riis's corpus. These studies of male desire glance at an ever-elusive gratification as they remain rooted in a form of hero worship that depends upon enforced limits. Riis's narrators acknowledge a gap between the primary object of their fantasy – the affection of Teddy; a Oneness of the candidate and "the people" – and the utter (im)possibility of ever possessing the presumed bliss of permanent peace. The titillation comes from deferred gratification.

Riis's campaign biography is replete with partial objects, missing objects, and acute differences. In each of these intervening moments, Riis undercuts his own fetishism. Upon telling a tall tale of Roosevelt in a Wild West brawl, Riis's narrator confesses:

> Now that I have made use of my privilege to put things in as I think of them, let me say that brawling was no part of (Roosevelt's) life in the West. I thought of it first partly because of some good people who imagine that there was nothing else on the frontier. (*TR* 84)

To unpack Riis's storytelling maneuver a bit: the singular part (Roosevelt) poses as the whole of America's vastness before being reduced once more to a part, a non-representative figure. Moving dialectically, Riis stresses a degree of separation between his various "romanticistic" fixtures and the Real that these fixtures cannot adequately encompass. "One man sees the glorious painting, priceless for all time," Riis's mouthpiece muses, "the other but the fly-speck on the frame" (170). *TR The Citizen* cuts from a factual report of the narrator scanning the sea for Roosevelt's vessel to a poetic daydream in which "I see him now riding away over the hill in his Rough-Rider uniform" (173–174). Elsewhere, Riis's narrator "glimpses" Teddy's childhood through the once and future President's recollections and, at the same time, presents Teddy's youth "as I like to think of it" (20). Riis therefore does not shy away from his role as iconographer; like Howells, he actively acknowledges his part in constructing the myth. Consequently, his contrived "romanticistic" comforts run up against something presumably more Real. "The President who walks through your pages is a very heroic and kingly figure," the narrator confesses, "but could I show you him as he really is … you would have to love him" (337). This oscillating pattern, from icon to iconoclasm and then back again, underscores the extent to which Riis, not unlike authors considered in earlier chapters, relishes in the excess as well as containment of his ideal candidate. On the one hand, the narrator asks himself: "Something very learned and grand had come into my head. But how can you analyze your friend? Men's minds and men's motives you may analyze … and a pretty mess you will make of it"; on the other hand, he boldly posits, "I shall tell you of him just as I knew him. I like him best that way, anyhow, – just as he is" (254). Hence the core contradiction of Riis's campaign biography: the (im)possibility of Riis – or the reader, for that matter – "really" knowing his friend, alongside the absolute certainty of transcendental connection – as if Riis's personal knowledge of Teddy is the only genuine knowledge because he sees the man "just as he is." Riis juxtaposes "something very learned and grand" with a Real that eludes representation, an underlying mess that cannot be analyzed or possessed.

Through its political and aesthetic contradictions, Riis's campaign biography of Roosevelt enables readers to make better sense of the uneven and unsettled contributions to the campaign biography as a genre. For Riis, the preferred candidate appears to be both fully satisfying and a reminder of the perpetual dissatisfaction that defines heterogeneous societies. As some of his recent critics suggest, albeit in a different register, Riis captures the slipperiness that defines American democracy at its most foundational level.[22] Although Riis can appear to be guilty of fetishism – his authoritarian President; his magical consensus; his mythical universality – for critics to reach such a conclusion means ignoring how Riis incessantly deconstructs "the establishment" in order to evoke new political horizons, with greater numbers of immigrants that hold an even bigger stake. In this way, Riis's output choreographs the weaknesses as well as strengths of populism as a political style: "Any emerging 'people', whatever its character, is going to present two faces: one of rupture with an existing order; the other introducing 'ordering' where there is basic dislocation" (Laclau 122). Riis's tract written on behalf of Roosevelt possesses two faces as well – order and excess; an "empty fullness." The glaring surpluses of *TR The Citizen* thus reflect the peril and the promise of the campaign biography as a genre.

Notes

1 Some of the other influences on Riis's work include George Foster's *New York by Gaslight and Other Urban Sketches* (1850), while influential contemporaries include Ernest Ingersoll's *A Week in New York* (1891) and, more prominent still, Stephen Crane's *Maggie* (1893).
2 Important for my argument, Louis Fried similarly suggests that *all* of Riis's texts, even his campaign biography of Roosevelt, are "of a kind" (5).
3 Riis's racial taxonomy is more prevalent in early works like *How the Other Half Lives*, in which he insults Italian immigrants as "born gamblers," Arab immigrants as "a dirty stain, spreading rapidly," Chinese immigrants as "by nature as cunning as the cat," and Jewish immigrants as possessing a "natural talent … for commercial speculation" (40, 20, 71, 94). In this problematic text, the inherent dangers of Riis's fixed ideals are rendered quite obvious.
4 Eric Schocket likewise emphasizes the unsettled character of Riis's work by highlighting its "dual identity." Moving at times awkwardly between ethnicities as well as classes, Riis's "class-transvestite narratives" depict a society based upon constant difference, one that shifts ceaselessly across "fragile borders" (111, 119).
5 A host of critics acknowledge Riis's strong ambivalence. Joel Schwartz, for one, comments: "Riis was fully aware of the moral ambiguities of the attempt to reform others" (29).

6 To this end, another "man of letters" was commissioned by the Roosevelt camp to pen campaign materials: Edward Stratemeyer, the prolific creator of such popular children's series as the Hardy Boys and Nancy Drew.
7 See Slavoj Žižek's "Against the Populist Temptation," *Critical Inquiry*, vol. 32, no. 3 (Spring 2006), pp. 551–574.
8 Dominiek Hoens writes, "The realm of politics can only function at a distance from what it is supposed to represent, to take care of, and listen to, i.e., the people ... democratic political power is by essence finite... (it) consists in abandoning any claim on truth ... the aim of psychoanalysis – to be able to deal with castration as a lack of being that gets located and operative via signifiers – coincides with the kind of political subjects democracy needs" (107).
9 Of course, the exploitation of Christmas in realist texts predates Riis's contributions to the conversation – earlier writers in this mold include the British writer, Charles Dickens, with whom Riis shares a good deal in common stylistically. Later, Henry James will use Christmas as a framing device in *Turn of the Screw* (1898), while William Dean Howells, Willa Cather, Sarah Orne Jewett, and Mary Wilkins Freeman repeatedly reference the traditions of Christmas in their fiction. For a heartier discussion of this trend, see Ann Romines's "After the Christmas Tree: Willa Cather and Domestic Ritual," *American Literature*, vol. 60, no. 1 (March 1988), pp. 61–82. See also George C. Carrington Jr.'s "Howells' Christmas Sketches: The Uses of Allegory," *American Literary Realism, 1870–1910*, vol. 10, no. 3 (Summer 1977), pp. 242–253.
10 This pattern persists long after Riis's career. Maria Sachiko Cecire argues, "Cultural texts from movies to literature to family anecdotes enshrine Christmas Eve and Christmas morning as moments of real-world passage from the mundane into the marvelous" (129).
11 Critics of Riis outline his gradual shift from "realism to sentimental portraiture" (Tuerk 259).
12 Early in his autobiography, Riis espouses a deep investment in the ideals of Christmas: "I am a believer in organized, systematic charity upon the evidence of my senses; but – I am glad we have that one season in which we can forget our principles and err on the side of mercy, that little corner in the days of the dying year for sentiment and no questions asked" (*Making* 4).
13 It is important to remember that critics have long struggled to achieve consensus regarding the parameters of realism, as we have discussed throughout this book. Miles Orvell reminds us, "The word itself – realism – meant different things to different people, and was variously high or low, uplifting or vulgar, idealistic of literal" (103). I would add that these differences do not only occur between people, but sometimes within a given text.
14 It is important to remember that Santa Claus in America remains, throughout the nineteenth century, anathema to the heavily commercialized version that we recognize today. Santa is "an invented tradition" of two major New Yorkers, Washington Irving and Clement Moore (respectively), and he is meant to embody a "pseudo-Dutch folk identity" that ran counter to urban commerce – and went on to serve as a countermeasure against the "corruptive cultural effect of consumer capitalism" (Nissenbaum 64–66, 178). A toast from the New York Historical Society in 1809 conveys this counter-cultural function: "May the virtuous habits and simple manners of our Dutch ancestors be not lost in the luxuries and refinements of the present time" (qtd. in Flanders, 101).
15 Here we see another popular genre from the era bleeding into Riis's campaign biography: the self-help tract. Myths function as an invitation for young men to idolize certain heroes and model their behavior after them: "It is a good story for all American boys to read. For they can do the same, if they choose to" (Riis *TR*, 18). Later in the biography, in chapter XVI: "A Young Man's Hero," Riis extends his treatise on hero worship as a spring board for self-help by providing a running list of pithy sayings for young men to read and follow.

16 In another example, Roosevelt proves to be in complete sync with "the people": "The hall rang with their cheers ... his trust in his fellow man was justified" (Riis *TR*, 153).
17 In another story, "Rent Baby," Riis reveals the normative aspect of his universalism by tying it to an indirect sort of evangelism. The story tells of a Jewish protagonist that hates Christmas because the holiday only brings him more "hatred and persecution." By the end, however, his Christian neighbors have saved the day and rescued him from ruin. Their final cry sounds less benevolent and more hostile: "This is Christmas, and don't you forget it!" (6, 8). Although Riis's tales claim to prefer sekf-described Christian principles, they never come very close to advocating conversion; instead, they strip Christmas of its religious connotations and promote America's "melting pot."
18 For a more robust discussion of Roosevelt's associations with "manliness," see Neil Cogan's *Theodore Roosevelt: A Manly President's Gendered Personal and Political Transformations* (New York: Routledge, 2020).
19 See Laura Fisher's *Reading for Reform: The Social Work of Literature in the Progressive Era* (Minneapolis, MN: University of Minnesota Press, 2019).
20 E. Anthony Rotundo explains why submissiveness and self-abnegation serve as mainstays in this genre: "The most dramatic instances of male submissiveness involved the cult of the leader ... deference to a heroic leader" (238). Fodder for the cult of the leader, the militant Roosevelt exists as both bosom friend and, at the same time, master and commander.
21 Boyd adds that the two most representative writers of this mode are Herman Melville – in both his stories of male bonding and his personal letters to Nathaniel Hawthorne – and, later, Henry James.
22 Thomas Heise observes a parallel ambivalence: "Slumming literature established social, physical, and moral boundaries for the city even as it trespassed through them by way of pleasure in a dark doorway" (49–50). Riis's campaign biography upholds a similar sense of excess and release at odds with an illusion of wholeness that forecloses open perspectives.

Works Cited

Boyd, Sarah. *Masculinity and the Highly Wrought Style in Nineteenth-Century American Fiction*. 2017. PhD Dissertation, Chapel Hill, NC, University of North Carolina.
Budd, Louis J. "W. D. Howells' Defense of the Romance." *PMLA*, vol. 67, no. 2, 1952, pp. 32–42. *JSTOR*, www.jstor.org/stable/460085. Accessed February 17, 2021.
Carter, Christopher. "Writing with Light: Jacob Riis's Ambivalent Exposures." *College English*, vol. 71, no. 2, 2008, pp. 117–141. *JSTOR*, www.jstor.org/stable/25472312. Accessed March 5, 2021.
Cecire, Maria Sachiko. *Re-Enchanted: The Rise of Children's Fantasy Literature in the Twentieth Century* (Minneapolis, MN: University of Minnesota Press, 2019).
Farooq, Nihad M. "Of Science and Excess: Jacob Riis, Anzia Yezierska, and the Modernist Turn in Immigrant Fiction." *American Studies*, vol. 53, no. 4, 2014, pp. 73–94. www.jstor.org/stable/24589398. Accessed March 5, 2021.
Ferber, Michael. *Romanticism: A Very Short Introduction* (Oxford: Oxford University Press, 2010).
Flanders, Judith. *Christmas: A Biography* (New York: St. Martin's Griffin, 2019).
Forbes, David Bruce. *Christmas: A Candid History* (Los Angeles, CA: University of California Press, 2005).
Fried, Lewis. "Jacob Riis and the Jews: The Ambivalent Quest for Community." *American Studies*, vol. 20, no. 1, 1979, pp. 5–24, https://journals.ku.edu/amsj/article/view/2253.

Greenberg, David. "Theodore Roosevelt and the Image of Presidential Activism." *Social Research*, vol. 78, no. 4, 2011, pp. 1057–1088. *JSTOR*, www.jstor.org/stable/23349843. Accessed March 4, 2021.

Heise, Thomas. *Urban Underworlds: A Geography of Twentieth-Century American Literature and Culture*. *JSTOR*, www.jstor.org/stable/j.ctt5hj8t4. Accessed March 8, 2021.

Hoens, Dominek. "Objet a and Politics," in *Jacques Lacan: Between Psychoanalysis and Politics*, ed. Samo Tomsic and Andreja Zevnik (New York: Routledge, 2015), pp. 101–113.

Hug, Bill. "Walking the Ethnic Tightwire: Ethnicity and Dialectic in Jacob Riis' *How the Other Half Lives*." *Journal of American Culture*, vol. 20, no. 4, 1993, pp. 41–53. Accessed March 5, 2021.

Jackson, Gregory S. *The Word and Its Witness: The Spiritualization of American Realism* (Chicago, IL: University of Chicago Press, 2009).

Laclau, Ernesto. *On Populist Reason* (London: Verso, 2007).

Lane, James B. "Jacob A. Riis and Scientific Philanthropy during the Progressive Era." *Social Service Review*, vol. 47, no. 1, 1973, pp. 32–48. *JSTOR*, www.jstor.org/stable/30020802. Accessed March 5, 2021.

Mouffe, Chantal. *On the Political* (New York: Routledge, 2005).

Mouffe, Chantal. *The Return of the Political* (London: Verso, 1993).

Nissen, Axel. *Manly Love: Romantic Friendship in American Fiction* (Chicago, IL: University of Chicago Press, 2009).

Nissenbaum, Stephen. *The Battle for Christmas: A Social and Cultural History of Our Most Cherished Holiday* (New York: Vintage, 1997).

O'Donnell, Edward. "Pictures vs. Words? Public History, Tolerance, and the Challenge of Jacob Riis." *Public Historian*, vol. 26, 2004, pp. 7–26. doi:10.1525/tph.2004.26.3.7. Accessed March 5, 2021.

Orvell, Miles. *The Real Thing: Imitation and Authenticity in American Culture, 1880–1940*. Chapel Hill, NC: University of North Carolina Press, 2014. *JSTOR*, www.jstor.org/stable/10.5149/9781469615370_orvell. Accessed February 1, 2021.

Restad, Penne. *Christmas in America: A History* (Oxford: Oxford University Press, 1995).

Riis, Jacob. *How the Other Half Lives: Studies Among the Tenements of New York* (Torrington, CT: Martino Press, 2015).

Riis, Jacob. *Is There a Santa Claus?* (Victoria, Australia: Leopold Classic Library, 2015).

Riis, Jacob. "The Little Dollar's Christmas Journey," in *Children of the Tenements* (Scotts Valley, CA: CreateSpace, 2013), pp. 27–32.

Riis, Jacob. "Merry Christmas in the Tenements," in *Children of the Tenements* (Scotts Valley, CA: CreateSpace, 2013), pp. 57–70.

Riis, Jacob. "Nibsy's Christmas," in *Children of the Tenements* (Scotts Valley, CA: CreateSpace, 2013), pp. 35–39.

Riis, Jacob. "The Rent Baby," in *Children of the Tenements* (Scotts Valley, CA: CreateSpace, 2013), pp. 5–8.

Riis, Jacob. *Theodore Roosevelt, The Citizen* (New York: Macmillan, 1904).

Rotundo, E. Anthony. *American Manhood: Transformations in Masculinity from the Revolution to the Modern Era* (New York: Basic Books, 1993).

Saveth, Edward N. "Theodore Roosevelt: Image and Ideology." *New York History*, vol. 72, no. 1, 1991, pp. 45–68. *JSTOR*, www.jstor.org/stable/23175177. Accessed March 5, 2021.

Schocket, Eric. "Undercover Explorations of the 'Other Half', or the Writer as Class Transvestite." *Representations*, no. 64, 1998, pp. 109–133. *JSTOR*, www.jstor.org/stable/2902934. Accessed March 8, 2021.

Schwartz, Joel. *Fighting Poverty with Virtue: Moral Reform and America's Urban Poor, 1825–2000* (Bloomington, IN: Indiana University Press, 2000).

See, Katharine Allyn, "The Christmas story in American literature." (1943). Electronic Theses and Dissertations. Paper 2167. https://doi.org/10.18297/etd/2167.

Tigchelaar, Jana. "The Neighborly Christmas: Gifts, Community, and Regionalism in the Christmas Stories of Sarah Orne Jewett and Mary Wilkins Freeman." *Legacy*, vol. 31, no. 2, 2014, pp. 236–257. *JSTOR*, www.jstor.org/stable/10.5250/legacy.31.2.0236. Accessed March 4, 2021.

Tuerk, Richard. "The Short Stories of Jacob A. Riis." *American Literary Realism, 1870–1910*, vol. 13, no. 2, 1980, pp. 259–265. *JSTOR*, www.jstor.org/stable/27745953. Accessed March 4, 2021.

Twigg, Reginald. "The performative dimension of surveillance: Jacob Riis' *How the Other Half Lives*." *Text and Performance Quarterly*, 12:4, 1992, pp. 305–328, doi:10.1080/10462939209359654. Accessed March 5, 2021.

Watts, Sarah. *Rough Rider in the White House: Theodore Roosevelt and the Politics of Desire* (Chicago, IL: University of Chicago Press, 2003).

7
ROSE WILDER LAND AND THE FRONTIER CANDIDATE

Rose Wilder Lane publishes *The Making of Herbert Hoover* in 1920 under the assumption that Hoover will decide to enter the Presidential contest – although he ultimately defers his run until 1928. Lane's text offers a loose constellation of ideological postures; part libertarian tract, part frontier myth, and part rags-to-riches yarn, Hoover's campaign biography reflects a confluence of diverse cultural and counter-cultural impulses from the period.[1] Specifically, Lane depicts her ideal candidate as a Janus-faced figure caught between the role of economic manager – eager to maximize efficiency – and economic risk-taker, one willing to innovate and tap into the nation's entrepreneurial zeal. In this way, Lane forecasts the sort of candidate that would become quite familiar to American citizens living through the neoliberal moment. From aesthetic as well as political perspectives, Lane's account of Hoover straddles a line between closed forms – the system manager; the self-made man – and open forms – the plotless rogue; the Romantic potential of the frontier. That is, her chosen candidate serves as a conflicted site for the American imaginary, and in turn campaign biographies like *Making* must be read not as straightforward cultural histories but as literary interventions in their own right.

Lane remains a prominent albeit under-analyzed figure in two distinct areas of American culture: as a progenitor of what comes to be known as prairie fiction and a keystone for the libertarian movement.[2] Indeed, it is "impossible to discuss (Lane) apart from the history of the American frontier" (Beito 554–555). Contemporary readers likely know Lane, if they know her at all, for her long-hidden contributions to *The Little House on the Prairie* series that she co-writes with her mother, Laura Ingalls Wilder. Lane extensively re-shapes her mother's manuscripts before sending them to Harper and Row, thereby serving as a critical interloper in the formation of her mother's endearing fiction for young adults. Lane's own fiction routinely

DOI: 10.4324/9781003132448-8

returns to issues linked to homesteading as well as the trials and tribulations of life on the frontier.[3] It is not exclusively as a ghost writer for her mother that Lane rises to fame; in truth, she stands out as one of the best-paid and most popular American writers of the 1920s and 1930s. She writes for a wide array of publications, from *Ladies Home Journal* to children's literature to biographies of purportedly self-made men like Charlie Chaplin, Henry Ford, Jack London, and, our focus herein, the future Commander-in-Chief, Herbert Hoover.[4] Throughout her fiction as well as her creative nonfiction, Lane promotes what she defines to be the values of American pioneers by infusing many of her stories with the gritty struggles of prior generations.

Of course, Lane is not really writing in the age of the homesteaders. Frederick Turner declares the closure of the American frontier nearly half a century before her ascent.[5] Nevertheless, Lane capitalizes upon a set of tropes that she links to the open prairie in order to advance her strongly held political and economic principles. She reportedly coins the term libertarian and plays a vital yet frequently ignored role in the spread of libertarian beliefs through her book *The Discovery of Freedom* (1943), which unpacks libertarianism for a mass audience. In addition to serving as a valued correspondent for the free-market ideologue Hoover throughout his life, she also mentors Roger MacBride, the first libertarian Presidential candidate who runs in 1972. As she grows older, Lane becomes increasingly extreme in her positions, eventually drawing the ire of the FBI for her sharp critique of the New Deal as well as America's war efforts. This chapter does not, however, focus at length upon Lane's later extremism due to the fact that *The Making of Herbert Hoover* appears in the year 1920, when Lane was only beginning to develop her ideas. But certain threads do run throughout her entire corpus of biographies of so-called self-made men, her journalism, and her novels – including, most famously, *Let the Hurricane Roar* (1933) as well as *Free Land* (1938). "She built (her corpus) around certain themes – freedom, respect for free markets, and love of nature and the natural order" (Woodside xiii). Placing her disparate texts into conversation with one another, this chapter highlights how Lane's unique campaign biography informs – and is informed by – the fictional devices that she employs in her influential depictions of the American frontier.

Lane initially receives the call to craft a Hoover biography in 1919 from editor Charles K. Field, who wishes to exploit her novelistic approach to writing biographies in order to elevate Hoover's political standing. In response, perhaps more than almost all of her predecessors in the genre of the campaign biography, Lane curates a novelistic experience for the reading by endowing her "facts" with a healthy dose of fiction. Holtz describes Lane as "a writer of lives, both biographical and fictional, and at times a blend of the two" (62). This generic blending eventually raises concerns among her biographical subjects. Chaplin, for one, derails her biography of him because it handles the concrete events of his life with very little fidelity to what he would call the truth. Likewise, when she composes the biography for London, she shows a willful "disregard for accuracy" as well as a propensity to "draw on her own background" in order to dramatize London's life (Campbell 177). Because Lane routinely leans upon "character types familiar to popular fiction" in her many biographies of so-called self-made men, we must read *Making* not only as an object of historical interest but also as a distinctly literary artifact.

In sum, Lane struggles to walk the thin line between fiction and the construction of political tracts. Her London biography, for instance, fails because it cannot decide whether it wants to be "a serious piece of art" or a "bestselling potboiler" and so it ends up being a little bit of both (Campbell 187).[6] Her libertarian sensibility reflects this ideological bromide, as radical as it is conservative. She notes of her critical reception that she stands outside of both partisan poles and eventually winds up "damned by both" (Holtz 91). In his study of the American frontier in popular culture, Richard Slotkin comments upon "the capacity of mythology to contain and reconcile conflicts within an ideological system" (610). Lane's ambivalent style illustrates Slotkin's point. In turn, to acknowledge this ambivalence as it appears in *Making* is to reconsider the campaign biography as a genre that cannot be discarded as mere easy-to-digest propaganda, fed by manipulative elites to a gullible electorate. Although *Making* remains at times formulaic, we must not overlook the degree to which Lane elsewhere generates a "new genre" – namely, the pioneer story. For a handful of critics that actually give her prose the time of day, some of Lane's output actually comes very "close to high art" (Woodside 69, 34). Her critics have gone so far as to assert that Lane "has a (contested) claim to popular literary fame even greater than (Ayn) Rand's" (Doherty 125). Since she contributes extensively to the development of literary and political alternatives in early twentieth-century America, we must not too hastily dismiss Lane's campaign biography of Hoover as a text written by an ideologue with a uniform purpose. In actuality, *Making* requires that we reconsider the campaign biography as an ideological constellation: a hodge-podge as dependent upon fictional strategies as it is upon Lane's counter-cultural economic and political perspectives.

Lane's imaginary candidate, not unlike candidates imagined in previous chapters, provides formulaic enclosure – a sense of wholeness associated with many of the dominant social values of the day – as well as generic openness – a sense of incompleteness that also fuels the dynamism of a functioning democracy. Lane maintains this slippery signification thanks in no small part to her literary inventiveness, as she imbues Hoover's campaign biography with tropes that she derives from Gothic treatments of frontier life. At the same time, Lane assists in shaping a type of foreclosed candidacy that endures today: a neoliberal prototype entangled in the tenets of the free market, exuding a managerial ethos, and less willing to consider political input from the masses. Lane's vision of Hoover thus complicates the latent openness that we have been tracking throughout the preceding chapters. What happens when the uncertainty of American politics, punctuating the campaign biography since at least Nathaniel Hawthorne's treatment of Franklin Pierce, pivots into the uncertainty of American economics? Of what value will the genre of the campaign biography be in this increasingly depoliticized context? Lane's *Making* upholds the political tensions of its predecessors while at the same time drawing these tensions to a close through an appeal to excessive economic calculation. In the final tally, *Making* anticipates a fundamental shift in the genre of the campaign biography – in fact, in American politics as well as American literature more broadly speaking – as candidates for higher office begin to lose their uniquely political character and become something else entirely.

"The Ache of Incompleteness"

In her biography of Hoover, Lane advances her belief in the intrinsic merits of uncertainty, which is to say, her evolving libertarian ethos infuses her campaign biography with an acceptance of endless change and a near constant re-assessment of risks and rewards. Just as Lane romanticizes the imaginary free market by aligning it with her otherwise generic depictions of the American frontier, in *Making* she similarly utilizes the idea of a democratic candidacy as a site in which to work out the glaring inconsistencies of her nascent libertarian model. We witness once more the ritualistic "contradictions and paradoxes of the West" on display in American popular culture (Paul 313). *The Making of Herbert Hoover* therefore serves as an invaluable bridge between Lane's literary legacy and her arguably much more enduring impact on American thought (her libertarianism). Whether she's outlining a mining expedition in the Wild West, or championing greater financial speculation, Lane interweaves a wide array of threads in American life into the fictionalized figure of Hoover, and she does so with one overarching purpose in mind: to promote the poetic beauty of incompleteness.

To convey the poetic beauty of incompleteness, Lane's biography starts with Hoover's ancestors in sixteenth-century France as they defy the dominant order of the day: "The need of man's soul," one of Hoover's ancestors purportedly declares, "is to be free." In response, "for the sake of that freedom which he valued more than all his possessions (Lane's ancestor) tore up the roots of his life." In this way, Lane establishes her lifelong working thesis almost immediately in her campaign biography: "The need of the human soul for freedom" (*Making* 3–5). From her vantage point, Hoover serves as only the latest icon to represent this human constant, an existential constant that pushes us to reject all efforts at claiming stasis or permanent authority. But how is Lane to depict this impetuous freedom, this beautiful incompleteness, for a mass audience in the 1920s – an audience that has rarely seen this position advocated in mainstream discourse? Lane answers this question by turning to literary tropes associated with the frontier, many of which she was simultaneously cultivating in her fiction, to outline her vision of libertarianism as well as her hopes for a different kind of Presidential candidate.

Hoover "grows up" in Lane's story, certainly, but not in the manner that characters typically mature. She dwells upon Hoover's time at Stanford in the early years of that university. Hoover categorizes himself as a member of the Pioneer Class. By stressing the utter newness of Stanford, Lane treats the knowledge that Hoover gains during his time there not as an accumulation of information attained through communal effort, but as yet another extension of the frontier experience, articulated by yet another supposedly self-made man: "Everywhere activity, creating, building toward the future, hopeful, hurrying. No traditions, no past. Only today, and today flung back in the race toward tomorrow. America. Stanford!" (103). For Hoover, change is the only abiding law of the universe. Lane's fictional characters paradoxically enjoy a similarly rootless sort of freedom. In her novel *Free Land*, for instance, the patriarch James Beaton "started out, at twenty-one, with nothing but his freedom." When he at last realizes the demands of this kind of freedom, the elder Beaton releases his son to the frontier with precious little support: "Maybe he had been too easy on his boys, spoiled them" (9). Lane's characters – including, prominently, her version of Hoover – are born into a radical state of freedom, which is to say, they stand out as disembedded sketches, unfinished and always awaiting something else. More than any of the preceding campaign biographies, Lane relentlessly pushes her would-be President into new territories and literally as well as figuratively forces him to be "born again" in order to realize the inherent value of existential incompleteness: an incompleteness that provides him with a reason to struggle ever anew. "The past was a ball-and-chain on their feet. Youth was the conquering spirit" (206). In another scene, Lane recounts how one of Hoover's business associates runs off with his money and Hoover must "begin again" at the ripe old age of 28 (300). Lane's persistent restoration of a *tabula rasa* for her candidate suggests a vision of American society that ostensibly invites near total revision at a moment's notice.

Ironically, to convey this innate openness, *Making* draws upon formulaic thrills associated with the American frontier, a literary topography that Lane simultaneously develops – both alone and alongside her mother – in the realm of American fiction. Across multiple genres, Lane references the transcontinental railroad and the spectacles that it produces. Her reader follows Hoover as he boards an awe-inspiring locomotive: "The strange life to which he was going ... the circling, climbing train ... a new world; he was not yet able to move freely in it, but he would be some day" (99). Lane's descriptive passages dress Hoover's campaign biography in the laurels of a scenic wonderland: "A country bewildering in its beauty ... a country such as he had never imagined" (101). We might parallel the formation of Hoover through his *Bildungsroman* with the unfolding of the frontier in Lane's fiction. In particular, Hoover and the frontiersman, in their race to "grow" (in multiple sense of the word), each depend upon a fundamental lack. The portrait of Hoover shares a good deal in common with the figuration of the frontier, in that both imaginary points resist the allure of fulfillment and so they reiterate Turner's anxiety about the closure of the frontier. Embodying the frontier spirit, Hoover requires ongoing dissatisfaction to propel him outward to greater innovation. The young David Beaton in *Free Land* feels "exhilaration ... a sense of unlimited freedom, in so much space" (20). One of David's neighbors rhapsodizes, "I like it where there aren't any people, where it's big and new – and fresh" (92). Meanwhile, in Lane's novel *Let the Hurricane Roar*, David – for some reason, Lane recycles the same handful of names throughout her fiction – delights in "the vast, unconquered forest" and relishes in how "the whole land was exuberant with change and promise" (4, 16–17). Like her campaign biography, Lane's novels advance the premise that youthful individuals as well as aspiring nations will only thrive if they can maintain the "ache of incompleteness" that they initially encounter on the uncultivated prairie, be the encounter in person or, more realistically in the year 1920, upon the written page (102).

To illustrate this drive for dissatisfaction, let us consider Molly's personal trial in *Hurricane*. Left alone on their homestead, Molly must come to terms with her "bare existence" – a state of being that eternally calls for what is missing in order to sustain an ever-unfinished habitus. Absence defines her budding work ethic. Molly "confronted space ... she knew the infinite smallness, weakness, of life in the lifeless universe. She felt the vast, insensate forces against which life itself is a rebellion" (99–100). However, according to Lane, this smallness – this sense of futility – is a gift, not a burden. It is her maintenance of an "infinite smallness" that empowers Molly to confront, in the novel's climax, an ominous gathering of cattle out on the frozen tundra. "Was this too great a risk?" she wonders to herself. Risk becomes at this climactic moment a vital part of her experience. "Some dangers," she finally recognizes, "must be faced" (105, 111). She kills one of the bovines that she deems too ineffective to survive, before claiming one of the heifers for her own. The lesson for Lane's readers remains clear: the uncertainty of the frontier, with its lack of comfort or security, ultimately empowers resilient characters like Molly as well as Hoover. To somehow resolve this incompleteness would prove a detriment: "It was great to think of all there was ahead ... the atmosphere was alert with expectancy" (*Making* 110–112).

Lane similarly crafts her incomplete candidate through gestures at the well-trodden territory of the American frontier. *Making* spends an enormous amount of time gazing at uncultivated landscapes because their sheer emptiness offers an ideal blank canvas upon which to paint yet another variation of the so-called self-made man. Lane plants her reader's footing firmly in the frontier to explain away Hoover's training as a geologist – a discipline not immediately relevant to political office – and so to embed the value of open-endedness quite literally into the landscape itself. Indeed, sliding from factual information to literary metaphor and back again, Lane dwells upon the "ceaseless flux and change" of the strata that Hoover studies. She never loses sight of this terrestrial metaphor as she details how "generations of men were like the waves of the sea" and, subsequently, how world history offers a surface on which we can measure the undulations of "free men."

When a young Hoover unearths strange stones in Iowa, he notes: "What other mysteries they might reveal no one could say" (160, 49). Lane therefore emphasizes the landscape of the frontier in order to naturalize her libertarian vision. In so doing, she creates a candidate that embraces the unpredictability of a volatile free market as well as the specific skills that enable individuals to interpret seismic flux and change. That is, Hoover as geologist bows down before the incompleteness of the figurative strata of human existence while simultaneously mastering its diverse geological formations, thereby adding a concrete layer of significance to already-familiar signifiers associated with the American frontier.

What may surprise contemporary readers about *Making*, though, is how utterly inefficient Lane envisions her future President to be. Perhaps we ought not be so surprised: we have seen in previous chapters how literary interventions in campaign biographies routinely generate a democratic surplus of meaning, an incompleteness that cannot be easily wrangled into neat-and-tidy narratives. In Lane's hands, this beautiful incompleteness takes on a distinctively wasteful yet redemptive visage. Readers are once more led to uncover the absence of efficiency within the material earth: "Its secrets were open to (Hoover): he saw disclosed the vast epochs of time, the aeons of nature's blind, wasteful endeavor to create a world and people it" (120). When faced with this excess, Hoover demonstrates his acumen because he alone – as geologist and financier – seems capable of comprehending the secrets buried within man's nature. But why is this version of nature so "blind," so "wasteful"? For Lane, the answer lies in her libertarian belief that first, man cannot forecast the free market or plan for financial success, hence Hoover's "blindness," and second, man must take risks in order to accrue wealth – hence Hoover's acceptance of appropriate "waste." Both a part of the world and somehow hovering above it, Hoover must prove periodically wasteful if he wants to be victorious in the long run. In other words, his overall efficiency depends upon his willingness to be temporarily inefficient. Lane's libertarian sentiment directly shapes the contours of her future Commander-in-Chief: a figure that must remain open in his response to shifting conditions so as to avoid foreclosing the opportunity to take greater risks in pursuit of greater reward.

The story of Hoover's life proves to be a story of productive mistakes. Whereas previous campaign biographies generally avoid excavating the candidate's past life for errors, focusing instead upon moments of obvious triumph that reflect the calcified values of the present, Lane's *Making* understands errors to be invaluable components of a campaign's larger narrative. From childhood, Hoover demonstrates a propensity for "romps," a "longing to run, to jump, to shout in the joy of ... release" (21, 26). As a boy in attendance at Quaker meetings, "an infinite boredom descended upon his spirit" (25). In response, Hoover takes chances by doing things that his elders tell him to avoid, activities that Lane describes as "innocent experimenting." For Hoover, then, to embrace danger means rehearsing the actions of America's early pioneers and confronting "the immensity of the unknown" (29–30). This paradox of "efficient wastefulness" defines Hoover's development as a character since, like the strata upon which he stands, he blindly gropes for answers and sometimes stumbles into precarious situations.

This habitual risk-taking takes on acutely economic dimensions in Lane's fiction as well as her campaign biography. David from *Hurricane* announces his presence as "laughing and bold, a daring hunter," a man brave enough to take chances (3, 11). More explicit still, *Free Land* can be described as a nothing more or less than a series of transactions in which David negotiates his own risks and rewards. One of the initial lessons that a neighbor bestows upon the young man underscores the need for bouts of profligacy: "There's such a thing as being too saving," his neighbor insists (74). Examples of "good excess" abound: to beat a blizzard and haul in some hay, David repeats his motto: "I'll try anything once" – a sentiment affirmed by his friend's response: "Nothing ventured, nothing gained" (159). After he beats the blizzard, Lane's reader is meant to understand that sometimes the benefits for risk-taking overrule the prudence practiced by David's Puritan ancestors. David consistently invests in farming machinery, observing along the way that "there's a lot of stick-in-the-muds that don't know they're living in these progressive modern times"; he wisely invests in a risky crop of turnips to offset some of his other risks, holding a "trick up his sleeve" – language that suggests Lane's ambivalent relationship to the art of gambling. Elsewhere in the novel, Lane appears to condemn, half-heartedly, a "dandy" named Gay for his gambling, although Gay walks away in the end virtually unscathed for his "transgressions" (166, 223). Finally, David falls unexpectedly into ownership of a flock of sheep: "It was taking a risk, to go deeper into debt, but maybe with sheep he could pull out" (299). And so he does. Simply put, Lane's protagonists must take risks so that they can open up unrealized parts of the country – and themselves. Again, the cultural context for Lane in the 1920 and 30s remains far less agrarian than the fictional nineteenth century that she depicts. In *Making*, Hoover unequivocally dismisses the notion of becoming a farmer. Through the convenient imagery of the unrealized prairie, Lane asks her reader to take risks not on the open plains but in a starkly different arena: namely, in the speculative chaos of the stock market.[7] *Free Land* leaves little gray area on this point: "Any man that tried to be safe instead of going ahead and taking his chances was a fool" (256). David's wayward sister presumably gains the reader's admiration when she decides to go even further west, "where chances are big ... (and) anybody with the gumption to take the risks, lawful risks, can make himself a millionaire!" (288).

Lane's Hoover pivots from prudent conservative to risk-taking libertarian in tandem with lessons learned by her literary pioneers. She encourages her readers to comprehend these moments of excess, risk, and waste as innocuous and even necessary. When Hoover cannot afford to attend the Stanford football game, he opts to spend money that he does not have to invest in his "personal growth" and attend the game. When he has spent all of his money, he decides that such an expenditure was "worth it" (125). Later, when he wishes to attend the senior ball, he takes out a loan, demonstrating to Lane's audience the need to invest – that is, to take certain risks – in the pursuit of career advancement (163). In a more figurative sense, when Hoover later goes to work mining in the deserts of Australia, he accepts the cost of living in a barren wasteland for the long-term benefit of wealth and power: "One must pay for success" (217).[8] For much of *Making*, Lane presents Hoover as a shrewd risk-taker emboldened by his own youthfulness and the youth of his nation. He comes to loathe the cloddish posture of bureaucrats and traditionalists: "Ever notice that it's old people who care about customs and forms?" (243). In lieu of social planning, Hoover ostensibly seizes upon the highly-individualized agonism of pioneers on the frontier, upheld by actors that prefer to take chances today and engage in battles that they might well lose for the sake of profitability down the road. Lane calls it the "Great Game" and plots its rules as "the matching of wits; quick mind against quick mind ... seizing unguarded openings" (234). Her incomplete candidate thrives at the outermost edge of an imaginary frontier and, rather than embody the fullness of American accomplishment, Lane this figure with an existential lack that endows him with a healthy appetite for uncertainty and perpetual risk-taking.

In sum, Lane does not merely use fictional tropes associated with the American frontier to supplement her campaign biography; rather, she employs these tropes to mark for her readers the glaring gap at the core of the future President. Ever the imperialist, Hoover the candidate must move ceaselessly from frontier to frontier: from the Midwest, to the shores of California, to Australia, to China.[9] In Lane's fiction as well as her campaign biography, a beautiful incompleteness functions at the intimate level of narrative form, transposing the lacuna that we have seen in earlier campaign biographies between Romance and realism into a more overtly economic register. Lane quilts into the tapestry of *Let the Hurricane Roar* this internal pattern of open-endedness when she notes that the Bible shared by the young protagonists contains "pages for Births and Deaths (that) were still blank, waiting to be written upon" (5). Lane then bookends her novel with a scene in which Molly writers a letter concerning the alluring promise of frontier life as blank page waiting to be filled, and tucks the missive into the same Bible, where it will remain "never mailed" (94). What are readers to do with these blank pages and uncirculated letters? Lane's novel gestures at what is consistently lacking: life-giving chasms that leave individuals unsatisfied, hungry, and forever in pursuit of some better tomorrow. This missing piece is folded into the text itself as a Derridean reminder that the missive always, mercifully, evades its final destination. To refashion Turner's thesis, we can continue to pursue meaning only if the figurative frontier endures in a state of being "uncivilized" and our imaginations do not come to rest on any conclusive figuration. We see a similar sensibility throughout Lane's campaign biography of Hoover – a text that, despite its aims at overall coherence and systemic thought, returns incessantly to the holes in its own supposed logic. Hoover must acknowledge that "the human factor, that inexplicable and erratic element ... preventing all organizations from becoming perfect machines ... prevents them also from becoming static and holds the door open to that endless change that is called progress" (221–222). Meta-formulaic in the sense that it refuses its own rigidity, *Making* declares itself to be (im)perfect and so the work maintains an essential schism between Hoover as emblem of advanced organization and Hoover as an always-already temporary, which is to say, democratic figure, one designed to "hold the door open" for future changes. Whether the sketch of Hoover does prove, in truth, to be all that democratic will be explored in the final section of the chapter.

The inherent incompleteness of Lane's candidate marks an intersection of the pioneer tale, the libertarian tract, and ongoing permutations of the campaign biography. By promoting uncertainty as well as risk-taking, *Making* recalibrates the unstable underpinnings of the genre that this book has been tracking. It preserves a hole in the reader's knowledge to advance a relatively novel understanding of the American economy. Her vision of the Hoover's candidacy advances this understanding by appealing to the reader's love of adventure: "Change was not without its excitements and pleasures" (*Making* 59). At the dawn of the Roaring Twenties, Lane claims that her audience requires an invigorating dosage of "pioneering adventure ... to stir the blood ... American energy, American imagination and initiative, American organizing ability ... a young man at the edge of it" (204). Here, however, the problem at the Hoover as a symbol at the frontier's edge comes more fully into view: given the overarching drive for incompleteness that we have charted, what are we to do with Lane's parallel desire for the future President to act as a sort of enclosure, an ubermanager, a source of stability to counter the abject openness of the Wild West? What are readers to make of this young Executive, with his exceptional "organizing ability," as he erodes the "mystery" of the strata, thanks to his erudition and his otherwise deft handling of social concerns? To come to terms with this paradox, we must turn our attention to the fictional strategies seen throughout Lane's corpus.

Gothic Frontiers and the Organization Man

As odd as it may seem, one of the best ways to make sense of Lane's managerial message may be to begin with her reliance upon Gothic literary tropes, typically categorized as excessive in nature. Lane practices what Jerrod Hogle describes as "Gothic oscillation": a shift from the thrills of frontier openness, discussed in the previous section, to a conservative refuge that closes off such terrors.[10] Although, as we have already seen, the character of Hoover depends upon a necessary, at times beautiful, sense of incompleteness, Lane also uses incompleteness as an occasion for organizational repression – as an invitation to suppress the chaotic impulses of a society shifting into heavy-handed forms of managerialism. This oscillation between repression and return parallels what Richard Hofstadter describes as the "dual identity" of homesteaders in American culture: "(The homesteader) had long since taken from business society its acquisitive goals and its speculative temper, but he was still practicing the competitive individualism that the most advanced sectors of industry and finance had outgrown" (59). Lane's literary frontier remains open and closed, released and contained, and so her ideal candidate capitalizes upon moments of sublime dread on the prairie as an excuse to institute control via her preferred economic calculus.

Lane's best-known short story from this period, "Innocence" (1922), reveals how the author paradoxically employs Gothic imagery to advocate for greater managerial oversight. The story comes in second place in the O. Henry Short Story prize, and many critics at the time describe it as one of her finest works. It depicts the darkness that accompanies Prohibition: underground economies and moral swamplands that cry out for a return to "law-and-order." The young protagonist Mary visits her uncle in Florida only to discover that her relative has been lured into this macabre world by her aunt, a shape-shifting succubus that embodies the grotesque side of any rebellion from authority. After Mary awakens from a particularly disturbing nightmare in which she dreams of "moon shine," her mother calms her: "Moonshining is a bad word" (582). Lane's *mise-en-scene* is unmistakably Gothic – the woods, plagued by snakes and "thick and moldy with smells," are designed to make the reader shiver. "Nothing was safe. Terror and strangeness reached out of the gray woods and seized (Mary), and she shrieked, and there was nothing anywhere but sobbing and screams" (578–579). A host of menacing creatures populate this forest at the edge of civilization, including a Venus flytrap as well as ravenous ants that busily devour a moth: "The piney woods were shadowy in the moonlight and things without shapes moved through them" (538). Eventually, her tyrannical aunt attempts to murder Mary, causing her family to flee from this sinister place. In typical Gothic fashion, the transgressive nature of the borderland cries out for a return to "normalcy," that is, to a more well-defined social order. Mary's mother pleads with her brother: "You don't belong with such people. You used to be the finest boy in Webster County" (581). Despite her pleas, Mary's uncle remains mired in America's dark economy. Much like the works analyzed in the preceding section, "Innocence" incorporates the utterly unexpected into its formal structure: it begins with Mary (and the reader) waking on a train; momentarily disoriented, she forgets where she is and where the train is going. Throughout the story, the reader shares Mary's perspective as well as her inability to understand the ominous world that suddenly surrounds her. Mary's trip into this uncivilized corner of the universe provokes a reactionary posture. Throughout Lane's fiction there appears to be a glaring difference between the "thrill" of industrial progress and the "thrill" of seedy underground economies. Lane's managerial candidate Hoover plays an invaluable role in sorting out these cultural distinctions.

To probe further into these distinctions, we might also consider some of Lane's many isolated "damsels in distress" left to fend for themselves on the foreboding frontier – a staple of the Gothic genre. *Free Land* and *Let the Hurricane Roar* both highlight female protagonists in extremely vulnerable positions, under siege by Gothic forces that surround them and threaten to invade their sanctuaries. Hardly a land of opportunity, Molly in *Hurricane* views the prairie as indifferent and "inhuman" (14). When locusts descend upon their field, she is overcome by dread, an unsettling sensation that "the whole earth (is) scaly and crawling" (46). In this heightened moment of horror, she recognizes the frontier as a distinctly Gothic space: "Grasshoppers, going west – like the railroads, like the people, like cities and settled lands ... as alien, as indifferent to human suffering, as wind or cold" (49). An uneasiness with the Gothic side of westward expansion continues for Molly in the pages to come: "She feared trains. When she slept she saw the monstrous, inhuman things of steam and iron, swiftly coming, roaring, panting, staring with the headlights like eyes; things that seemed alive, but were not alive" (64). Molly must eventually face this nightmare of "progress" in order to declare herself a "proper" frontier woman, one that has been appropriately hardened by the affair and thus found a newfound respect for self-discipline. Left alone at the homestead, she at last confronts the "shapeless, dark thing" outside of her door (98). In *Free Land*, Lane's other Mary feels an oppressive sense of dread when she braves an empty void that almost swallows her homestead whole: "Something was watching her ... the dark shapes of things" (88). Lane's novel frequently augments this titillating horror by racist means, as when it exploits the image of a forest full of mummified "Indian" babies hanging from branches, or a faceless mass of "Indians" that blend into the daunting landscape: "The mist seemed full of ... brown bodies, paint-streaked chests and faces, goblin-like, impossible" (109). Mary and David stand up to a plethora of abject elements: they are overwhelmed by a cyclone, with its "black tentacle groping"; they find themselves stranded in blizzards that disorient them at a profound level: "Nothing had been like this terror, this knowing that his own mind was not sure, not safe" (201, 143). While we have already seen how this uncertainty remains a fundamental part of life within a volatile financial arena – because "no one knows the weather," which is to say, no one can forecast with total accuracy the swings of the mercurial marketplace – these Gothic moments sound an alarm and force readers to confront the anxieties associated with a "frontier mentality," even as Lane ties this mentality to speculative markets instead of agrarian pursuits (273). By novel's end, the horrors of Lane's imaginary frontier demand stronger management as well as more elaborate organizational mechanisms. This tension between the Gothic frontier and the acumen of Lane's geologist-financier reflects the inconsistency of a managerial mindset that can somehow hold onto the libertarian hypothesis of absolute freedom from oversight. For every "wider vista" opened by David, a bog of "unknown depths" manifests and, in turn, Lane's readers are led to recognize the two-sidedness of the frontier as a Gothic space – its promise as well as its peril (*Hurricane* 25).

The figure of Hoover enables Lane to suture the two sides of her Gothic frontiers by sustaining an innate incompleteness and, at the same time, bolstering a sense of managerial prowess. Said another way, Hoover's campaign biography embodies Gothic oscillation by wavering at the border between yawning, progressive openness and the security of conservative enclosures. It concurrently demonstrates the changing concept of winning candidates at the dawn of the twentieth century. Like Lane's fictional works, *Making* (re)contains the idea of the ideal candidate in very specific ways: he appears to be the beneficiary of a long lineage tied to the mythical notion of industrial "progress," part of the Romantic ideal of a vast web spun by Adam Smith's "invisible hand," and a self-made manager that improbably exists outside of these vast systems while controlling them from on high.

As the preceding chapters illustrate, campaign biographies frequently wrestle with questions of the candidate's lineage. This focus upon lineage is of course not literal in these cases, but metaphorical – it gestures at broad cultural values that have supposedly endured for generations. On behalf of Pierce in the mid-nineteenth century, Hawthorne points to ancestors including, most prominently, Revolutionary War veterans in order to establish a sense of continuity in certain American beliefs such as military valor. Like Hawthorne, Lane stresses lineage to promote a set of specific values. Hoover stems from Quaker roots, which – according to Lane – implies a faith in the divine impetus of industrial "progress." Hoover speaks on behalf of his Quaker ancestors because "their spirit had made his"; upon his "small affairs was the touch of hands that had been dust for years" (5, 115). Lane highlights Hoover's great-grandmother in particular because she can spin the character to stress the same capitalist tenets that a Hoover administration would privilege: "an extraordinary executive ability" and, ironically given Lane's propensity for useful waste elsewhere in her works, the absence of "waste" when anything was placed into her hands (7–8). The Quaker lineage upon which Lane lingers could have been used to stress any number of principles, such as pacifism, but she opts to underline instead a Protestant work ethic purportedly idiosyncratic to the Quakers in a manner that renders Hoover's ideological agenda all the more visible.

Stretching Hoover's lineage from sixteenth-century France into a presumably prosperous future, Lane endorses the vast and quite familiar, at least for American audiences, metaphysics of Western "progress." She pauses regularly to chart the metaphysical tides: "Modern industry was well started on that course destined inevitably to lead to the growth of great cities and corporations, and tremendous concentration of wealth and power" (14). In this manner, Lane utilizes the candidate as an avatar for the stability of American society, even amidst the upheavals that she recognizes must continue in order to foster feelings of productive precarity among the populace. Lane accomplishes this effect through a complicated understanding of what "family" means. Lineage anchors everything to a common core while, at the same time, it explains unexpected events as variations upon a dependable theme by "building a secure future on the firm foundations of the past" (356). In other words, Lane's uneasy reconciliation of conflicting Gothic impulses sets the stage for a convoluted conservatism that takes a much firmer hold nearly a century later under neoliberal orders – a contemporary conservatism torn between traditionalism and a reliance upon restless financial markets that instigate periodic seismic shifts.[11] The concept of lineage conveniently encompasses both elements, the stable and the uncertain, into a relatively coherent whole. For example, *Making* celebrates Hoover's aunt and uncle for their disciplinary efforts "to control (Hoover's) actions for his own good," while simultaneously championing Hoover's resentment toward any and all "discipline from without" (74). The head of the Hoover family acts as a temporary manager without, importantly, suppressing the adventurous spirit of youth – an entrepreneurial spirit that leads the young candidate from acceptable risk to ever greater innovation. By encapsulating Hoover's lineage as closed off from deviation as well as open to child-like release from oversight, Lane's candidate effectively embodies the central paradoxes of America's industrial "progress."

Lane's fiction similarly re-contains the threat of incompleteness, which remains part and parcel of the frontier experience, through an appeal to lineage. While Lane highlights the Gothic edges of civilization – tied to the thrill of freedom – she concurrently tamps down upon all of this unsettling openness: "It has never been easy to build up a country, but how much easier it is for us, with such great comforts and conveniences" (*Let* 93). Her fiction thus speaks out of both sides of its mouth, admitting that it is not really "pioneer times" anymore and self-fashioned settlers should be grateful for the fruits of industry that have set them up to succeed (*Free* 78). Perhaps no more intelligible example of the synthesis between familial lineage and industrial "progress" exists in Lane's fiction than in the framing device of *Free Land*. The novel opens with David's father, James Beaton, deciding to release his son out into the western territories, and it closes, strangely enough, for a text written by one of the founding mothers of libertarianism, with James visiting David's family to gift him an advance on his inheritance because he wants David "to have an easier time than (he) did" (332). *Free Land* starts with the thrill of an incomplete life yet to be lived, a libertarian adventure, and ends with the imposition of a father's inheritance – James's managerial move to dictate the outcomes of his son's efforts, a move seemingly at odds with the tenets of libertarianism. The father oversees his son's life even as he outwardly refuses to "regulate" him. In these conflicted moments, the metaphor of familial lineage provides a conceptual tool with which Lane can compensate for her Gothic oscillation, since lineage depends upon the excitement of youth, evolutionary ruptures, and the security as well as coherence that comes from a stoic father-figure. In short, by enfolding industrial "progress" into an intergenerational *Bildungsroman*, Lane mitigates the unruly surplus produced, of necessity, by her Gothic sensibilities. Lane's vision for the Hoover Presidency likewise compensates for moments of utter openness with a call for (im)possible wholeness – that is, the synergy of a cohesive body politic or, more appropriate still, a cohesive body economic.

Making conveys the global economy through the symbol of a singular, interconnected web. By so doing, Hoover's biography re-enforces the premise that the metaphysical "progress" behind American industry is always-already predetermined. No frontier, in Lane's estimation, is ever truly open because it remains always-already foreclosed within the vast web. Echoing the circularity of Lew Wallace (see Chapter Five), Lane articulates this reassurance through multiple references to actual webs in the organic world, a natural phenomenon not unlike the strata discussed earlier: "A spider swung to and fro, laboriously weaving with invisible silken strands a web that would be ready when dawn brought the day's opportunity for spiders ... (Hoover's) mind toiled over geometric lines and calculations" (91). Lane parallels Hoover with the weaver of the web, thereby placing him at the epicenter of a growing global economy: "Someday (Hoover) would be in the center of ... that machine, that giant organization of human lives and material things" (197–198). Although Hoover weaves the web, he also does its bidding; the web remains woven more often by an "invisible hand" than by Hoover himself. This web – a "vast impersonal organization" – weaves itself with little input from the individuals involved, including Hoover, who apparently has "no choice" when it comes to his participation (224–225).[12]

Lane's web metaphor reflects her Gothic proclivity for excess – the ominous, "impersonal" threads that call to mind the literary phrasing of Jonathan Edwards' "Sinners in the Hands of an Angry God" – in tandem with her Gothic proclivity for a conservative (re)containment of the threat. While the frontier that Hoover inhabits remains at times blessedly incomplete ("a world unorganized, chaotic, wasteful; a mass of men tumultuous with conflicting desires; without order, reason, or definite purpose"), it retains a crucial sense of orderliness, anchored to very particular economic principles: "(Hoover) was entangled in the web of a world commercialism" (307, 312). Unwilling to embrace wholesale the internal logic of a *laissez-faire* system, Lane's ideal candidate serves as a link between chaos and conformity, between the "stockmarkets of London" and the "mazes of Oriental intrigue" (252). Her would-be President provides a confounding amalgamation of freedom and authoritarianism that would later characterize libertarian influence between 1972 to 2016. Hoover himself actively resists management and embraces it without hesitation. The spider's web, like Smith's "invisible hand," aids readers in imagining intangible threads that presumably bind together the diverse elements of a society that has, paradoxically, been atomized under the pressures of free enterprise that have now been sent to save it. In this sense, the ideal candidate can be both godlike engineer as well as a relatively powerless organizer, beholden to a grand force that transcends him. Lane's web metaphor similarly allows her to repress the Gothic sensationalism that periodically (re)surfaces in her fiction. In *Free Land*, the web of business organization promises to tame malevolent entities that roam the frontier: "No telling what would happen to all of us, out here with no law," a character laments, before confidently asserting that "it will be different when the country's organized" (91). The economic web that gradually entangles the prairie, "world commercialism," enfolds every ragged, disparate piece into a coherent whole. As proof, Lane's modern-day settlers are impressed by the speed of novel shipping methods:

> We've living in the greatest age this planet ever knew or ever will! ... The whole future of this country's part and parcel of railroads, railroads and telegraph. If it wasn't for them, not one of us'd be sitting here today. (122)

A meticulous sense of management, alongside the innate inner-connectivity of commerce, blankets Lane's imagined frontier with reassurances to counterbalance the Gothic menace of her chosen *mise-en-scene*. And Lane visualizes this invisible web in distinctively economic terms – be it the railroad, telegraph, commercialism (specifically, trade), or in the capital loaned to young risk-takers. In *Free Land*, David learns to appreciate his banker because his banker continues to lend him money in risky circumstances, even though the banker might lose out on the deal. We are all connected, he paternalistically proclaims; the lender needs the recipient of the loan, who needs the railroad, which needs the bank, etcetera. Molly – that most distressed of Gothic maidens – finds her heart strings equally entangled in the intricate web of a swelling economic system: "Her expanding heart seemed to enclose the enormous land, the great sky, the whole West with its outpouring of abundance of joy, of freedom" (29). In dialogue with Lane's seminal pioneer tales, the Hoover campaign biography (re)contains the thrill of risky investment within the comforting matrix of the marketplace, and it thus affirms a libertarian mythos that Lane continues to develop throughout her career.

The idea of the candidate as a business manager was given perhaps its fullest expression to that point in Lane's *Making*. Like her pioneer tales, *Making* advocates for the diminution of regulatory efforts, social planning, and excessive prudence – yet, again like her pioneer tales, *Making* promotes an organization man to oversee a specific sort of "progress." In *Let the Hurricane Roar*, Molly quickly takes comfort in "the feeling that the country was setting up rapidly," a promise that the industrial schema was being erected to make their lives less unpredictable; in *Free Land*, although the text establishes that "on the edge of an abyss ... there was no certainty," David proves himself to be a highly competent manager, a quick study of basic economic principles like supply and-demand that he applies expertly in every transactional encounter (*Hurricane* 68; *Free* 27, 150–151). The concept of an open prairie shrinks dramatically as Lane tames it by forcing the fictional construct to conform to her own ideological preferences: "The third wave in the development of the West was rising: first the forests, then the wheat, now the orchards" (*Making* 83). In other words, as the West advances into new "frontiers" – for Hoover, it is the Midwest, West coast, Australia, and finally China – each incomplete void is supposedly filled by a manager that maximizes profits. At times pushing against the sense of incompleteness described in the previous section, Hoover embodies a mythical consensus. He serves as master of the "wild" elements that he eventually domesticates and subsumes within the emerging organizational model of the United States.

Lane's chosen candidate appears as an ideal business manager most visibly during his time at Stanford. She tracks Hoover's desire to centralize the student government because, after three years of "pure individualism," there was a need for the student body to form a "compact unit" (151). Deemed an "organization shark" by his peers at the university, Hoover sharpens his "merciless pencil," sparing no one, in order to consolidate the wasteful energies of his disorganized fraternity (138, 152). Lane unconsciously reveals the irony when she admits that, although Hoover is "against group control, any group, anywhere," in this case, administrative acumen proves a necessity: "It was *his group* that would bring about the reform" (147, emphasis mine). Once more, Lane's vision for the American Presidency contains a range of conflicting impulses: to release from oversight *and* to manage the masses meticulously; to send sons westward *and* to ensure that they receive a healthy inheritance; to dismiss the merits of bureaucracy *and* to peddle a vast, faceless hegemonic order to encapsulate nearly every aspect of American lives. In Lane's hands, Hoover serves as a communal signifier that captures a national desire for security as well as stability and, at the same time, preserves the drive for Gothic dissolution required of any democratic – or perhaps a better term in this context might be "liberal" – citizenry looking to avoid the stasis of tyranny.[13] Hofstadter adds, upon examining Progressivism in early twentieth century America, that the fictional world of homesteading allows audiences "to keep the benefits of the emerging organization of life and yet to retain the scheme of individualistic values that this organization was destroying" (217). However, an important question remains: when one takes into account the managerial ethos of Lane's future President, what are the significant differences, if any exist, between the ideal candidate as liberal, economic facilitator and the ideal candidate as a vital part of a democratic, open-ended political imaginary?

"The New American Manager"

As the previous section illustrates, some of the most acutely political moments of Lane's corpus also happen to be its most Gothic. Her campaign biography stimulates and then stifles this sense of abject openness by packaging the unknown within her chosen ideological framework – namely, free-market idealism. Once more, she utilizes unpredictability on the frontier as an essential part of the libertarian calculus rather than its antithesis; meanwhile, managers like Hoover remove the necessity of communal input in favor of economic expertise. Pointing to the historical moment in which America's frontier myth intermingled with the genre of the campaign biography, Slotkin describes "a classless ruling class at once plebeian and aristocratic, born to its virtues but earning them nonetheless, and emerging from a democratic infancy to the maturity of bureaucracy and empire; an alternative to commercialism, but nonetheless its product" (637). Indeed, in Lane's treatment, Hoover appears to be both plebeian and aristocrat, as he develops from his supposed birth in a democratic crucible – anybody is somebody on the frontier – to sacrificing on behalf of a vast, bureaucratic empire. However, despite this obfuscation, does Lane's winning candidate actually signify the values of democracy? Can Lane's readers salvage the candidate as an open-ended figure – a reminder that no embodiment of the nation could ever fully enclose its diverse peoples or plurality of interests?

Like so many of Lane's characters, the Hoover of *Making* views his entire existence through a transactional lens and subsequently runs all of his choices through a cost/benefit analysis. Lane's candidate argues that no aspect of human life should be exempted from this algorithm. Hoover understands education and religion to be investments that enable individuals to reap rewards in the future. Whereas young Hoover remains fascinated by the magical "secrets" of geology, the older Hoover can only comprehend his world in exclusively economic terms: "Mining engineering paid" (92). As a result, Hoover does not approach philosophical and moral issues of "truth" or "right" as ideals to be considered without the pressures of profit margins, but as practical concerns: things that work; things that pay. "Work," he observes, is nothing less than "life." Life is not about enjoyment, but "the concrete task completed" (190). Consequently, Lane's candidate reserves little patience for democracy with its messy, inefficient, and political (as opposed to economic) attitudes. Her Executive-in-waiting still acts as a supervisor with a monomaniacal focus upon the bottom line. Like Lane's fictional homesteaders, Hoover accrues "authority as an expert" by emphasizing efficiency over morality (314).

The Hoover campaign biography is quite clear on this point: the masses, when left to their own devices, will always prove terribly wasteful and unable to improve their society. The character of Hoover models a faux openness to change yet, in reality, the managerial campaigner actually marshals popular sentiments as well as resources in a specifically libertarian direction. Writing two years later in 1922, the real Hoover trumpets a similar need for discipline and guardianship over the feckless "people":

> The crowd only feels: it has no mind of its own which can plan. The crowd is credulous, it destroys, it consumes, it hates, and it dreams – but it never builds … Popular desires are no criteria to the real need; they can be determined only by … constructive leadership. (19)

Lane's Hoover too stands apart from the crowd by championing economic foreclosure over political engagement.

In his diagnosis of the neoliberal shift of the past 50 years, Jacques Rancière aids us in understanding better the dangers of a candidate that acts like an Executive over the masses instead of a placeholder to temporarily represent the presumed will of "the people." "The political begins precisely when one stops balancing profits and losses," he argues, "and worries instead about distributing common lots and evening out communal shares and entitlements to these shares" (*Disagreement* 5). According to Rancière, political demands disrupt the dominant order of the day to remind us of the contingency inherent to any social order. Hoover-as-CEO polices "the people" and, in turn, upholds corporate hegemony, which is to say, he refutes the incompleteness of democracy by unapologetically policing the body politic in the name of increased profits for a select few. The character of Hoover accomplishes this disciplinary function by declaring his own expertise and downplaying the importance of the democratic impetus. Hoover's training as a geologist further sustains his illusory prowess because it suggests that his style of management is always "scientific," and so he purportedly maintains the wherewithal to solve any problem though tangible, material means. Rancière tracks

> the growing equivalence of the production and relationships of law and management of market forces, in endless cross-referencing of law and reality whose final word is pure and simple identification of democratic 'form' with the managerial practice of bowing to commercial necessity. (112)

As Lane deploys the idea of the managerial candidate to cross-reference market forces and "natural law," she starts to cover up the lack of political as well as aesthetic determination that she initially exploits. Without this abiding lack, Lane's campaign biography mutates into a sort of accounting ledger, a work of one-directional propaganda not unlike the hagiographies of Parson Weems and others that appear during the germination of America's political imaginary. Fading is the intangible shadow of Romance or realism that has haunted the democratic machinery; in its stead, Lane posits the clinical precision of an expert manager. In this sense, Lane's *Making* perhaps marks the terminus the genre of the campaign biography as a politically and aesthetically complex commentary upon America's democratic consciousness.

Nonetheless, contemporary readers can still benefit from re-reading Lane's campaign biography, because the text forecasts a condition that, especially between the years 1972 and 2016, has become all-too-familiar. Citizens during this era watch the "colonization of political reason by management reason" as "executive decision overrides public justification and critique" (Davies 121, 148). Proving the thesis of Lane's text, candidates today more frequently resemble corporate bosses, beholden to stockholders and relatively distanced from their democratic constituencies. Wendy Brown, who has offered some of the most trenchant analyses of this cultural shift, contends that the late twentieth-century elevates "management, law, and technocracy in place of democratic deliberation, contestation, and power sharing" (57). American politics, she insists, (d)evolves into a set of economic metrics as monied actors strip away the value of shared governance until society appears to be nothing more than a profit-driven organization. From Brown's perspective, Lane's sort of libertarian rationality ultimately results in a "profoundly antidemocratic political culture" (86).[14] Lane's campaign biography of Hoover anticipates these concerns with her frontier-manager amalgamation.

Yet the fictional and political frontier continues to linger in Lane's text because it cannot be fully contained. Despite the managerial drift of her text, the word democracy endures throughout Lane's campaign biography, as when Lane declares that Hoover maintains faith in democracy, "a belief in the intelligence and honors of humanity," and perceives himself to be "part of a big, democratic undertaking" (308, 105). Since the democratic candidate is always to some extent fictional, this conceptual figure invariably falls prey to the constitutive law of language: specifically, a candidate acts as an ever-slippery signifier, a map for arbitrary emplotment, and a generic invention that must be forever modified to suit the times. Even though Lane pushes to give "precedence to the science of experts over the passions of the multitude," and even though she reflects the intense wish of "the oligarch ... to govern without politics ... to banish the democratic supplement," the political supplement lurks always in wait (Rancière Hatred 75, 80–81). Lane's desire to transform Washington, D.C. from an "old political organization" to a "conglomeration of enormous economic machinery" fails to eradicate entirely the democratic openness that accompanies her symbolic renderings of the American frontier (Lane *Making*, 338). That is, Lane simply cannot suppress the thrills – for better or worse – of a world teetering eternally at the brink of uncertainty. Although the fantasy structure of *Making* implies that Lane is "all for the great complex of science and business and industry that grows in American freedom," Lane herself concedes that "human beings are living souls. Science is knowing, and life is unknowable ... infinitely various and variable" ("Don't" 115). The powerful engine of self-reinvention that runs throughout her prairie fiction injects the Hoover biography with a sense of beautiful and unsettling incompleteness that will not be readily extinguished by an economic calculus.

The impression of variability in commerce or finance can never be made synonymous with genuine variability, which requires no seed money to manifest – only conviction and a voice with which to speak. The experience on the prairie levels all men in a democratic fashion; it teases the revelation that anyone – even a poor, orphaned son of Quakers – can rise to help guide society. The interruptive egalitarianism of a democratic campaign cannot for long be paralyzed by the rigid confines of expertise or scientific managerialism because images of the candidate have historically been drawn by the likes of Lane from the volatility of fictional borderlands. No market algorithm could completely harness this volatility for an exclusionary purpose.[15] Due in part to literary interventions in the campaign biography, portraits of democratic candidacies remain mercifully open to aesthetic as well as political renewal.

Notes

1 Lane was not the only "literary" figure tapped for this purpose. Other writers included Herman Bernstein, a widely-read poet, playwright, novelist and translator, for Hoover's 1928 campaign, as well as Clement Wood, a poet and major contributor to pulp fiction of the period, for Hoover's 1932 campaign.
2 Brian Doherty writes that the "modern libertarian movement can convincingly be traced back to the work," in part, of Rose Wilder Lane. Throughout her life, she maintains a "voluminous correspondence" with libertarians of all ages (113, 131).
3 Lane is hardly the only writer of frontier fiction that contributes to the genre of the campaign biography. On behalf of William McKinley in 1901, Edward Ellis pens a glowing biography of the candidate. He is better known, however, for his frontier tales and, in particular, for the first science fiction dime novel – another story set on the frontier – *The Steam Man of the Prairies* (1868).
4 In his study of Abraham Lincoln's campaign biographies, Thomas A. Horrocks writes that, in these sorts of texts, candidates often "overcome modest or humble environments – many were born in log cabins or simple cottages – in which they were raised and achieved success as a result of hard work, innate ability, and dauntless ambition. In other words, they were self-made men" (42). The same can certainly be said of Hoover's biography.
5 For extended studies concerning the complex role of the frontier as a symbol in American popular culture, see seminal works such as Henry Nash Smith's *Virgin Land: The American West as Symbol and Myth* (Harvard University Press, 1950), Richard Slotkins' *Fatal Environment: The Myth of the Frontier in the Age of Industrialization, 1800–1890* (Atheneum, 1985), and Leo Marx's *The Machin in the Garden: Technology and the Pastoral Ideal in America* (Oxford University Press, 1964).
6 Indeed, Lane later disavows *Making* in similar terms: "I'm not particularly proud of it ... I think it is, really, a cheap bit of work" (qtd. in Holtz, 190). Of course, we might read this disavowal with a healthy degree of skepticism, as campaign biographers habitually distance themselves from the genre, seemingly in an attempt to retain their reputations as impartial artists.
7 Richard Hofstadter writes that the Homestead Act (1862) was, itself, not as "agrarian" as it may have seemed in popular culture; rather, it proved to be "a triumph for speculative and capitalistic forces, and it translated cheap or free land into a stimulus." In other words, by 1862, frontiersmen had already become "dependent upon the vicissitudes of the world market" (Hofstadter 55, 58).
8 See Gary Becker and cost-benefit analysis of human capital in, for example, Becker's *The Economic Approach to Human Behavior* (Chicago, IL: University of Chicago Press, 1976).
9 Lane names this course "the world-pioneering movement of America" (*Making* 355).
10 See Jerrold Hogle's "Introduction: the gothic in western culture," from *The Cambridge Companion to the Gothic*, ed. Jarrold Hogle (Cambridge: Cambridge University Press, 2002), pp. 1–21.
11 Richard Slotkin, in his discussion of the contrast between Frederick Turner and President Theodore Roosevelt, notes "a division of sentiment between nostalgia for the lost world of the frontier past, and an optimistic determination to see the progressive dynamic of the frontier carried forward into the new century." In turn, nostalgia and progress become "the twin motifs of the frontier myth" (609–610). Lane's synthesis of the frontier myth with the campaign biography produces a similar division of sentiment.
12 Lane writes, "The whole system needed thorough reorganization from top to bottom ... American methods, American enterprise and energy and standards of business honesty" (*Making* 257).
13 Lane's fiction similarly conveys this ambivalence. In *Free Land*, David's father acknowledges: "In one way everything always changed, and in another way, nothing

did" (6–7). Meanwhile, David must reconcile himself to the need for oxen – who are "no pleasure" to work with, and who stupidly drool – to coexist with his team of horses, colts that are spirited, free, and not easily yoked. The manager needs to encourage risk-taking "romps" as well as the burdensome but essential work done by oxen – in this case, the breaking of sod, a job that cannot be done by freedom alone.

14 I have written about neoliberal popular culture extensively, especially in my book *Mass-Market Fiction and the Crisis of American Liberalism, 1972–2017* (New York: Palgrave Macmillan, 2018).

15 Of course, this fact does not stop many forces from trying to do so. According to William Davies, in the neoliberal context "planning for the new represents an alternative – and paradoxical uncertainty, that is a further example of a market-based ethos that can be extended into non-market domains" (Davies 115). On this front, Lane's generic amalgamation of the frontier, the free market, and the campaign biography appears to be quite prescient of conditions in the early twenty-first century.

Works Cited

Beito, David, and Beito, Linda. "Isabel Paterson, Rose Wilder Lane, and Zora Neale Hurston on War, Race, the State, and Liberty." *Independent Review*, vol. 12, 2018, pp. 553–573.

Brown, Wendy. *In the Ruins of Neoliberalism: The Rise of Antidemocratic Politics in the West* (New York: Columbia University Press, 2019).

Campbell, Donna M. "Fictionalizing Jack London: Charmian London and Rose Wilder Lane as Biographers." *Studies in American Naturalism*, vol. 7, no. 2, 2012, pp. 176–192, www.jstor.org/stable/23431446. Accessed March 9, 2021.

Davies, William. *The Limits of Neoliberalism: Authority, Sovereignty and the Logic of Competition* (Newbury Park, CA: SAGE Publishing, 2017).

Doherty, Brian. *Radicals for Capitalism: A Freewheeling History of the Modern American Libertarian Movement* (New York: Public Affairs, 2007).

Hofstadter, Richard. *The Age of Reform* (New York: Vintage, 1960).

Holtz, William. *The Ghost in the Little House: A Life of Rose Wilder Lane* (Columbia, MO: University of Missouri Press, 1993).

Hoover, Herbert. *American Individualism* (Stanford, CA: Hoover Institution, 2016).

Horrocks, Thomas. *Lincoln's Campaign Biographies* (Carbondale, IL: Southern Illinois University Press, 2014).

Lane, Rose Wilder. *"Don't Tell: The Rediscovered Writings of Rose Wilder Lane*, ed. Amy Lauter (Columbia, MO: University of Missouri Press, 2007), pp. 113–117.

Lane, Rose Wilder. *Free Land* (Lincoln, NE: Bison Books, 1984).

Lane, Rose Wilder. "Innocence," *Harper's Magazine*, April 1922, pp. 577–584.

Lane, Rose Wilder. *Let the Hurricane Roar* (New York: Harper Trophy, 1985).

Lane, Rose Wilder. *The Making of Herbert Hoover* (Los Angeles, LA: HardPress, 2013).

Miller, John E. "Rose Wilder Lane and Thomas Hart Benton: A Turn toward History during the 1930s." *American Studies*, vol. 37, no. 2, 1996, pp. 83–101. JSTOR, www.jstor.org/stable/40642822. Accessed March 9, 2021.

Paul, Heike. *The Myths that Made America: An Introduction to American Studies* (London: Transcript Verlag, 2014).

Rancière, Jacques. *Disagreement: Politics and Philosophy*. Trans. Julie Rose (Minneapolis, MN: University of Minnesota Press, 2005).

Rancière, Jacques. *Hatred of Democracy*. Trans. Steve Corcoran (London: Verso, 2014).

Slotkin, Richard. "Nostalgia and Progress: Theodore Roosevelt's Myth of the Frontier." *American Quarterly*, vol. 33, no. 5, 1981, pp. 608–637, www.jstor.org/stable/2712805. Accessed March 9, 2021.

Woodside, Christine. *Libertarians on the Prairie: Laura Ingalls Wilder, Rose Wilder Lane, and the Making of the Little House Books* (New York: Arcade, 2016).

8
THE CAMPAIGN AUTOBIOGRAPHY

In the 1920s, the trend of commissioning popular or prestigious literary figures to compose campaign biographies begins to wane.[1] One might consider a number of plausible explanations for this shift, including evolving attitudes toward literature, changing electoral strategies, and realignments in the technological as well as media landscapes. Although certain aspects of the campaign biography endure in later adaptations, the overall contours of the campaign biography undergo a significant reappraisal. Perhaps most importantly, different stewards take charge of the campaign biography: instead of "men of letters," prominent journalists including Arthur Schlesinger, Jr. and T.H. White caretake the genre.[2] Eventually, by the dawn of the twenty-first century, the candidate seizes the reigns of his or her own narrative, often alongside ghost writers – an important point to which we will return. The "literariness" of the genre fades or, more to the point, it becomes easier to overlook the residual literary qualities of campaign materials. The purposes of this chapter are twofold: first, to survey the historical and political context of these post-1920s alterations, and second, to analyze the most recent iteration of the genre, what I will be calling the campaign autobiography. While the campaign autobiography extends some of the core issues surveyed throughout this book – including ongoing tensions within American realism – it also poses novel questions about the importance of literature within the field of American politics.

Let us start by briefly surveying a handful of campaigns near the *fin-de-siècle* to track major developments in electoral politics. In the 1880 election, General Winfield Hancock opts to stay silent during much of the campaign, while his opponent James Garfield renders himself more available by entertaining voters on his front porch. This front porch style of campaigning subsequently becomes hugely popular. The days of remaining aloof to avoid appearing too eager to

DOI: 10.4324/9781003132448-9

attain the office come to an end; candidates now increasingly appeal to the public directly. In 1888, Benjamin Harrison – the subject of Chapter Five – continues the trend, utilizing a more robust marketing strategy to cover up his less than affable demeanor, and thereby instigating a Cult of Personality that continues to characterize contemporary campaigns. At the *fin-de-siècle*, then, the ideal character is less frequently painted as an archetype, and ritualistic, predictable tropes from the campaign biography lose their luster. In place of the formulaic stories of old, new candidates look to increase their perceived accessibility. William Jennings Bryan famously takes his case to "the people" with what Gil Troy describes as "unprecedented directness" (105). Teddy Roosevelt, learning a good deal from Bryan, shatters what remains of the mold, using his spellbinding personality to bypass party leadership and attain greater power for himself. In short, by the 1920s most democratic candidates enact a crucial pivot from comforting-yet-distant archetype to greater personal appeal.

Early twentieth-century campaigns accentuate this shift. In 1908, for example, William Howard Taft and Bryan engage in a heated campaign – the first in which both seekers of the Presidency actively stump for their own cause. Soon afterward, voters in 1916 witness the rise of professional ad campaigns and more sophisticated sloganeering. Quite suddenly, the powerbrokers in a given campaign are trained in marketing, not backroom dealings at party headquarters. When we arrive at the campaigns of Calvin Coolidge and Herbert Hoover, the state of Presidential politics appears to be dramatically different from the days of Andrew Jackson and the first "literary" campaign biographies. For a multitude of reasons, voters no longer look to prominent "men of letters" to filter out noise and present the unvarnished character of the candidate; instead, campaigns must compete with new and exciting media for the spectator's attention, and the key to doing so effectively, or so many biographers seem to believe, is to pursue the Real behind the candidate – that is, to circumvent artistic middlemen and claim access to the "man himself" as well as the Truth that he purportedly represents. As this book has sought to demonstrate, the "realer-than-thou" propulsion of American letters explains a great deal about the transformation of the campaign biography. This propulsion clarifies how the campaign biography evolves into something else, something ever more Real, something that supposedly does not depend upon any literary artifice to accomplish its aim. In a word, the campaign autobiography intends to fulfill the promise of greater authenticity made by American realists during the late nineteenth and early twentieth centuries.

From a technological standpoint, the explicitly literary interventions in the campaign biography lose effectiveness as the media landscape transforms. The presence of the radio, for one, enables candidates to enter into a voter's living room, to offer her an unfiltered, magical connection without the endless train rides to targeted cities. Thanks to the radio, American politics looks – for a time – less staged and more genuine. Audience expectations concurrently change as fickle voters grow more readily exhausted by generic candidates. Indeed, for modern readers, the campaign biographies of William Dean Howells or Nathaniel Hawthorne, driven in part by a predictable formula, can feel painfully boring, since media savvy voters now possesses the option to listen instead to a baseball game or a dramatic production.[3] Suddenly the mass audience can be catered to by specialists within the ever-shrewder apparatus that Theodor Adorno and Max Horkheimer name the "culture industry." As early as 1896, candidate William McKinley's political manager, Mark Hanna, is asked if he is related to Herman Melville because Hanna's brother has the middle name "Melville." Unaware of, or indifferent to, the world of literary prestige, Hanna snaps, "What the hell kind of job does Melville want?" (Kazin 23). We have already seen inklings of this trend in the campaign biographies of Lew Wallace and Jacob Riis – with their proto-cinematic prose – as well as Rose Wilder Lane, with her increased sensationalism and deployment of tropes derived from other avenues of popular entertainment. Citizen-consumers learn to view the candidate for public office through a different, less overtly "literary" lens as the kinds of tension that make Howells's biography of Lincoln compelling – that is to say, the kinds of tension that may be said to characterize literature itself, a dynamic interplay of closed icons and iconoclastic innovation – are superseded by the arguably less intellectually engaging platforms of radio and film. We will return to the socio-political cost that accompanies this loss in "literariness."

Certainly, one should not too quickly dismiss the cultural value of the new media in American politics. Radio, after all, helps to dismantle the oppressive stranglehold of partisan newspapers and listeners gradually hear the world of the campaigner "not as embalmed text, but as living things" (Jamieson 24). Yet certain negative consequences do follow. No longer as dependent upon personal audience reactions, the campaign increasingly relies upon polling data, an obsession that carries over into the twenty-first century and turns politics into a numbers game for calculating politicos rather than a participatory activity for a democratic populace. Rather than tap a family friend with literary prestige to compose a spirited defense, engaging readers and forging a narrative that correlates a persona with a "people," by the 1920s the candidate must instead spend exorbitant sums to purchase air time across the nation. Money starts to play a significantly larger role in elections as media consultants trump political operatives. The "nobility" of the winning candidate – its status as a fixture, an emblem of national character – appears increasingly degraded by the relentless pressure to be popular. To be sure, the campaign biography has always wrestled with the issue of stasis. Previous chapters consider how representative texts are aware of their own myth-making function. In the realm of American literature, though, the question of stasis serves a vital purpose, as we have seen when some of the more interesting contributors to this genre explore the line between fixity and flux. Writers like Hawthorne and Howells seem, by temperament, unable to "turn off" nuance and serve as mere propagandists; forged in the fires of Romance and realism, they intuitively understand that American democracy, like its literature, is a restless sort of thing. In contrast, most electoral spectacles of the twentieth century lose sight of the critical function of "literariness" as they probe into private lives in pursuit of the white whale known as "greater access."

Following the 1920s, well-known journalists compile campaign biographies. While the journalistic variant does not discard wholesale the hobbyhorses of the genre explored in prior chapters, it rarely asks its reader to consider the role of fiction in the creation of a candidacy. The average journalist-biographer tends to embrace wholesale the "realer-than-thou" initiative: namely, a completely objective presentation of candidate – one that encompasses the Real of American life, which is to say, the essence of a "people" that can only be captured in words that are (im)possibly unflinching, honest, and transparent.[4] These biographies are still occasionally bound in book form, certainly, but they start to materialize more often as televised interviews, documentaries, and eventually, viral clips on social media. While an entire monograph could be dedicated to the journalistic intervention in the history of the campaign biography, I wish to close this book by racing a bit further ahead, to the present day and the genre's autobiographical turn.

Scholars of the autobiographical turn in late twentieth and early twenty-first century America view an increased obsession with autobiography as the dissolution of a Romantic sense of self that still attempts to retain some semblance of orderliness and control. In the postmodern age, due to a variety of economic, political, and cultural factors, subjects experience rampant fragmentation and their sense of self undergoes dramatic upheaval. To avoid this loss of coherence, critics conjecture, many readers look to the soothing balm of autobiography – a genre which generally upholds the illusion of a whole self, even as subjectivity mutates into data points and well-calibrated Internet avatars. Sidonie Smith and Julia Watson summarize the broader argument: "The disappearance of an unproblematic belief in the idea of true selves is everywhere compensated for and camouflaged by the multiplication of recitations of autobiographical stories" (7). In other words, ever more Real depictions of the candidate are partially informed by a growing desire to compensate for a widespread loss of belief in "true selves."[5] Howells himself praises autobiography for its ability to preserve what he would not outwardly recognize as a Romantic sense of self. Because of their frankness and their levelling effect, "all autobiographies are good," Howells remarks, "for one reason or another" ("Autobiography" 798). Increasingly couched in a confessional mode that claims to speak for itself, the autobiographical candidate provides a sense of stability despite an increasingly prevalent fear that the self is being supplanted by a simulation of subjectivity.

The "realer-than-thou" trend, as much a part of campaign biographies as it is constitutional of American realism, thus arrives, perhaps inevitably, at the campaign autobiography. The campaign autobiography ostensibly allows a candidate to speak with his or her own voice, uninterrupted by the interpretations of a third party. Philippe Lejeune distinguishes autobiography from fictional prose by describing an "autobiographical pact" in which readers comprehend the obligations and conventions of the genre, or "the conditions of the reading of the text" (*On Autobiography* 128). That is, readers of the campaign autobiography typically pick up these texts under the assumption that they present only "the facts." Notably, recent campaign autobiographies are not entirely without precedent; for instance, earlier candidates like Horace Greeley (1872) and Hoover (1931) attempt to tell their own narrative, followed in more recent years by Hubert Humphrey (1976). Yet the campaign autobiography undoubtedly reaches its high-water mark at the turn of the twenty-first century. Rather than entrust literary giants or popular writers to craft a portrait of the candidate, contemporary campaigns posit that readers prefer the illusion of hearing from the candidate him or herself.[6] Therefore, most of the prose generated by campaigns today remains autobiographical in nature – or, it is at least marketed as such. To conclude this study, I gesture at the latest iterations of a quintessentially American genre in order to understand better which elements from earlier campaign biographies endure and, of even greater relevance, what might happen if we overlook the continuously widening chasm between American literature and American politics.

Writing Self as Nation

Autobiography is one of America's foundational genres.[7] As Robert Sayre notes, "Autobiography may be the preeminent kind of American expression" (1). When we think of Henry David Thoreau's *Walden*, or Ralph Waldo Emerson's self-exploratory essays, or Benjamin Franklin's *The Autobiography of Benjamin Franklin*, or the poems of a multitudinous selfhood composed by Walt Whitman, we summon to mind a formative set of texts that cumulatively develop the unique premise of American individualism. But these works never perform a solely solipsistic function; rather, they connect the individual's narrative to the broader narrative of a nation.[8] "American autobiographers have generally connected their own lives to the national life or to national ideas," Sayre elaborates. The United States as an abstract entity offers an ideal for these autobiographers "to embody" (1, 11). In short, American autobiography historically encourages readers to link their private lives to the fulfillment of national ideals, thereby acting as a sort of bridge between self and community. By acknowledging an interplay between life writing and nation writing, we understand better the scope of the campaign autobiography, a subgenre that parallels the careful crafting of a candidate's personal story with the story that his or her candidacy wishes to construct for a select "people."[9]

Right away, we must acknowledge that the campaign autobiography, instead of radically departing from the campaign biography as it has been defined in the preceding chapters, maintains a number of its identifying tropes. For instance, the campaign autobiographer – like the campaign biographer – relies extensively upon letters, news clippings, speech excerpts, and interviews with supporters to round out his or her case, a tendency that highlights the form's preferred *heteroglossia*. Moreover, campaign autobiographies as well as campaign biographies construct a chronological, orderly image of the subject that is only occasionally interrupted by an acknowledgment of the complexities associated with personal memory or public perception. Finally, today's campaign autobiography, much like the campaign biography of old, tracks a dynamic process rather than resting upon a static portrait. That is, even as they claim to memorialize a transcendent figure, both iterations remain entrenched in the business of democracy – the negotiation of "a people" with its chosen representative – and so it cannot simply settle into a detached or aloof state of admiration (recalling the Federalist idolatry of Washington Irving explored in this book's first chapter). The relatively recent proliferation of campaign autobiographies therefore should not be mistaken for a radical departure, but viewed instead as an extension of many of the formal qualities that germinate in the genre from which they were derived.

Yet the campaign autobiography also augments the template of the campaign biography. It aims to dig even deeper, into what Paul John Eakin classifies as the "corporeal substratum of identity" (*How* 67). Although various campaign autobiographers remain understandably anchored to "larger-than-life neo-Byronic posturing" – the lifeblood of self-promotion, which remains the paramount pillar of any campaign for public office – they must, given the democratic underpinnings of the exercise, engage with previously sanctioned boundaries between self and community. In other words, because a candidate must be intimately connected to the electorate, her story of necessity poses as an autobiography of an entire "people." Eakin posits that American autobiography reveals "assumptions about the way in which boundaries between 'I' and 'we', between self and other, are customarily drawn" (74). Perhaps no critic examines this interaction in greater detail than Albert E. Stone, who describes autobiography as being fundamentally relational, which is to say, designed to connect "a self to the 'extensive totality' of the world … (a) thick web of text and context" (5). Unpacking the dialectical underpinnings of the genre, Stone views autobiography as "transforming an individual story into cultural narrative … (forming) bridges between public life and private experience" (16). Although contemporary discourse conditions subjects to segregate a false public image from a Real private being, the distinction proves an illusory one: "Jeremiads against inauthenticity rest on the faulty assumption that images are distinct from reality. They aren't … they emerge from a dialectical or collaborative process between politicians and their audiences" (Greenberg xxiv). Even as contemporary readers are conditioned to conceptualize the autobiography as a display of "the self's uniqueness, privacy, and interiority," the genre remains always-already tied up in relationships between the subject of the autobiography and the world around her. The campaign autobiography heightens this sense that the life writing of a given candidate provides an interface between the self and its culture, a coalescence of "representative" and "stubbornly singular" stories (Stone 18). In pursuit of a candidate's narrative stripped of literary artifice and embellishment, readers of the campaign autobiography seek the Real at the center of their own lives as well: the yet-unspoken core of who they are as a "people," unearthed from private confessions. The campaign autobiography, then, reveals the extent to which autobiographical selves always orbit around collective selves, forming a rich and complex constellation.

To examine this extension of the "realer-than-thou" phenomenon in concrete detail, let us begin with the 1987 campaign autobiography of George H.W. Bush, *Looking Forward*. This campaign autobiography reflects an evolving conservatism in American politics through the lens of a singular man. Specifically, the story of Bush Sr. revolves around a delicate, and paradoxical, balance between bureaucratic safekeeping and a greater appetite for risk-taking (see once more Rose Wilder Lane's campaign biography for Herbert Hoover, analyzed in the previous chapter). One can partially explain this balancing act by attending to the distinctive circumstances surrounding the campaign in question: one of Bush Sr.'s greatest strengths in the public eye – his nonpartisan posture; his managerial gravitas as business owner, U.N. ambassador, and head of the Central Intelligence Agency – doubles as one of his perceived weaknesses, because many critics of Bush Sr. paint him as boring and tepid. And so the candidate, alongside his cadre of advisors, revises his image to bolster his credibility as a no-nonsense leader and, at the same time, stress his own aptitude for risk-taking. This precarious equilibrium reflects a conservatism that must maintain its tried-and-true traditionalist ethos – "family values"; existing social hierarchies – while embracing a more volatile economic outlook: the shift into financialization and Reaganomics that remains the legacy of the 1980, the decade in which Bush Sr. initially ascends into prominence. *Looking Forward* thus presents the personal struggles of an individual in order to appeal to the needs of potential voters as well as to envision the political possibilities to come – an abstraction that Bush Sr. memorably describes as "the new world order."

The ambivalence of *Looking Forward* underlines a particular personal and political outlook. Autobiographically, Bush Sr. opts to go into business for himself instead of becoming a Rhodes scholar because he has a "family to support" and he does not want to seek financial help from others (43). Time and time again, the autobiographical candidate emphasizes the importance of self-discipline and dispassionate rationality, as when he recalls being gunned down during the Pacific War in order to stress how "tedious hours of emergency training paid off" (37). Concurrently, though, Bush Sr. includes the Pacific War story because it demonstrates his fitness for office, and it establishes that he can handle high levels of stress. He recalls moving to Texas. "I didn't want to do anything pat and predictable" after graduating from Yale, he notes; he prefers something challenging, "outside the established mold" (22). To offset his bureaucratic sensibilities, Bush Sr. relies heavily upon the frontier imagery of Texas: "Whatever we wanted, we'd have to earn … we wanted to make our own way, our own mistakes, and shape our future" (23). From high-flying quests on his grandfather's lobster boat to his diplomatic time in Beijing – in another interesting historical parallel, Hoover too spends formative years in China – Bush Sr. depicts himself in pursuit of "a challenge, a journey into the unknown" (128). Through his countless adventures, Bush Sr. presents himself to his audience as a risk-taker with the capacity to stay even-keeled in the face of possible danger. For a nation living through the halcyon days of globalization, Bush Sr. positions himself as a representative of the very best of American conservatism: a strong manager with a corporatist mindset, willing to take financial risks in far-flung corners of the globe without sacrificing the deathless values of middle America – namely, vigilant maintenance of the status quo.[10] The life writing of Bush Sr. doubles as the life writing of a nation both "on the move" and intent on standing still.

Perhaps unsurprisingly, the campaign autobiography of Bush Sr.'s son, *A Charge to Keep* (1999), follows a similar template. Bush Jr., after all, serves on his father's campaign in 1992, and so he cultivates his own political voice within that distinctive world. Each text recycles personal family stories to frame a larger national narrative. In *Looking Forward*, Bush Sr. exploits his daughter Dorothy's baptism in China as an event that parallels the uneven road of globalization, right down to a "militant atheist interpreter" that resists involvement in the family's "special moment" (142). Bush Sr.'s campaign autobiography highlights the overlap between a deeply personal anecdote and the ideological narrative that a nation tells itself: "In a low-key, informal way, we'd made progress breaking down some of the barriers" (153). In *A Charge to Keep*, Bush Jr. evokes similar frontier imagery to affirm that his adventures too are the stories of an imperial country in the process of outgrowing its borders: "Tumble weeds blew into our yard. Once it rained and frogs came our everywhere, like the biblical plague, covering the fields and front porches" (16). If anything, Bush heightens his father's Texas persona by attempting, at once, to sustain his father's healthy degree of risk-taking ("I've never plotted the various steps of my life") while, at the same time, carving out his identity as his own man. Even as Bush Jr. must navigate the precarious line between adventurer and manager, just like his father, he must also distinguish himself as a candidate, especially given the political reality that Bush Sr. was a one-term President and not an obvious success story in the political arena. To accomplish this feat, whereas Bush Sr. never fully abandons his roots in white-collar New England, Bush Jr. infamously generates greater distance from the exclusively corporate arena: "I wanted to show off for my eastern professors," he laughs at himself. "So much for trying to sound smart" (20). A campaign operative informs Bush Jr. that his father "got to Texas a little late" and Bush Jr. does not disagree (182). In turn, while *Looking Forward* reads as a fairly nuanced balancing act between traditional conservatism and the nascent demands of rampant globalization, *A Charge to Keep* reads as much more doctrinal, filled with platitudes and black-and-white prescriptions meant to alleviate exaggerated social ills. Nonetheless, Bush Jr. still utilizes his family history to narrate his version of the nation's story. In fact, the two tales are so entwined that they ultimately become difficult to tell apart:

I had been there then, too, the son of the candidate, and now I was in the same place more than thirty years later as Governor, my own daughters at my side. It was a sentimental moment, *weaving a thread of politics and history through the Bush family*. (170, emphasis mine)

The text goads the reader into sentimentality by filtering American history and politics through the personal trials and tribulations of the Bush clan.

Bush Sr. and Jr. employ a love of sport to encapsulate American cultural beliefs in a way that presumably speaks to "the people." Bush Sr. recounts his time as a baseball player for Yale to emphasize the message that both he and his nation had to be willing to accept more risk, usually of the financial sort: "I'd been so wound up in batting techniques," he admits. He decides to "put more practice into attacking the ball" (43). *A Charge to Keep* adopts and then doubles down upon the baseball metaphor. Recalling his time as part owner of the Texas Rangers, Bush Jr. exhausts his reservoir of baseball yarns to tell the tale of his own candidacy as well as his imagined future for the United States: "I'm a traditionalist when it comes to our national sport … reverence and respect for its history and traditions" (207). Put a bit differently, Bush Jr.'s campaign autobiography entangles the threads of the candidate's personal life with his professional life as well as the political movement that he hopes to inspire. "Baseball is a pursuit for optimists, just like drilling for oil or running for office … you have to believe you can win." He later adds: "Baseball was a great training ground for politics … you have to attract customers … and you have to keep the, with you and bring them back" (207). When read carefully, this amalgamation of mixed metaphors suggests a confusion in American life between democracy and the world of business, one that can be dated back to Lane's campaign biography for Hoover. What is the difference, if any exists, between elected officials and corporate leaders? "A Governor is a chief executive officer," Bush Jr. observes (118). By blending the candidate's relationship with business and sports, *A Charge to Keep* reveals a prominent sensibility in American politics: being an American means participating in a grand competition, and decisions should be made by competent managers rather than a democratic electorate. Government appointments are like a "start-up business"; the way to run a government is obvious: "I believe in results … wins or losses are right there in black and white" (101, 70). Politics, business, and sports bleed together as Bush Jr.'s private proclivities sustain a cultural shift into corporate governance.

Although he offers a different vision of self and community, Barack Obama's *The Audacity of Hope: Thoughts on Reclaiming the American Dream* (2006) continues to build upon the trend of conflating self-discovery with a revised national identity. Arguably, Obama's book blurs self-actualization with an abstract search for rapidly fading "American values" to an even greater extent than the Bush examples. *Audacity* presents an individual wrestling with himself in tandem with a narrative about what the country wishes to become next. The narrator confesses a desire to "ponder positions" more deeply and "to reflect on the meaning of America, the meaning of citizenship, and my sometimes conflicted feelings" (120, 261). Obama's introspective self conducts an intimate inquiry into his own story and its parallels with America's story, thereby tapping into the imaginary essence of himself as well as his culture at the very same moment. To amalgamate his life writing with the nation's life writing, he cites the rift between Jefferson's republicans and Hamilton's Federalists as proof that he, like the rest of us, has "always been in a constant balancing act" (193). Unlike the two Bush examples, *Audacity* probes a good deal more into internal tensions and uncertainties. Obama depicts himself re-reading the Constitution ahead of an important meaning; he later visits Iraq on an evidence-gathering mission because he reportedly feels compelled to understand these issues better before governing on the matter: "I find myself poring over the evidence, pro and con, as best I can" (129). His life writing seemingly leaves no aspect of his own narrative unplumbed and, in turn, his campaign autobiography follows Obama as well as his reader through an active process of self-affirmation. "I am answerable mainly to the steady gaze of my own conscience," Obama insists. He acknowledges his "painful process of trial and error, a series of difficult choices" (134, 150). This emphasis upon personal identity formation is no less indicative of social and political trends than the Bush autobiographies; specifically, Obama's text supplements a cultural shift into enhanced identity politics, self-entrepreneurship, and the concomitant "memoir craze" of the late twentieth and early twenty-first centuries. It remains important for us to underscore that *Audacity* is, in the final tally, no more introspective or "honest" than the Bush tracts. Quite the opposite: Obama's campaign autobiography simply sells the intrinsic value of self-analysis over the more strictly autocratic impulses of the Bush texts, which remain committed, in varying degrees, to a hyper-hierarchical outlook. Neither approach could be described as truly counter-hegemonic.

Audacity argues that the closer readers get to the "core" of Obama as a person, the closer they get to the Real of American life – that is, to the kernel of an ever-elusive "American Spirit" that eternally resists permanent symbolization. Obama writes: "In me, one of those flaws had proven to be a chronic restlessness ... endemic, too, in the American character" (2–3). With its rapaciously internal gaze, Obama's campaign autobiography models the ideal neoliberal subject: an individual that must constantly re-assess himself, therapeutically, without settling on a firm set of absolute convictions. Subjects in the early twenty-first century increasingly view themselves as transactional sites. The subject constructs and dismantles itself, most regularly in the digital sphere, according to the demands of specific situations.[11] As such, *Audacity* channels iconoclastic energy into an auto-deconstruction of selfhood. The story of Obama's unending reinvention of himself as a man and a candidate purportedly mirrors the American democratic experiment which proves, in truth, to be an economic experiment. We will return to this self-abdication in the final section of the chapter; for now, it may suffice to say that Obama's text upholds dominant social guidelines drafted at the turn of the century, once more drawing significant correlations between life writing and nation writing. By its close, *Audacity* does not suggest a genuinely novel mode of reinvention; instead, it enforces the imposed need in the neoliberal period for a "pragmatic, nonideological attitude" that conjures once more a sense of imaginary consensus. "How much we share: common hopes, common dreams, a bond that will not break" (34, 25). That is, like the Bushes before him, Obama returns to a fictional bedrock of American society, summoned in a fantastic yet palpable form: "A rising, Shakespearean rhythm – the clockwork design of the Constitution and the Senate … almost a specter, the spirit of Senates past" (74). Just as Obama comes to understand himself not as a construction or a famous façade, but as Real self that remains constantly under revision, his reader is meant to find in the crux of his personhood a shared sensibility, one that reflects the dominant ideological features of early twenty-first century America. The restless narrative of Obama's rise as a self-declared man of mixed races, who remains rooted to a plurality of places, purportedly echoes the restlessness of the "American Dream" itself. Obscuring the role of the external biographer in meticulously mediating this bond for readers, *Audacity* may at times feel more Real than the campaign biographies considered in previous chapters. However, precisely because of its apparent transparency, this illusion requires even more careful analysis.

To expand our understanding of this illusion of synthesis between a candidate's personal journey and the national narrative, let us consider Hillary Clinton's 2014 campaign autobiography, *Hard Choices*. Rather than delve immediately into the prose, we ought to begin with what literary critic Gérard Genette describes as the "paratextual" elements, which are not typically given much attention: the cover, preface material, the famous endorsements, and so forth. The cover and spine of *Hard Choices* include a reproduction of Clinton's actual signature – a visual cue intended to elicit stronger belief in the authenticity of the account as well as the candidate herself.[12] Moreover, Clinton's campaign autobiography includes a number of colorful, glossy pictures from her travels around the globe to simulate a tourist's slideshow upon her return from far-flung travels. Earlier chapters contemplate an increasingly pictorial focus in campaign biographies through the contributions of Lew Wallace and Jacob Riis, respectively. This pictorial emphasis secures a greater sense of transparency, unlike the perceived manipulation that accompanies the written word. Clinton's book similarly opens, for reasons that are never made explicit, with a map of the world. Readers might reasonably surmise that Clinton yearns to be associated, thanks to her stint as Secretary of State from 2008 to 2012, with the role of America on a global stage. Indeed, her preface describes the stint as "a personal journey … visiting 112 countries and travelling nearly a million miles," a statistic that she repeats several times over the course of the book (xiii). The opening pages display praise for *Hard Choices* – a not uncommon practice for publishers, certainly, but this time the praise comes not from a domestic audience, but "From Around the World." In no uncertain terms, Clinton posits a correlation between her "personal journey" and America's significant investment in the tenets of globalization. A final paratextual element of Clinton's campaign autobiography reveals the degree to which Clinton hybridizes her private narrative with the narrative of the American people during the age of globalization: the title of the book was supposedly decided upon not by Clinton, but by readers of the *Washington Post*. The book therefore opens with a seemingly democratic gesture – the story of her life symbolically belongs to the entire nation, or, more accurately, to the entire globe.

Hard Choices depicts the act of travelling not as a mere part of the narrative, but as an end-in-itself. Clinton adorns her petition for greater global connectivity with exotica and impressive tales of her personal bonds with other cultures. For example, Clinton recalls meeting the Empress of Japan: "We greeted each other with a smile and a hug. Then she welcomed me into her private quarters. The emperor joined us for tea and a conversation" (45). Later, she remembers how she once shared breakfast with de Klerk and lunch with Mandela on the day that "the entire history" of South Africa changed (248). She then regales the reader with accounts of a "lavish lunch" with the Sultan of Oman, against the backdrop of the Royal Oman Symphony Orchestra (347). It nearly goes without saying that these luxurious tales do not serve to make Clinton any more relatable to the average reader; instead, they bolster the desired impression that Clinton's life writing cannot be extricated from the ballyhooed plot of America's engagement with the rest of the world. Put differently, Clinton's global memories are entangled with the thrills of globalization experienced – or at least, fantasized about – by America's reading public.

Like the Bushes and Obama, Clinton dwells upon lines of continuity that run between her family history and the history of the United States. She waxes poetic on the pleasures of being a mother and a grandmother, and she marks the "progress" of her consanguinity alongside the "progress" of nations under the "familial" guidance of America. For every reference to her pride in her daughter, Clinton includes a reference to her maternal pride in the development of other countries: "We marveled at how far the country had come" (221). In *Hard Choices*, her trips as Secretary of State double as trips down memory lane, as Clinton underscores her personal growth through a parallel discussion of globalization's apparent successes. For instance, she associates her own transfer of power to John Kerry, her successor as Secretary of State, with Hamid Karzai's impending transfer of power in Afghanistan as well as George Washington's "selfless" abdication of the Presidency (156). Like a nesting doll, her personal journey reveals layers upon layers of international influence, as the text leap through space and time to craft a purportedly universal narrative. Her epilogue makes this case quite clear: "Charlotte's birth seemed to strike a chord with a lot of Americans ... *the true miracle here is universal*" (493, emphasis mine). In a word, Clinton's campaign autobiography renders abstract ideals like globalization quite intimate by revealing private moments through which bulky geopolitical ideals can conceivably refract. She deftly weaves her daughter's wedding into a narrative about the Trans-Pacific Partnership in a fashion that forges not-so-subtle connections between "the elaborate diplomacy" of wedding planning and the promise of the TPP: unity, progress, development. The reader cannot quite decide if Clinton refers to the wedding or the TPP when she summates: "This, I thought, is why Bill and I had worked for so many years to help build a better world" (73). *Hard Choices* effectively abolishes any lingering division between the personal and the political. This text – along with the works considered above – demonstrates how campaign autobiographies provide national narratives with a convenient, easy-to-understand set of individualized reference points. *Hard Choices* tracks a first-person "I" engaged in the never-ending search for a third-person "we."

In interesting ways, then, the campaign autobiography allows us to rethink Mikhail Bakhtin's account of classical autobiography. According to Bakhtin, the loosely defined art of autobiography begins in ancient Greece not as a "literary" exercise, composed from a place of aloofness, but as a form of writing that "was first laid bare and shaped in the public square" (131). Constructed within the commons, classical autobiographies highlight an intimate relationship between the individual and her community. On the one hand, today's campaign autobiographies speak to a swelling insularity as well as a fundamental disconnect between the subject and her surroundings; and yet, on the other hand, something lingers in the campaign autobiography, indeed, throughout many variations of the campaign biography: a dialectic between the singular subject and an (im)possible notion of public wholeness. In this way, the genre retains a residue of a characteristic first brought to light in the Greek *demos*. For all of the apparent novelty of campaign autobiographies in the twenty-first century, a central aspect of the genre carries over from ancient archetypes.

The Political Biography

Perhaps the most interesting aspect of the campaign autobiography remains its internal unrest, since this turmoil reflects a long-standing tradition in campaign biographies of all stripes. The campaign biography as well as autobiography are always, in the final tally, a story of becoming rather than being, which is to say, they tell the story of a national selfhood under construction, in pursuit of the Real, and enduring countless visions and revisions. Most campaign autobiographies are not simply about consensus or continuity; they grapple, however unconsciously, with gaps in knowledge and so reveal, beneath their ostensible desire to promote a coherent self, a drive to dissolution. Lejeune realizes, "Telling the truth about the self, constituting the self as complete subject – it is a fantasy" (*On Autobiography* 131). While the campaign autobiography sustains the "realer-than-thou" ethos described in the preceding chapters, it also sustains a living character: a restlessness that simultaneously fuels democratic open-endedness. Once more, campaign biographies and autobiographies stand out as uniquely democratic texts.

Outsider in the White House, the campaign autobiography of Bernie Sanders, retooled for his 2016 campaign for President, departs from a number of the expectations surveyed in the previous section. Sanders spends precious little time presenting a descriptive portrait of himself; readers only receive snippets, as when he describes how he kept a bathing suit in his car during his early campaigning days in Vermont, or when he remarks of an official meal he had in Congress, "in case you're interested, the food was terrific" (115). But these insider snippets are rare, and Sanders seems more keen to downplay the importance of his personal presence in his own campaign narrative. To qualify an anecdote with "in case you're interested" suggests that even Sanders doubts the relevance of the private details that he appears compelled by convention to include. By temperament and, of course, design, he appears to care much more about detailing a political movement. Although his infrequent private moments confirm that in recent campaign autobiographies "petty details of private life (still) begin to take on an importance," the Sanders text sustains that ancient democratic practice of giving shape to the individual in dialogue with the public (Bakhtin 144). To convey this public character, *Outsider* focuses almost exclusively upon the nuts and bolts of political campaigns. Undoubtedly, Sanders does not abandon claims of authenticity; after all, as a politician in the populist mold, he depends upon a distinction between "down-to-earth people" and the "corrupt establishment," and so he routinely wishes he could stop being "so political" in favor of what he presents as common-sense solutions (62). Nevertheless, the generally impersonal tone of *Outsider* stresses a fundamental aspect of the campaign autobiography: even as it chronicles the intention to declare an authoritative "I," one that unifies an individual story with his or her communal story, it must remain open to renegotiation, because neither the winning candidate nor the individual self can ever achieve permanent stasis. Paul de Man writes:

> The interest of autobiography, then, is not that it reveals reliable self-knowledge – it does not – but that it demonstrates in a striking way the impossibility of closure and of totalization (that is the impossibility of coming into being) of all textual systems. (922)

According to Sanders, his book should be cataloged as "a political biography" (4). This term proves highly useful in untangling the art of autobiography from the art of campaigning. A "political biography" is, by definition, a life writing of the political. Yet how does a subject record, or even begin to articulate, the life of "the political"? Since the concept of the political constitutes an inexhaustible recalibration of the social order, that is, the unending realignment of groups with shared interests as well as the endless selection of different representatives, we cannot enclose the life of the political by endowing it with a rigid form, a coherent "life." To be political is to recognize that social arrangements, like life itself, can always be changed, and as long as a given arrangement cannot please every citizen – and such a utopia remains [im]possible, given the variegated desires expressed by members of any populace – the promise of the political forever returns to unsettle the status quo. Since it appears as though the life writing of Sanders cannot be extricated from the life writing of the political (specifically, his campaign), his "political biography" reveals the deconstructive vitality of the genre. Neither his private life nor the public life that he attempts to articulate can achieve consensus or a sense of unbroken continuity. "Somebody else will always want my job," Sanders comments. "That's democracy. Okay" (43). The only intimate glance of Sanders that the reader receives is a portrait of a harried candidate that may never be satisfied: "We'd better get moving," he tells his readers on several occasions (178). The restlessness of the political unceasingly drives his narrative: "A major political struggle ... everything was partisan. Nothing came easy ... The struggle never ends. If it's not one fight, it's another" (78, 152). Although Sanders clearly admires the dynamism of a political process that writes itself – for Sanders, the crowds are "a beautiful sight" – he remains hyper-aware that democracy is a "fragile" thing (264, 287). In turn, his campaign autobiography, or political biography, underscores how the concept of the political is given life through writing, but it remains a very precarious kind of writing. It hints at a Real that resists symbolization, a formlessness that achieves only periodic, and illusory, moments of stability. The democratic campaign and the genre of the autobiography both convey in related ways how democracy is driven by dissatisfaction instead of the attainment of an (im)possible end.

Eakin tarries around this unsettled line between the restless self and the futility of its articulation:

> We are always out of sync with our selves, always lagging behind, always trying to catch up ... but self, of course, which we take to be experiential fact, is also finally a fiction, an elusive creature that we construct even as we seek to encounter it. (*Living* 125)[13]

Eakin describes the autobiography as a relentless process, never a final product; unlike memoir, autobiography discovers the self "in the making," not through retrospection. Autobiography choreographs the "mapping of our living in (real) time," which is to say, because it differs from the objective commemoration at work in biography, autobiography tracks a self that evolves always in dialogue with its context (170). It makes sense that a campaign might gravitate toward the autobiography, then, due to the fact that both entities are not impartial, detached, or empirical – rather, they involve writing out a life that must resonate with others, imminently. Since autobiography charts an individual's voice as it seeks the pitch and frequency of a larger community, it suits contemporary political campaigns quite nicely. However, the intrinsic slipperiness of this process remains vital to its function in American society. William Epstein calls the reader's expectations, when approaching an autobiography, "biographical recognition." He goes on,

> Biographical recognition would seem to encourage (more or less self-consciously) a relatively naïve collaboration with the 'natural' that locates it outside (or to the side) of contemporary theoretical discourse and maintains it as one of the last strongholds of empirical knowledge. (38)

Although we tend to treat biography as "monumental or inflexible," Epstein points out, "biographical recognition is always biographical (mis)recognition" (84). In other words, readers ignore at their own peril the intrusive role of the biographer, and the role of biography as an art form, as artifice, as text. Previous chapters demonstrate how biography's rather imprecise transposition of a nondiscursive figure into discourse – especially a candidate for public office – exudes "fullness and emptiness," all at once (84). The winning candidate supposedly embodies the Real, the essence of a "people," and yet the candidate also relies upon language, upon (im)perfect words that can never fully capture things-in-themselves. As biography slips into autobiography in an ever more heated chase to attain the Real, readers risk losing sight of the literariness behind this move, convinced once again that the candidate on display is "a cold, hard, silent thing ... (that simply) exists" (46). In effect, readers risk falling into the trap of a presumed "naturalness" and "authenticity": this is not the story *of* Barack Obama, it is a story *by* Barack Obama. Here is a story told without barriers: "The economy of symbolic exchange through which we (mis)recognize the biographical subject will then shift, artlessly and craftily" (89). The fetishized biographical object erodes, replaced by the increasingly fluid autobiographical subject. And so on, ad infinitum, under dialectical propulsion, as the modern self tries in vain to recover its Romantic qualities. Epstein's discussion of this slippage remains invaluable for any consideration of the campaign autobiography because it reminds us of what remains eternally in process, eternally becoming: self, "people," candidate – always in conversation.

In actuality, the campaign autobiography is never the simple story of a single subject, "told from the heart"; in contrast, a conglomerate of stakeholders compose the campaign biography. Consider, for instance, the hidden presence of the ghost writer. Ghost writers assist the candidate in gathering materials and formalizing his or her life writing. At the same time, a campaign involves countless "invisible" voices behind the scenes, from donors to volunteers, and so to treat the campaign autobiography as direct access to the "soul" of the candidate remains utterly fallacious. Georges Gusdorf insists, "(The autobiography) is unquestionably a document about a life ... but it is also a work of art ... (the autobiographer) realizes himself in the unreal" (43). The campaign autobiography exacerbates a tension inherent to all autobiographies: in its thirst for the Real, it falls short; condemned to artifice, it returns invariably to what is unreal – that is, to the calculated efforts of an authorial entity that remains of necessity alienated from itself through its engagement with the symbolic order. The kernel of a pre-discursive Hillary Clinton recedes, eternally just out of reach, as the demands of the campaign, the voting public, and language itself compel the subject-in-herself into the background. By invariably turning the candidate into a missing object, the campaign autobiography does not foster consensus. Instead, it catalyzes the very desires needed for a representative democracy to function.

Because the campaign autobiography cannot avoid revealing, at some level, the gap between the subject and its articulation, it unconsciously allows readers to glimpse the degree of internal restlessness required by American politics. No portrait of a candidate, regardless of his charisma, can lay claim to the Real of a particular community, comprised, as it is, of individuals with variegated longings. Gusdorf argues, "Autobiography is therefore never the finished image of the fixing forever of an individual life: the human being is always a making, a doing" (47). This emphasis upon "becoming" marks the campaign autobiography as an invitation to difference – an openness which remains fundamental to any democratic order as well as any democratic consciousness. "The self is (like the autobiography that records and creates it) open-ended and incomplete," James Olney contends. "It is always in process or, more precisely, is itself a process" (25). Perhaps, then, we ought to read campaign autobiographies not only as delusions of wholeness, as illusory syntheses of self, candidate, and "people, which they of course are, but also as disjointed and (im)perfect placeholders that reflect a community in pursuit of a Real that it could never hope to contain yet remains condemned to pursue.[14] By reading the campaign autobiography in this way, we reaffirm the thesis of this book: the campaign biography – even in its later iterations, including the campaign autobiography – is an acutely political document. It offers a life writing infused with democratic sensibilities: "political biography," in the strictest sense of the term.

All that remains for us to do, then, is to locate evidence of a vital gap between the Real and artifice in specific campaign autobiographies. In *Looking Forward*, instead of exclusively stressing continuities that the text creates between candidate and electorate, we might consider the lack of such futile integration. In the middle of a straightforward narrative concerning Bush Sr.'s time as an ambassador at the U.N., Bush Sr. interjects an aside of great consequence: the death of his father. However, the text does not attempt to smooth out the transition or to capitalize upon the looming absence of the father for political meaning-making. The personal and the political do not seamlessly merge; there exists a lingering refusal of resolution. *Looking Forward* unwittingly exposes a schism between the Real – in this case, the presumably traumatic loss of a loved one – and strict obedience to campaign conventions. Later, Bush Sr.'s campaign autobiography ends with an atypical interview between the candidate and himself. As the candidate puts it, he has long "speculated how I would have raised ... questions if I were a reporter" (247). This unusual, self-enclosed bifurcation, in which Bush Sr. serves as candidate as well as candidate's biographer, reveals the awkward machinations of the genre. That is to say, as Bush Sr. schizophrenically separates his self-reflective narrator from the subject under scrutiny (himself), he acts as both object and subject.[15] For certain circles of literary critics, this tension within the autobiography is marked by with a visual cue – the slash in the term auto/biography – in order to express an inherent friction between self and self-as-biographer. In its solipsistic question-and-answer session, *Looking Ahead* watches the unfolding of a subject in dialogue with itself – an unfolding that resembles a dog in pursuit of its own tail.

Or, we might consider similarly disjointed moments from Bush Jr.'s *A Charge to Keep*, in which the candidate exposes the fictive nature of his own candidacy. For one, as we have already seen, the text relies heavily upon intertextuality with his father's *Looking Forward*. By recycling a number of well-known anecdotes from the first Bush campaign autobiography, *A Charge to Keep* stresses inheritance, a textual consanguinity. This overlap suggests something "unnatural," something constructed. These are not genuine, unfiltered memories, bubbling to the surface of an individual's mind, but artificial memories, written down in another text, for a calculated effect on the collective consciousness. So-called private memories provide mere fodder, grist for the mill of a campaign, and so they are both private as well as public, at the very same time. Said another way, the illusion of "naturalness" runs up against the unnaturalness of generic convention. Furthermore, Bush Jr.'s campaign autobiography highlights the tension of the auto/biography with a strange moment of confession in which the candidate acknowledges the unreal qualities of his own life writing. He critiques the national media for its "worship at the altar of public confession, demanding that candidates tell all … some parents of my generation make the mistake of telling their children too much … (I will) purge the system of its relentless quest for scandal and sensation" (134). Foreshadowing the widely criticized secrecy of the candidate's forthcoming administration, *A Charge to Keep* admits that it is not actually in pursuit of the Real; it wishes instead to preserve an unexposed kernel of Truth that evades the public eye – that which remains unsaid at the "altar of public confession." Whether openly acknowledged or not, the campaign autobiography tarries with an imagined essence, personal as well as political, that it refuses to utter. The genre is built not upon ultimate satisfaction for the reader/voter, then, but upon an ever-receding horizon that it must pursue yet never reach. This futile pursuit reveals much more about the longings of the body politic than it does about flesh-and-blood members of the Bush clan.

Or, let us consider the disjointed moments in Obama's *The Audacity of Hope*, in which the candidate expresses suspicion of his own fictive presentation. "I am a prisoner of my own biography," he laments. Due in part to his experiences as a black man in the United States, the object-subject of this auto/biography admits to feeling a degree of separation from the "American experience." This alienated existence compels the text to interrogate its own conventions: "The telling of the story is too neat, I know" (9, 36). These moments of estrangement illuminate the constructedness of Obama's life writing as well as the life writing of American politics. Charlotte Linde writes of autobiographical form:

> A distinction (remains) between the narrator and the protagonist … the narrator can observe, reflect, adjust the amount of distance, and correct the self that is being created. The very act of narrating creates the occasion for self-regard and editing. (105)

The campaign autobiography therefore depends upon a constant renegotiation that remains predicated on necessary failure. Obama frequently lifts the curtain to show his reader a constitutional friction: "How long before the committee of scribes and editors and censors took residence in your own head … how long before you started sounding like a politician?" (123). He remarks, "I often wonder what makes it so difficult for politicians to talk about values in ways that don't appear calculated or phony … scripted … standardized … harder for the public to distinguish between honest sentiment and political stagecraft" (64). Here again we return to the "intimate theme" of Obama's campaign autobiography: a split between the Real Obama and Obama as the calculating biographer of his own candidacy – the internal editor or censor that resides in his own head; the political biographer and the apolitical self, wrapped into one authorial entity. As readers witness a man hunting down his own Truth, they engage in a process not of unblemished being, the function of basic hagiography, but of becoming (interestingly enough, the title of Michelle Obama's 2018 autobiography). And the (im)possibility of this exercise resolving itself, of readers arriving at some pre-discursive Obama, separated from the artifice of fastidious campaign management, evokes a uniquely political undercurrent. Readers caught up in the narrative of a campaign are trained to run tirelessly after the supposedly fixed essence of "who they are," which is to say, the point at which they intersect with the confessional subject on display. Yet this long-sought communal essence is always imaginary and only ever temporary because consensus, the illusion that America = Obama, could never be fully attained. Personal desires change in perpetuity based upon mercurial circumstances – "the people" will, indeed it must, eventually synchronize with a different candidate. Obama himself acknowledges, in tenuous alignment with Sanders, "No law is ever final, no battle truly finished" (76). In short, a "political biography," the life writing of the political, remains necessarily unstable and short-lived. How else could democracy adopt a substantive narrative form?

Given the nature of democracy, the heavy-handedness of the campaign autobiography cannot help but undermine its own illusion of wholeness. Clinton's *Hard Choices* strains to connect the candidate's claim of middle-class roots – her "babysitting gigs" – as proof that "middle-class values" should be universal values: "The rise of a global middle class will be good for the world … (a world) more likely to share our values" (440). Clinton's declaration of universal values and global interdependence, her grand gestures at the farthest-reaching kind of consensus, feel increasingly forced, as the text rummages through Clinton's personal memories for concrete support of her political vision. Is a thread between babysitting gigs and global free trade really believable, or effortless – or is it a sign of a narrative apparatus that cannot quite accommodate the scope of its broadest ambitions? Similarly, *Hard Choices* concludes with Clinton receiving a "memory quilt" made from widely circulated pictures of Clinton's daughter, Chelsea. Although the text does not balk at the opportunity to synergize Clinton's personal memories with collective recollections of her family, a sense of disjointedness persists: how can Clinton's readers be expected to weave together these disparate private/public memories, like the discomfort of babysitting and the tenets of international finance? How can readers plausibly stitch together Clinton's private consciousness with a figurative tapestry of consciousnesses, in which an individual's desires are sutured to the holistic, homogeneous desires of an entire community? The futility of such a task speaks to the inner turmoil of the campaign autobiography as a genre.

The ancient roots of democracy as well as autobiography re-emerge in tandem at the dawn of the twenty-first century. The quilting points meant to hold together the self, the biographer, and the citizen-reader cannot hold; the strain is simply too great. Very much like the totem of the "memory blanket" to which it clings, *Hard Choices* reveals how campaign autobiographies, in their attempt to knit a neat-and-tidy sense of cohesion between self and "people," are highly seductive promises of connectivity that remain mercifully (im)possible. The constitutional chasm between a candidate and "the people" cannot be elided by confessional texts like the works that we have examined from the Bushes, Obama, Clinton, or even Sanders. In fact, I would argue that the underlying disjointedness is precisely what propels these narratives forward in the first place, as they emphasize, however unconsciously, the process of becoming. In the end, the campaign autobiography exposes a complex relationship between democracy and life writing – the crucial connection that this book has sought to illuminate.

Over the course of this book, we have surveyed the genre of the campaign biography as it emerges in the wake of American Romance, dovetails with the "realer-than-thou" energies of the Progressive Era, and arrives at last at the autobiographical restlessness of the present. We have defined and clarified the parameters of this genre by placing it into conversation with the major literary and political occupations that continue to inform it a century after its birth. At our conclusion, I wish to petition briefly for the sustained relevance of these strange works.

A successful candidate remains a necessarily tenuous ideal. While it seems as though American citizens increasingly view candidates with a strong degree of absolutism – the cultish reverence of Trump's followers; the utopian liberals that lionize Obama – the innate imperfections of the campaign biography remind us that any given candidate remains a fetish intended to fasten us together as well as a temporary placeholder that signals, albeit on a lower frequency, the vital openness of a democratic order. The careful scrutiny of this dialectical quality remains the providence of both American literature and its critique; indeed, this quality can be viewed as one of American literature's most identifying traits, because it habitually grapples with similar concerns, witnessed perhaps most vividly in the culture's long and winding relationship with realism, from Hawthorne to *Hard Choices*. The multiple iterations of the campaign biography present us with an occasion to revisit the interesting intersections of American politics and literature, and to question the absolutism of political candidates in today's popular imagination.

Chantal Mouffe explains how art and politics are not "separately constituted fields" and so they must be studied in dialogue with one another:

> There is an aesthetic dimension in the political and there is a political dimension in art ... artistic practices play a role in the constitution and maintenance of a given symbolic order, or in its challenging, and this is why they necessarily have a political dimension. The political, for its part, concerns the symbolic ordering of social relations, and this is where its aesthetic dimension resides. (*Agonistics* 91)

As we have seen throughout the preceding chapters, the artifice associated with a candidate's depiction for the public underscores a democratic surplus: "The open nature of the social (stems) from the impossibility of managing a total fixity" (Laclau, *New* 28). When Obama's campaign autobiography cannot manage to fix the candidate's image, it reveals our political iconography to be under constant revision. Yet the politician as well as the artist must still offer something, some form to which readers might cling, a temporary portrait. As Ernesto Laclau insists, "The response to the dislocation of the structure will be its recomposition around particular nodal points of articulation" (40). The life writing of American politics cannot be deconstructed without pause, or without quilting point; American democracy returns incessantly to an (im)permanent fixture, one meant to offer stability and coherence. In its eager pursuit of fullness and its occasional admission of emptiness, the campaign autobiography embodies this dialectical movement. "Social myths are essentially incomplete," Laclau elaborates. "Their content is constantly reconstituted and displaced" (63). However, despite its endless reconstitution, the campaign biography never tires in its hunger for the Real, that promise of absolute realization, that proverbial City on a Hill. The futility and fulsomeness of American realism continues to inform the nation's political imagination. The preceding pages have wrestled with the question of how this restless democratic lineage moves through the quiet corners of the under-appreciated campaign biography, in all of its chameleonic iterations.[16] And in the end we discover a useful lesson for ourselves within our larger story as a nation: if democracy once required literary voices to articulate itself, those voices may be required now – at the brink of democracy's dissolution – more than ever.

Notes

1 Of course, the end of a trend is never completely clean-cut. For instance, in 1940, the Thomas Dewey campaign asks the respected poet, short story writer, and Academy Award nominated screenwriter Rupert Hughes to pen Dewey's campaign biography. But I would argue that, despite occasional exceptions to the rule, we can still chart an overall decline.
2 T.H. White famously utilizes novelistic techniques in his treatment of Presidential campaigns: "American politicians … were such vivid characters and the mix among them was an entertainment to be enjoyed" (432).
3 A similar shift occurs with television in the middle of the century. "Television has caused an upheaval in political campaigning," Jules Abels writes. "It has changed the content of campaigns, it has changed the style, it has altered all previous canons of judgment … the viewer judges (the candidate) as he judges all else on television. He needs no experts or higher authorities to guide him" (45).
4 David Greenberg writes, "As politics become increasingly staged – with makeup and lighting in the 1950s, refined polling methods in the 1960s, slick campaign ads in the 1970s, sound bites in the 1980s, focus groups in the 1990s – public awareness kept pace, incorporating each innovation into its storehouse of knowledge. In this upward spiral of sophistication, the authentic appeared to recede, like the earth as seen from a space capsule hurtling skyward … the public's greater knowledge forced the professionals to innovate further" (xxii–xxiii).
5 Perhaps the most famous example of this tension surfaces in the controversy surrounding Jonathan Franzen's book *The Corrections* (2001), upon its selection as a part of the Oprah Winfrey Book Club. Whereas Oprah pushes the book as an unvarnished tale of a suffering soul, the text is in fact a mixture of fact and fiction. The outrage that follows this debacle suggests that many Book Club members were pining for a "true self" and could not easily come to terms with the futility of such a notion.
6 This "realer-than-thou" approach, perhaps unsurprisingly, pleases that arch-realist, William Dean Howells. In 1909, Howells calls autobiography the "most delightful of all reading" due to its supposed lack of artifice ("Autobiography" 796).
7 For an intellectual history of the genre, see Karl Joachim Weintraub's *The Value of the Individual: Self and Circumstance in Autobiography* (Chicago: University of Chicago Press, 1978).
8 As James Olney argues, "They seem very different things, study of the self and study of the world, yet the two cannot be ultimately separated" (*Metaphors* 14).
9 In *The Gay Science*, Friedrich Nietzsche comments that the autobiographer considers "as his *own* history the history of all humanity" (268, author's emphasis).
10 For analysis on the Bush family's managerial approach to American politics, see James Bennet's "C.E.O., U.S.A.," in *New York Times Magazine*, January 14, 2001. Archived at https://archive.nytimes.com/www.nytimes.com/library/magazine/home/20010114mag-bennet.html. Accessed April 7, 2021.
11 For a full treatment of this phenomenon, see Ulrich Brockling's *The Entrepreneurial Self: Fabricating a New Type of Subject*. Trans. Steven Black (New York: SAGE, 2015).
12 Tonya Blowers expands upon the concept of the signature in autobiography. While a signature may appear to testify to the Truth of the account, it also resonates as a "flourish" – that is, as a calculated rhetorical move. In turn, "the reader holds on to a sense of 'the Real' outside the text whilst simultaneously aware of the representative nature of reality within the text" (115). Clinton's text is not the only candidate to utilize the signature in this fashion; Charles Wolcott Balestier's 1884 campaign biography of James G. Blaine includes, in its opening pages, a facsimile of Blaine's handwriting (a copy of a handwritten to be unfolded) while the cover itself includes the candidate's indelible signature.
13 Of note, despite his dalliance with poststructuralism, Eakin stills invest in "prelinguistic" self-experience (*Living* 66).

14 Hermione Lee underlines the emancipatory possibilities of a biography that capitalizes upon these moments of disjuncture: "Alternatives, missed chances, roads not taken, accidents and hesitations, the whole 'swarm of possibilities' that hums around our every experience, too often disappears in the smoothing biographical process" (*Body* 2–3). While this open-endedness may be suppressed in most campaign autobiographies, traces of it remain.
15 In truth, this technique simply accentuates a long-standing trend in autobiography. Philippe Lejeune argues, "The first person, then, always conceals a hidden third person, and in this sense every autobiography is by definition indirect" ("Autobiography in the Third Person" 32).
16 Todd McGowan contends that "contradiction is not anathema to thought but what animates both thought and being" (*Emancipation* 6). In its unfolding from fullness to emptiness (and back again), McGowan might argue, the campaign biography reveals how this contradiction endures as "the engine behind all political movement" (197). Thanks in part to its indebtedness to American realism, this genre recalls a defining aspect of the democratic candidate in the popular imagination: an illusion of wholeness that retains a kernel of incompleteness, to preserve hope for dissatisfied citizens and to keep the furnaces of democracy lit.

Works Cited

Abels, Jules. *The Degeneration of Our Presidential Election: A History and Analysis of an American Institution in Trouble* (New York: Macmillan, 1968).
Bakhtin, M.M. *The Dialogic Imagination: Four Essays*. Trans. Caryl Emerson (Austin, TX: University of Texas Press, 1982).
Blowers, Tonya. "The Textual Contract: Distinguishing Autobiography from the Novel," in *Representing Lives: Women and Auto/Biography*, ed. A. Donnell and P. Polkey (London: Macmillan, 2000), pp. 105–117.
Bush, George H.W. *Looking Forward: An Autobiography* (New York: Bantam, 1988).
Bush, George W. *A Charge to Keep* (New York: William Morrow, 1999).
Clinton, Hillary. *Hard Choices* (New York: Simon & Schuster, 2015).
De Man, Paul. "Autobiography as De-facement." *MLN*, vol. 94, no. 5 (1979), pp. 919–930.
Eakin, Paul John. *How Our Lives Become Stories: Making Selves* (Ithaca, NY: Cornell University Press, 1999).
Eakin, Paul John. *Living Autobiographically: How We Create Identity in Narrative* (Ithaca, NY: Cornell University Press, 2008).
Greenberg, David. *Nixon's Shadow: The History of an Image* (New York: W.W. Norton & Co., 2003).
Gusdorf, Georges. "The Conditions and Limits of Autobiography," in *Autobiography: Essays Theoretical and Critical*, ed. James Olney (Princeton, NJ: Princeton University Press, 1980), pp. 28–48.
Howells, William Dean. "Autobiography, A New Form of Literature," *Harper's Monthly*, 119, 1909, pp. 795–798.
Jamieson, Kathleen Hall. *Packaging The Presidency: A History and Criticism of Presidential Campaign Advertising*, 3rd edn (Oxford: Oxford University Press, 1996).
Kazin, Alfred. *On Native Grounds: An Interpretation of Modern American Prose Literature* (Boston, MA: Mariner Books, 1995).
Laclau, Ernesto. *New Reflections on the Revolution of Our Time* (London: Verso, 1990).
Lejeune, Philippe. "Autobiography in the Third Person." *New Literary History*, vol. 9, no. 1, 1977, pp. 27–50. *JSTOR*, www.jstor.org/stable/468435. Accessed March 17, 2021.

Lejeune, Philippe. *On Autobiography*. Trans. Katherine Leary (Minneapolis, MN: University of Minnesota Press, 1989).
Linde, Charlotte. *Life Stories: The Creations of Coherence* (Oxford: Oxford University Press, 1993).
McGowan, Todd. *Emancipation after Hegel: Achieving a Contradictory Revolution* (New York: Columbia University Press, 2019).
Mouffe, Chantal. *Agonistics: Thinking the World Politically* (London: Verso, 2013).
Nietzsche, Friedrich. *The Gay Science: With a Prelude in Rhymes and an Appendix of Songs*. Trans. Walter Kaufmann (New York: Vintage, 1974).
Obama, Barack. *The Audacity of Hope: Thoughts on Reclaiming the American Dream* (New York: Vintage, 2008).
Olney, James. "Autobiography and the Cultural Moment: A Thematic, Historical, and Bibliographical Introduction," in *Autobiography: Essays Theoretical and Critical*, ed. James Olney (Princeton, NJ: Princeton University Press, 1980), pp. 3–27.
Olney, James. *Metaphors of Self: The Meaning of Autobiography* (Princeton, NJ: Princeton University Press, 1972).
Sanders, Bernie. *Outsider in the White House* (London: Verso, 2015).
Sayre, Robert. "Autobiography and the Making of America." *The Iowa Review*, vol. 9, no. 2, 1978, pp. 1–19.
Smith, Sidonie, and Julia Watson. "Introduction," in *Getting a Life*, ed. Sidonie Smith and Julia Watson (New York: Routledge, 2004), pp. 1–27.
Stone, Albert E. *Autobiographical Occasions and Original Acts: Versions of American Identity from Henry Adams to Nate Shaw* (Philadelphia, PA: University of Pennsylvania Press, 1982).
Troy, Gil. *See How They Ran: The Changing Role of the Presidential Candidate*, revised and expanded edn (Cambridge, MA: Harvard University Press, 1996).
White, T.H. *America in Search of Itself: The Making of the President, 1956–1980* (New York: Harper & Row, 1982).

INDEX

Abels, Jules 17, 25, 94n3
American Romanticism 7, 43, 47, 51–2, 72, 83, 90–1
The Audacity of Hope: Thoughts on Reclaiming the American Dream see Obama, Barack

Badiou, Alain 111–8, 120n16
Bakhtin, Mikhail 12, 143, 185–6
Balestier, (Charles) Wolcott 1, 103, 106, 119, 132, 194n12, *see* Chapter Four
Barrish, Phillip 15, 99, 119, 120n3
Beecher, Henry Ward 109
Bell, Michael Davitt 15–6, 120n10
Benefits Forgot see Chapter Four
Benfey, Christopher 84, 97n2
Ben-Hur: A Tale of the Christ see Chapter Five
Bercovitch, Sacvan 47, 59n4
Berthoff, Warner 13–4
Blaine, James *see* Chapter Four
The Blithedale Romance 53
Boller, Paul 6, 8
Borus, Daniel 16–7
Boyd, Richard 53
Brooks, Van Wyck 59n7
Brown, Wendy 168–9
Brown, William Burlie 2, 10–1, 59n1, 69,
Bryan, William Jennings 6, 174
Bush, George H.W. *see* Chapter Eight
Bush, George W. *see* Chapter Eight

Cady, Edwin 62, 64
Canby, Henry 27

Casper, Scott E. 2, 11–2, 24–5, 30, 45, 52, 58, 63, 65, 81n13
Castronovo, Russ 4, 14,
Cawelti, John 11, 20n9
"The Celebrated Jumping Frog of Calaveras County" 86
A Charge to Keep see Chapter Eight
Child, Richard Washburn 1
Christmas tales *see* Chapter Six
Civil War 7, 33, 35, 44–7, 51, 57, 60n12, 100, 102, 107
Clinton, Bill *see* Chapter Eight
Clinton, Hillary *see* Chapter Eight
Cole, Thomas 134
Coolidge, Calvin 6, 174, 120n1
Crane, Stephen 145n1
Cult of the Image 103–6, 108, 111

Darwinian 117
Davies, William 168, 171n15
Derrida, Jacques 12
De Tocqueville, Alexis 20n7
Dickens, Charles 37, 40, 78, 127, 146n9
The Discovery of Freedom see Chapter Seven

Eakin, Paul John 178, 187, 194n13
Eaton, John 5
Ellis, Edward S. 7–8, 170n3
Emerson, Ralph Waldo 15, 24, 177
Era of Good Feelings 4–6, 19, 25, 27

A Fair Device see Chapter Four
The Fair God; Or, the Last of the 'Tzins: A Tale of the Conquest of Mexico see Chapter Five
"Federalist style" 27, 30, 34, 36
Fisher, Laura 14, 135, 147n19
Fleetwood; Or, The Stain of Birth. A Novel of American Life see Chapter One
Foley, Barbara 100–1, 116, 118, 120n5
Foster, George 145n1
Franklin, Benjamin 177
Free Land see Chapter Seven
Frow, John 9
Fuller, Jaime 6, 11, 62

Garfield, James 16, 93, 102, 173
Genette, Gerard 5, 183
Gilded Age 85, 97, 100–3, 111, 116, 143
Gospel of Wealth 109–10
Gosse, Edmund 84–6, 91, 94
Gripp, Paul 105
Gusdorf, Georges 188–9

hagiography 16, 18, 31, 34, 191
Hamilton, Alexander 18, 33, 182
Hard Choices see Chapter Eight
Harrison, Benjamin *see* Chapter Five
Harrison, William Benjamin 6, 115
Hawthorne, Nathaniel 6–7, 13–4, 36, 62–78, 80n11, 83–91, 95–7, 107, 125, 132; *see also* Chapter Two
Hayes, Rutherford B. 16; *see also* Chapter Three
A Hazard of New Fortunes see Chapter Three
Hersey, John 20n1
Heteroglossia 12, 143, 178
Hildreth, Richard 20n1
Hirsch, Jr., E.D. 10
A History of New York 27, 29
Hofstadter, Richard 160, 166, 170n7
Hogle, Jerrod 159, 170n10
Holtz, William 151–2
Homestead Act 170n7
homiletic 101, 104, 109–11. 115, 117, 119, 120n14
Hoover, Herbert *see* Chapter Seven
Horrocks, Thomas 68, 80n2, 170n4
The House of Seven Gables 2–3, 7, 66
Howe, Irving 2
Howells, William Dean 7, 12–17, 44, 83–97, 108, 120n10, 124, 132, 176; *see also* Chapter Three
How the Other Half Lives see Chapter Six
Hutchison, Anthony 3

Ingersoll, Ernest 145n1
"Innocence" 160
"Invisible hand" 162, 164
Irving, Washington 1, 18; *see also* Chapter One
Is There A Santa Claus? 128

Jackson, Andrew 5–6, 25–6, 39–40, 41n2, 174
Jackson, Gregory S. 101, 104, 110, 120n7, 120n11, 120n14, 127, 142
James G. Blaine: A Sketch of His Life see Chapter Four
James, Henry 146n9, 147n21, 50, 84, 90, 120n10
Jones, Brian Jay 35–6, 41n1

Kaplan, Amy 66, 80n8, 104
Kipling, Rudyard 84, 95

Laclau, Ernesto 17, 96, 97n4, 139, 141–3, 193
Lane, Rose Wilder *see* Chapter Seven
Lee, Hermione 4, 26, 29, 56, 195n14
"The Legend of Sleepy Hollow" 28, 42
Lejeune, Philippe 176, 185, 195n15
Lepore, Jill 21n16, 63
Let the Hurricane Roar see Chapter Seven
libertarian 150–3, 156–7, 159, 161, 163–9, 170n2
The Life of Abraham Lincoln see Chapter Three
The Life of Franklin Pierce see Chapter Two
The Life of George Washington see Chapter One
The Life and Public Service of Henry Clay see Chapter One
Lincoln, Abraham *see* Chapter Three
"The Little Dollar's Christmas Journey" 131
The Little House on the Prairie 150
logocentric 113–4
London, Jack 151
Looking Forward see Chapter Eight

The Making of Herbert Hoover see Chapter Seven
Matthiesen, F.O. 49
McGowan, Todd 195n16
McKinley, William 6–8, 128, 133, 170n3, 175
Melville, Herman 1, 47, 80, 91, 132, 147n21, 175
"Merry Christmas in the Tenements" 128–9, 131

Mexican-American War 78
Miles, William 2, 20n3
A Modern Instance see Chapter Three
Mouffe, Chantal 17, 44, 51, 55–7, 59n12, 71, 124, 193

The Naulahka: A Story of West and East 95–6
neoliberal 150, 152, 163, 168, 171n14, 171n15, 182–3
"Nibsy's Christmas" 126–7
Nissen, Axel 135–6, 138
Nissenbaum, Stephen 143, 146n14

Obama, Barack 48, 181–84, 188–193
Olney, James 189, 194n8
Outsider in the White House see Chapter Eight
Ovid 52–3

Paul/Pauline 110–4, 117–8
picturesque 72, 79, 81n14, 85, 133
Pierce, Franklin *see* Chapter Two
populism 4–5, 39–40, 41n2, 95, 124–6, 130–1, 139–45, 186
Progressive Era 84–5, 110, 123, 125, 131–7, 192
Protestantism *see* Chapter Six

Rancière, Jacques 17, 44, 81n15, 168
"Rent Baby" 147n17
Reynolds, David 44
Reynolds, Larry 53
Riis, Jacob *see* Chapter Six
"Rip Van Winkle" 28–9
The Rise of Silas Lapham 7, 63, 67, 74, 92
Roberts, Kenneth L. 120n1
romantic friendship narratives 135–9, 141, 144
Roosevelt, Theodore *see* Chapter Six

Santa Claus 126–30, 140, 146n14
Sargent, Epes *see* Chapter Two
Schlesinger, Jr., Arthur 20n8, 173

scopophilia 103, 106, 108, 123
sensationalism 164, 175
Sheldon, Charles 109
"Sinners in the Hands of an Angry God" 164
Sketch of the Life and Character of Rutherford B. Hayes see Chapter Three
Skowronek, Stephen 14
Slotkin, Richard 152, 166, 170n5, 170n11
Smith, Adam 162, 164
Smith, Henry Nash 66, 170n5
Spengemann, William 2, 20n5
The Standard Fourth Reader 41n9
Stavrakakis, Yannis 18
Stowe, Harriet Beecher 20n1
sublime 72, 79, 132–4, 160
Sundquist, Eric 71

Theodore Roosevelt, The Citizen see Chapter Seven
Third Way 47–54, 59
Thoreau, Henry David 177
Todorov, Tzvetan 10
Trachtenberg, Alan 16, 64, 66
Trilling, Lionel 80n1
Troy, Gil 6–8, 20n8, 56, 174
The Turn of the Screw 90, 146n9
Twain, Mark 84, 86, 97

Van Buren, Martin 20n1, 25–6, 41n2
A Victorious Defeat: A Romance see Chapter Four

Wallace, Lew *see* Chapter Five
Washington, George *see* Chapter One, 184
Wealth and Worth: Or, What Makes the Man? see Chapter One
Weems, Parson 18, 29, 168
White, T.H. 173, 194n2
Whitman, Walt 101, 132, 177
Whittier, John Greenleaf 20n1
Williams, Raymond 18–9, 119
Wilson, Christopher 84–5
Wineapple, Brenda 59n10
Žižek, Slavoj 124, 146n7

Printed in the United States
by Baker & Taylor Publisher Services